WILTS & DORSET MOTOR SERVICES LTD 1915 – 1972

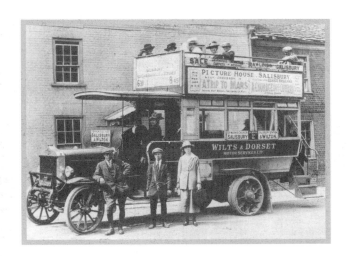

For David J.N. Pennels
— a Wilts & Dorset man through and through —

THE DEFINITIVE HISTORY OF
WILTS & DORSET
MOTOR SERVICES LTD

1915 – 1972

Colin Morris

and

Andrew Waller

First published in the United Kingdom in 2006
by The Hobnob Press, PO Box 1838, East Knoyle, Salisbury SP3 6FA

British Library Cataloguing in Publication Data
A catalogue record for this book is available from the British Library.

ISBN 10 0-946418-56-x
ISBN 13 (from Jan 2007) 978-0-946418-56-5

Typeset in 10/12 pt Scala
Typesetting and origination by John Chandler
Printed in Great Britain by Salisbury Printing Company Ltd, Salisbury

Contents

Note: Chapters 6, 7 and 8 depart from the general chronological structure of this history.

Colour plates will be found between pages 120 and 121. A reproduction of a destination blind and facsimile route maps in 1949 and 1952 will be found on pages 144-147

Introduction and Acknowledgements

A GLANCE at a population map of the British Isles, one of those which depict the degree of density by increasing shades of colour, quickly makes it apparent that Wiltshire and Dorset are both lightly coloured and populated.

All due credit therefore to those who set up and struggled to keep going a transport company in the midst of such territory. For the first 35 years of its existence, Wilts & Dorset Motor Services Ltd depended upon an unusual and unpredictable mix of agricultural performance plus a forceful British foreign policy.

Salisbury, the famous city at the centre of Wilts & Dorset's territory was no larger than a small market town. Its population when the company was founded was just 21,217. When Wilts & Dorset ceased trading some 58 years later, it had risen to little over 36,000. Against such a background, survival was the main theme at Wilts & Dorset until, from 1950, a large swathe of northern Hampshire was added to its territory by the British Transport Commission. As transport historian and author George Behrend once said to me: 'Ah, Wilts & Dorset; so-called because it operates in Hampshire and Berkshire'. Well, it had to find sufficient customers somewhere!

Thus the well-being and life-span of the company was improved and lengthened, until radical changes introduced piecemeal by the Transport Holding Company and, finally, the National Bus Company saw Wilts & Dorset subsumed under Hants & Dorset Motor Services Ltd – a fate it had previously escaped twice in earlier days.

To some extent, therefore, this book takes the form of a testimonial to those officers and staff of Wilts & Dorset who created and strove to maintain a characterful omnibus undertaking in a beautiful but far from ideal catchment area.

One such was David Pennels, chief traffic assistant with the company who, in the early 1960s painstakingly compiled a 151-page fleet history of Wilts & Dorset which was updated regularly after publication in 1963. This work set the bench-mark for the fleet histories published thereafter by the PSV Circle and the Omnibus Society.

Following publication of my first transport history ten years later, my then publisher had plans for a nation-wide regional history of the bus industry in Britain. In the event just two regions were covered, but by other publishers. My contribution was devoted to South-East England. On the grounds that a South-Central volume was planned, in 1974 I first met David Pennels, and discovered that, in addition, he was a highly talented and prolific transport photographer.

For reasons too complicated to explain, the notion of a single chapter about Wilts & Dorset in a 'regional' was replaced over the years by one of a volume devoted entirely to Wilts & Dorset Motor Services Ltd. In addition to enjoying the hospitality of David and Kathleen Pennels on numerous occasions, I corresponded with and met several officers with intimate knowledge of the company's affairs: they included Raymond Longman, David Deacon, Thomas Pruett, Douglas Morison, Harold Stevens (who was at school with my father), Colin Burt, Michael Wadsworth, Peter Hunt and Frank Pointon, the latter taking a particular interest in the wind-down history of Wilts & Dorset within a regional setting.

In the days when I enjoyed the use of a bolt-hole in Quality Square, Ludlow, this was used as a base for numerous daily visits to the Kithead Trust at Droitwich, where Peter Jaques provided access to the minutes of the Wilts & Dorset directors, the Executive Sub-Committee, the annual reports and accounts, and numerous other documents. From the same base I also commuted to the Omnibus Society's collection of transport memorabilia at Ironbridge.

Regular visits to the Pennels household continued as one treasure after another was forthcoming until 2003, when international journalist Andrew Waller, whom I have known well since our boyhood in 1948, and who now lives but 12 miles from David, kindly undertook the task of participating as co-author of this book. Accordingly he has liaised with David on a frequent basis and undertaken a considerable amount of research locally – not least by conducting interviews (such as a particularly delightful and informative one with Wilts & Dorset stalwarts Donald and Doris Bealing) – and compiled several of the appendices.

Practically all the captions to the illustrations were composed by Andrew, in consultation with David whose photographic collection forms the pictorial backbone for the work. Since Andrew's professionally economic style of writing differs noticeably from mine – 'Your sentences are longer', he says, the Contents page makes clear which of us wrote each chapter.

My thanks for hospitality over the years are also extended to Jacquie and Andrew Waller; also to Alan Lambert – founder of the Southdown Enthusiasts Club – for a considerable amount of technical work and advice for David, Andrew and me in relation to the production of this book. We owe a special debt of gratitude to Kathleen Pennels for tracking down Edwin Maurice Coombes, whose initiative in 1914 led to the creation of Wilts & Dorset. We thank Ian Scott, of the Salisbury Photo Centre in Catherine Street, for substantial assistance with photographic reproduction, and Roger Atkinson, of the Transport Ticket Society.

Finally, we are most grateful to John Chandler of the Hobnob Press who, upon the recommendation of David Pennels, readily agreed to add a book about Wilts & Dorset Motor Services Ltd to his much-praised list of erudite local histories. That is an honour indeed.

Colin Morris
Heswall, Cheshire
November 2006

1

Forerunners

Wilts & Dorset Motor Services Ltd was once described as having been so called 'because they operated in Hampshire and Berkshire'. Tongue in cheek of course, but Wilts & Dorset began moving southwards and eastwards into Hampshire in its earliest days, a process which culminated in its taking over responsibility for a very large area centred upon Basingstoke, previously the territory of Venture Ltd.

Nevertheless, the founding of the company at Amesbury, ten miles north of Salisbury, eight miles by the shorter up-and-down route, and on the edge of Salisbury Plain, reminds us that it was the presence of the military in that area which made the setting up of Wilts & Dorset a viable prospect.

Many good books about Wiltshire and Salisbury Plain, not least those published by the Hobnob Press, have touched upon roads, routes and travel facilities utilised in the area over the centuries – in particular the changes brought about by variations in the use of the terrain. Since much of the low-lying land was – both before and after the Roman occupation – covered by largely impenetrable woodland, going from one place to another meant travelling along the ridges of hills aligned in the appropriate direction. This also had the advantage of self-protection, for such 'ridgeways' gave their users the option of running easily downhill to take cover in those woodlands; a kind of 'early-warning' means of travel.

When the Saxons occupied the area, they used these very hills to defeat the Danes, set up their boroughs and counties and began clearing land for common agricultural use. Wilton on the River Wylye rose to great local importance and gave its name to Wiltshire. The Danes, still smarting, came back in 1003 and burned it to the ground. It was rebuilt – and today the Danes are remarkably pleasant people.

Came the Normans, who set about turning an already centuries-old hilltop fortification, called by the Saxons *Searobyrig* into a circular walled city which incorporated a cathedral and castle. The bishopric of Sherborne was transferred to this city of Sarum in 1072 – and for some 150 years this was the centre of all things that mattered in Wiltshire. Then, in the 13th century, when a suitable *modus vivendi* had been established, it was deemed safe to begin quarrying the whole site as a source of material for the construction of a new city nearly two miles farther south, on the banks of the river Avon – a place called New Sarum (Salisbury). The bishopric was once again transferred – to the new and beautiful Early English cathedral built there. The Old Castle Inn, where the hill of Old Sarum dominates the scenery to this day, was destined to see some 30 Wilts & Dorset bus journeys per day pass its door on the road between Salisbury and Amesbury.

Following the construction of New Sarum, three basic routes from London to the West Country passed through what was to become Wilts & Dorset territory. To the north of the area a road through Newbury and Marlborough branched off at Beckhampton (via Chippenham or Devizes) for Bath. Two basic routes to Exeter forked at what became Basingstoke, the more northerly going via Whitchurch, Andover, Weyhill, Amesbury, past Stonehenge, Wylye, Hindon, Mere and Wincanton; the more southerly – in the days before stage-coaches – via Popham Lane, Stockbridge, along a particularly difficult and hilly route to Lopcombe, to Salisbury, Wilton, Shaftesbury, Sherborne and Yeovil. A lengthier route from Salisbury to Exeter involved a journey through Coombe Bissett, Blandford, Dorchester – and on through Axminster, joining up at Honiton.

In the heyday of stage-coaches, the early 19th century, the route through Newbury and Marlborough saw the Comet, Monarch, New Company, Old Company, Regulator, Star and York House going to Bath through Chippenham; whilst the Emerald, Regent, White Hart and Royal Blue (no, not Elliott's, who never ran proper stage-coaches) went there via Devizes. The 'Exeter Mail' was the flagship coach on the route through Amesbury and across Salisbury Plain. Many sections of route ran across some of that well-worn high ground, which in winter became bitterly cold and windswept. More than one coachman lost fingers to frostbite crossing terrain from which even the large flocks of sheep had been taken into shelter on lower ground.

One such section, that between Barford St. Martin and Ludwell (between Wilton and Shaftesbury) was, as a result, rebuilt at a lower level, leaving the telegraph poles running along the crest of the ridge beside the

The Exeter to London mail coach towards the end of its career, in 1843.

now grass-covered original – and visible in motion parallax from the replacement road. To the east of Salisbury, the 22-and-a-bit miles long former Roman road between Popham Lane and Lopcombe Corner, sparsely populated and 'extremely lonely', was abandoned early by coach proprietors, who diverted their vehicles instead through Overton, Whitchurch, Andover and Wallop en route to Salisbury, finding considerably more custom and avoiding a notorious 'lurk of highwaymen' in the process. In relation to Wiltshire's need to export its wool-based products and import in return some of the Continental niceties which the resultant revenue made possible, the road from Salisbury to Southampton also became an important route for carriers and stage-coaches conveying businessmen. In the early 19th century, before the coming of the railways – somewhat late to Salisbury it transpired – the York House Coach from Bath, the Bristol Royal Mail, the Red Rover Brighton and Bristol coach, and the aptly named Salisbury Packet provided the necessary link with the port.

Meanwhile, how came the military to Salisbury Plain? In the early 18th century, Daniel Defoe found that the greatest market for Wiltshire sheep was at the eastern edge of the open down country – over the border in Hampshire, at Weyhill near Andover. It was not uncommon to find that several hundred thousand head of sheep had been sold at just one Weyhill Fair. Extra income for the local populace came from cottage industries such as handloom and girth-web weaving and the production of pillow-lace. Then, as William Barnes famously wrote, 'the common was a-took in!' The downlands became heavily enclosed in favour of arable cultivation. Corn crops are only seasonally labour-intensive: whole families began to emigrate as sheep-farming went into steep decline. By the 1870s many tenant farmers had simply given up – their workforces having discovered that there was more money to be made constructing railway cuttings, embankments and bridges. Abandoned farms and cottages were in many instances simply demolished by the landlords, who in turn looked to reduce their outgoings, if not make a handsome profit from the situation. As James (1987) and Chapter 8 describe, several eventually found a timely purchaser – Her Majesty's War Office.

The retreat of agricultural labourers from the indigent hill country of Wiltshire served further to concentrate the cultivation of local produce into the valleys formed, in the area destined to become the cradle of Wilts & Dorset Motor Services Ltd, by those rivers which joined the Avon in the vicinity of Salisbury – the Bourne, Nadder, Wylye and Ebble, each with its tributary streams.

From the communities which grew accordingly in each respective catch-meadow, village-based carriers brought harvested crops or saleable odds and ends to the weekly market at Salisbury. The vendors were found spaces among the goods – and returned likewise among their purchases in the city.

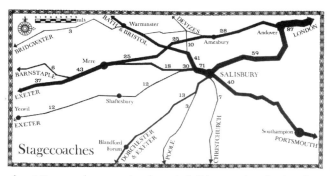

above] Stagecoaches operating through Salisbury and on the Amesbury road in 1839. The number of coaches traversing the road in each direction per week is given, and the thickness of the lines graded accordingly. JOHN CHANDLER (FROM ENDLESS STREET, 1983)

right] Carriers running into Salisbury in 1865. The numbers denote the carriers per week on each route (although their precise itinerary remains uncertain in some cases), and the lines have been thickened accordingly. JOHN CHANDLER (FROM ENDLESS STREET, 1983)

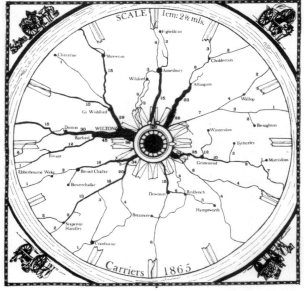

right] Representing the transition from the days of stagecoaches and horse-drawn carrier's wagons to motor traction is Thomas R. Lee of Winterbourne Gunner. Prior to becoming motorised in 1920, this was Lee's contribution to the Salisbury Market traffic. Less than a quarter of a century later, his widow Martha would be running one of his Winterbourne & Gomeldon Motor Bus Service vehicles to such high-tech establishments as the 'Gas School' at Figsbury.
DAVID PENNELS COLLECTION

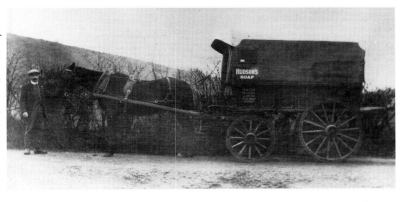

below] Until 1927 Wilts & Dorset did not reach as far up the Avon Valley as Upavon, leaving it to independents to provide bus services to Salisbury. Edwin Cave started his Upavon Motor Services in 1913 with this chain-driven Scout, AM2882, pictured on a weekend outing to Bournemouth. Cave ran to Salisbury on market days, and on different days to Devizes and Swindon. In about 1927 his services passed to Charles Mortimer's Upavon & District, and he in turn sold out to Wilts & Dorset in 1932. DAVID PENNELS COLLECTION

with bodywork ranging from the makeshift to accommodate about twelve people and some

With the advent of motor transport, several such carriers additionally provided vehicles which were primarily intended for passengers, but by no means all of them did so. As late as March 1921, the latter were criticised for their apparent lack of business acumen by a correspondent with *Motor Transport*.

> Anyone desirous of gathering first-hand information as to the use of motor vehicles by country carriers is recommended to pay a visit to Salisbury any day of the week, but preferably on a Tuesday, which is market day. Salisbury is the market centre for a very large number of villages within a radius of 20 miles and, in the majority of cases, the only means of conveyance is provided by the local carrier, who has forsaken the horse for the motor. The result is that on Tuesdays the market place is choked full...with country carriers' motor vehicles. The cars convey both passengers and goods, which consist entirely of market stock, to and from Salisbury.

Describing the vehicles as 'the most weird collection of road transport machines one could see anywhere',

goods, to those designed with some regard for the job for which they were used, he noted that some carried goods on 'glorified luggage grids at the back', others on top of the body, and others inside.

He found that most of the carriers, practically all of them owner-drivers, ran into Salisbury three or four times a week and that otherwise, apart from the odd job, the vehicles were idle. Worse, he thought, was that, on those days that they were used, they remained standing in Salisbury between 10 a.m. and 4 p.m. – with the effect that 'the average country carrier's car in the Salisbury district does not do more than about 24 running hours work a week'.

This 'brave young man' from 'Lunnon' then advised several of these doughty Moonrakers that they should use the time between arrival and departure by running some passenger-carrying services around the city. The unanimous response was that their customers had long used the vehicles as accumulative repositories for the items purchased piecemeal, and considered this part of the service, so they had to remain in the market place.

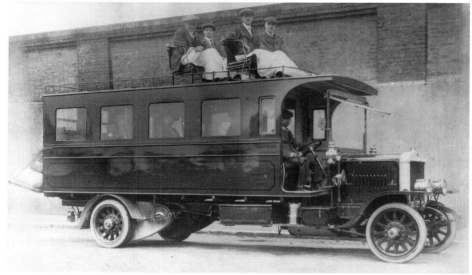

Harold Roy Bartley ran this chain-driven Scout bus between Sixpenny Handley and Salisbury before World War I, but then moved to Tidworth, where the big army garrison offered him a bigger market for his services. He linked up with Charles Avery to run buses to Salisbury and Andover, until Wilts & Dorset bought him out in 1929. His Handley bus, FX1578 – with seating for eight on the roof – was photographed outside Salisbury railway station.
DAVID PENNELS COLLECTION

His criticism overlooked such basic traffic issues as the likely response of the council to an interloping rush of vehicles, unsuited for the task, jostling for custom amidst people trying to conduct market business, the reaction of the local constabulary to such an attempt, the inevitable delays for the carriers' home-based customers – and the ensuing free-for-all at any central collecting station set up as a necessary alternative way of doing things. And who would be expected to pay for that anyway.

This patronising article also overlooked the fact that the majority of these carriers were also self-employed as farmers, market gardeners, grocers, coal merchants, blacksmiths, wheelwrights, hauliers or some such other useful activity in their local villages, which kept them well-occupied. Like as not many of them ran the road to Salisbury for the relative fun of it and to enjoy the comradeship of old acquaintances over a pint or two in the city hostelries; bringing their own purchases home into the bargain. This was a kind of lifestyle inherited from horse-drawn days and, in many instances, it took a subsequent generation of each family business to change it.

The bright young correspondent from *Motor Transport*, taking a last swipe at 'the miscellaneous junk heap of motor transport ... in the Salisbury district', concluded that 'what the carriers in the Salisbury area should do is to combine, scrap the dud machines ... and get an experienced transport man to organise a carrier's business on paying lines. If they do not they may find

M. Hall & Sons' Shrewton Motor Service was actually based in the next-door village of Orcheston. They bought their first bus in 1912 to run between Devizes and Salisbury on market days. AM5363, delivered in 1915, was their third Scout. By the time the business passed to Lavington & Devizes Motor Services Ltd in 1923, the Salisbury service ran every day and the Halls had another base at Hindon. The Bath Tramways Motor Co Ltd absorbed Lavington & Devizes in 1936, but handed over the Hindon-Salisbury route to Wilts & Dorset.
DAVID PENNELS COLLECTION

some enterprising firm come along and take all their trade away.' Well, his proposed solution to the perceived inadequacies of the local carriers was equally wide of the mark, but his final warning had at least some substance to it, even if that 'enterprising firm' achieved such an outcome, over a very lengthy period, by acquiring piecemeal the very activity he had opined the carriers should adopt – stage carriage services.

Apart from the horse bus services previously operated between the Salisbury railway stations and the local hotels, one of the first mentions of a (motorised) stage carriage operator in the area came in the summer of 1903, when it was reported that a motor wagonette service would start between Salisbury and Amesbury and the camps along the middle reaches of the River Avon. The following year the Great Western Railway's Road Motor Department started a motorbus route to the north of this area with a service between Marlborough, Avebury, Beckhampton and Calne. Eventually the GWR network of motorbuses was to include services to Pewsey, Upavon, Andover and even Basingstoke – territory which later became a Wilts & Dorset preserve.

It was at Tisbury, on the upper reaches of the River Nadder, that in March 1904 a decision was made, one from which the fledgling motorbus industry was to gain great benefit. In an attempt to preserve the rural nature of the area and its attendant natural beauty – and probably its funds also – the district council at Tisbury had claimed that the width of the roads under its jurisdiction was too narrow for motor traffic; but a local motorist consulted the Highways Act 1835 and discovered that justices of the peace were empowered to order that roads of inadequate width be widened to a breadth of as much as 30 feet. Accordingly, he requested two JPs to inspect Tisbury's roads – and the district council's workmen were soon to be seen widening them accordingly. The news spread, and emergent operators had less difficulty in getting some of the narrower lanes adjusted to suit their vehicles.

In the city of Salisbury the town clerk was invited in 1908 to write to the 'London Electric Omnibus Co Ltd' (properly the London Electrobus Co Ltd) to ask if it would undertake a trial run within the city, but no further developments seem to have been recorded. In 1911 a stage

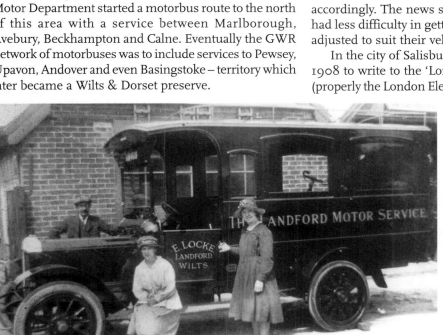

Ernest Oborn of Ebbesbourne Wake was the last of the small bus proprietors in the Chalke Valley to sell out to Wilts & Dorset in the 1930s. A decade or more before he did so this Ford T wagonette ran to Salisbury on market days, and took villagers on trips to the seaside on Sundays, like this one to Bournemouth. In the very month that World War II broke out Wilts & Dorset paid £250 to take over his thrice-weekly Berwick St. John-Salisbury service. No vehicles were involved. DAVID PENNELS COLLECTION

carriage service proper was established at Andover by T.A. Nicholls Ltd (see Chapter 6). It traded as T.A.N. with four Commer Car saloons which were run via Weyhill and Ludgershall to Tidworth, until mechanical problems put paid to the enterprise. At Orcheston, just off one of the most beautiful stretches of the road to Devizes, M. Hall & Sons set up their Shrewton Motor Service in 1912 and ran to West Lavington and Devizes on a through route from Salisbury Market Place. To their original Salisbury-built Scout 20-seater, they added two more by the early days of World War I, and opened a garage at Hindon to anchor a daily service to Chilmark, Dinton, Barford St. Martin and Salisbury.

A synopsis of operators like the latter, together with others who began as carriers, several in horse bus days, has been painstakingly brought together by Roger Grimley with the aid of other local historians, (see note in Bibliography).

Some of the official company records of the large territorial bus companies give the impression that it was the original directors – and, here and there, shareholders – of each undertaking at the time of its registration at Companies House, who were responsible for the original idea and initiation. In some cases – Devon General and Maidstone & District for instance – such a notion was actively pursued in official company literature. So it was with Wilts & Dorset, whose humble beginning in August 1914 could well have gone unrecorded but for preserved correspondence between David Pennels and Edwin Maurice Coombes which dates from 1961, when Pennels was painstakingly compiling his Wilts & Dorset fleet history (1963 – see Bibliography).

The original Wilts & Dorset Motor Company Coombes set up at his Amesbury address, a leasehold property at 46 High Street. A qualified motor engineer, his firm was described as a bus, taxi and garage business – although the premises seem to have included a cinema, presumably for the amusement of both the local people and troops from the nearby camps. He is known to have operated a Ford T taxi and a 3-ton Scout saloon bus in that manufacturer's preferred yellow livery, on a route between Amesbury and Salisbury along the Avon valley through Upper, Middle and Lower Woodford – rather than the sparsely populated up-and-down direct road between termini. Scout – Dean & Burden Bros Ltd of Friary Lane, Salisbury – had from 1904 been offering repair facilities to early motorists, turning to manufacture of goods and passenger vehicles which enjoyed a degree of popularity, particularly in Wiltshire, until 1921. Wilts & Dorset was to prove no exception at the outset.

I have learned by personal experience not to discount out of hand verbal information given by one generation to the next, et seq. So, I recall with appropriate interest that when (in 1972) I interviewed Lory, the daughter of William Wells Graham, founder of Hants & Dorset Motor Services Ltd, she told me that her great grandfather Francis had been, in his earlier years, a smuggler. He had provided a horse and cart for the nocturnal carriage of ankers of good Dutch brandy up into Dorset from the chines of Poole Bay. In this connection, it is fascinating

By 1924 Edward Charles H. Grant, of Middle Winterslow, provided a service to Salisbury for his fellow villagers four days a week. He was one of several small busmen serving this community east of Salisbury; the last of them survived until 1999. This little 1928 Chevrolet, MW2583, was with Grant's Kingston Coaches some years before he sold his stage bus operations to Wilts & Dorset in February 1939. DAVID GILLARD COLLECTION

Mark Ranger of Durrington was already running a bus to Salisbury two days a week by 1920. He used a well-appointed Alldays & Onions saloon bus, with electric lights and cushioned seats, for his market-day service. This Thornycroft charabanc, HR300, was available to run excursions into Salisbury for troops based at camps on the Plain. ANDREW WALLER COLLECTION

to note that, in the early 20th century, members of the Gulliver family, who lived in the Chalke Valley, were providers of local passenger transport services through Bowerchalke, Bishopstone and Coombe Bissett, to Salisbury. There is room for someone to discover if there is a family connection with the late 18th century smuggler Isaac Gulliver, who married the innkeeper's daughter at Sixpenny Handley (in Dorset) – just four miles south of Bowerchalke). Isaac had been involved in clandestine nocturnal journeys from that self-same part of the coast as had Francis Graham.

This romantic digression from the known facts about the founding of the 'Wilts & Dorset Motor Service' by Maurice Coombes in 1914 is justified as follows: recent research by Andrew Waller (2006) suggests that Coombes spent his childhood in Sixpenny Handley and may indeed have been born there. In which case he probably knew the Gulliver family – and what their (likely) forbears had been up to. Bringing together the separate information about both ends of this smuggler's-trail tale suggests that the Graham family of early Bournemouth knew the Gullivers – and if Waller's theory is right, the Coombes family as well?

Whilst it is more likely that Maurice Coombes met William Graham when he garaged his car in one of the latter's West Cliff premises on a holiday trip to Bournemouth, the connection just may have been much earlier. Whatever, in a letter (1961) to David Pennels, Coombes gives credit to William Wells (Dick) Graham for suggesting the title 'Wilts & Dorset' to him in 1914,

some two years before Graham himself became involved in the bus industry – and six before the latter adopted the name 'Hants & Dorset'. Nevertheless, smuggling had earlier been sufficiently rife in the county of Wiltshire (or, perhaps more accurately, the receiving and concealment of smuggled goods) for Wiltshire folk to be known famously, to this day, as 'Moonrakers'.

However, Coombes told Pennels that Graham's suggestion had been made following the acquisition by Lloyds Bank of the earlier Wilts & Dorset Banking Company Ltd (with branches as far afield as Southampton and South Wales) and was made in order to preserve a trustworthy local name. It would have appealed to Graham because, at the time, the registered office of his 'West Cliff Garages' was at Wilts & Dorset Bank Chambers, Bournemouth.

Maurice Coombes' chat with William Graham had taken place at a time when a combination of trade and naval (rather than army) rivalry between Great Britain and Germany was coming to a head. An outbreak of war in the Balkans, between Austria-Hungary and Serbia on 28 July 1914, provided the fatal spark. Germany declared war against France on 3 August and on the same day invaded a neutral Belgium minding its own business. The following day Britain declared war upon Germany, lining up beside France and Russia.

When Herbert Asquith's war minister Lord Kitchener appealed that September for UK volunteers, in the first month over 750,000 enrolled. Ironically (as events some seven years later will subsequently show), Britain's apparent willingness to go to war in defence of little Catholic Belgium initially won considerable moral

One of the first 'buses' to run between Salisbury, Amesbury and Bulford, before World War I, was little more than a carrier's van with windows, mounted on a Daimler car chassis. DAVID PENNELS COLLECTION

above right] Meanwhile, in far-away Worthing in Sussex, Bert Cooper was learning to drive a Milnes-Daimler motor bus – a combination of British and German technology which proved to be a major step forward for the emergent industry. When Alfred Cannon and Douglas Mackenzie gained control of Wilts & Dorset and turned it into a limited liability company, they brought several members of their already established Worthing Motor Services Ltd to Wiltshire. A.E. Cooper devoted the rest of his working life to Wilts & Dorset. LES COOPER COLLECTION

above] Edwin Maurice Coombes: originator of the name 'Wilts & Dorset' – so far as motorbuses were concerned – Coombes set up in business at Amesbury in 1914. Caught in thoroughly justified 'so there!' pose, some six and a bit years later; he'd been appointed manager by Wilts & Dorset Motor Services Ltd; was called to the colours in World War I – and told his job had gone when he returned. His revenge was sweet! DAVID PENNELS COLLECTION

support from both communities in a simmering Ireland – where partition was already upon the cards – and, as a result, many more Catholics than Protestants were among the early volunteers who came across the Irish Sea to join those flocking to the colours from Great Britain.

If the outbreak of World War I put a stop to house building in Salisbury, it had the opposite effect upon the encampments on Salisbury Plain. The rows of huts just grew and grew. Whether Coombes had foreseen this is highly unlikely, for his single saloon motorbus, which commenced operating in that fateful August of 1914, seems quickly to have proven inadequate to cope with demand.

According to Maurice Coombes' own account, it was his old friend Fred Sutton who introduced him to Alfred Cannon of Worthing Motor Services (WMS), together

with an important shareholder in that firm, Percy Lephard. Sutton was a Salisbury confectioner with a restaurant at 11/13 High Street and a bakery at 37/39 Crane Street. Perhaps they got to hear about Coombes' enterprise over lunch with Cannon's brother who'd 'stepped out for the day' as a young officer in training at Larkhill Camp. Maybe it is stretching the imagination a little to suggest that the latter had come down to Salisbury in Coombes' Scout, but clearly it was made apparent to the visitors from Sussex that there was a need for a larger and improved transport facility between Amesbury and Salisbury, to say nothing of the capital to fund it.

By late autumn 1914, Coombes was in formal discussions with Alfred Cannon – at the time a 31-year-old director of WMS – and his senior partner and fellow director, Douglas Mackenzie, the latter already something of a legend in the emergent motorbus industry. It seems that the young Lt Cannon at Larkhill was only interested in the provision of a taxi service from his camp – and since Worthing Motor Services had a sizeable fleet of taxicabs in addition to its omnibuses, it was arranged to send two old Napier cars along from Worthing to help out Coombes' original Ford T taxi.

2

Independent Wilts & Dorset

TAKING NOTE of the number allotted to each limited liability company when it was first registered at Companies House is extremely useful on several counts. First, it enables the historian to establish which of several similarly named companies it is, whose story is the subject of study – hence the qualified title of this book 'Wilts & Dorset Motor Services Ltd: 1915-1972'. So we avoid, for instance, any notion that the latter, and the Wilts & Dorset Bus Company Ltd (company no. 01671355), an offspring of Hants & Dorset founded in 1983, were one and the same thing – that they were not.

Secondly, the sequential allocation of company numbers enables a quick check upon the order in which companies in the same line of business were established. Thus Douglas Mackenzie cannot be described as 'having earned a good reputation with Southdown Motor Services Ltd' by the time of the founding of the subject of this book, because Southdown, upon its incorporation, was given company no. 140534 – as befitted the date of 2 June 1915. Advance notice of the intention to formalise the re-titled 'Wilts & Dorset Motor Services Ltd' was received in December 1914, and the company was registered on 4 January 1915, as no. 133876.

Although it does not apply to Wilts & Dorset, knowledge of the company number also provides a research key as to whether a company has undergone an official change of name, rather than being wound up or left to lie dormant.

Douglas Mackenzie did indeed enjoy a sound reputation in the road transport industry, however, founded in the late 19th century in the days of steam. No doubt, either, that 'Mac and Freddie' (Mackenzie and Cannon) saw Wilts & Dorset, from the outset, as part of a much larger scheme formulating in their fertile minds – of which more later.

Fortunately, Mackenzie was a prolific writer, drawing upon his accumulating experience to correspond with trade journals – which he also bombarded with letters – and record a fascinating series of reminiscences in *Tweenus*, the house magazine of Southdown Motor Services. Since Wilts & Dorset (the vehicles in particular) still bore the signs and symbols of his influence long after his death in 1944, an outline of the man is appropriate here.

Douglas Mackenzie, of Scottish descent, was born at Kensington in 1870. In his youth he was a 'train-spotter' and, lacking any ABC to help him with that hobby, devised a classification system into which he slotted the locomotive names and numbers which he saw. From this he assimilated what turned out to be a lifelong interest in numeration, and sequencing in particular – a methodology put to good use in the bus companies of which he became a director.

His first paid connection with any form of transport came as a trainee ship's engineer whilst apprenticed to

Douglas Mackenzie: better known for his work with Southdown, was a director of Wilts & Dorset from 1915 to 1927, secretary until 1919 and joint managing director until 1924. Manifestations of the Mackenzie 'style' were to remain with Wilts & Dorset – in one form or another – until after World War II, however. Pictured in his later years, it seems that his dress code did not match his innovations mechanical. COLIN MORRIS COLLECTION

a firm in Sunderland. As a result of his experience with steam engines, he was appointed in 1898 a member of the secretarial staff employed by the National Traction Engine Owners' Association. For some two years his task was to cycle around Wales and western England testing and reporting upon the suitability and strength of country roads and bridges for use by steam-driven road vehicles.

Apart from introducing him to the beauties of the countryside, this activity provided the impetus to search for some means to enable others to visit and enjoy the scenery he felt he had discovered. It also led to a job which was to give him his first experience of locomotion in Wiltshire. In 1901, Mackenzie joined Allen's of Cowley, Oxford, as the manager of a fleet of 80 steam-powered lorries, threshing and ploughing engines, and steam rollers. The 'Oxford Steam Ploughing Company' had won a contract to take building materials from Grateley Station, on the LSWR's Andover and Salisbury line, by road to new army camps being built at Bulford, pending construction of a branch railway line through to Amesbury via Newton Tony Junction. However, Mackenzie's allotted trucks were hauled by steam-powered traction engines with 12-inch-wide, nine-foot-high driving wheels. Despite the chalk base of the roads, these, plus the added weight of the cargoes, sank through or broke the surface of the road very frequently, and were 'never in good odour with the local authorities'.

Happily for those labouring on that part of Salisbury Plain, military traffic by rail reached Amesbury on 1 October 1901 – although it took until June 1906 to push that branch line through to Bulford itself. Meanwhile, apparently not held culpable, Mackenzie had become the London agent for Allen's at 2, Gloucester Road, Brownswood Park, Stoke Newington.

It was while based at Cowley that Mackenzie first met the young Alfred Cannon, who hailed from just down the road at Sandford-on-Thames, at the time serving his apprenticeship with the Great Western Railway at its Wolverhampton works. Like Mackenzie before him, Cannon was to make a smooth transfer from one mode of transport to another, by taking a first job with the London Power Omnibus Co. Ltd.

Earlier, Mackenzie's introduction to 'motorbuses' (a contraction which, in those days he disliked, as having a peculiar 'Yankee flavour that is distinctly unpleasant to British palates.'. . . E.S. Shrapnell-Smith, *Commercial Motor's* first editor, did not agree!) came in 1904, when he was employed by the Motor Traction Co. Ltd of London. The following year, he had set up as a consulting engineer in the Strand, and then at 109, Victoria Street, Westminster. In this he was highly successful, being engaged as an adviser by The Glasgow & South Western Railway Company, Clacton-on-Sea Motor Omnibus Company and the Isle of Wight Express Motor Syndicate Ltd – to which were added, among others, Kent Motor Services and Western Motor Coaches of Minehead.

Alfred Cannon: founding member of the Wilts & Dorset board, director from 1915 to 1952 and joint managing director until 1924. Cannon was also acting chairman from 1937 to 1939. Equally responsible, together with Mackenzie, for that discernibly 'Southdown-style' evident in Wilts & Dorset's first three decades, less is known about his innermost thoughts, because he was less prone to commit them to paper. COLIN MORRIS COLLECTION

When, in March 1907, the Isle of Wight company got itself into difficulties he was tempted into managing its affairs, which he sought to do from his Westminster office. This firm, however, proved beyond resuscitation, but Mackenzie in the meantime had opened an office in Ryde, IoW, whence he gathered DL motor vehicle registrations in careful numerical sequence for the last four companies listed, plus three others which he subsequently managed – the Sussex Motor Road Car Co. Ltd, Worthing Motor Services Ltd and – after the founding of Wilts & Dorset Motor Services Ltd – Southdown. The numerical sequencing was in-filled where necessary by employing BP (West Sussex) and CD (Brighton) registrations and, so Maurice Coombes told David Pennels, turning to County Armagh at one stage, the only authority prepared to grant him sequential numbers (IB series) which he could reserve in a block, but take up over a period of time. Thus his early vehicles were referred to by the numbers only of their registration, which were never duplicated.

This, then, was the methodical Douglas Mackenzie, who came along with his colleagues, Cannon and Lephard, to meet Maurice Coombes and discuss terms with him. Apart from his somewhat difficult experience with traction engines on Salisbury Plain in 1901, he brought with him the memory of a brief episode during 1908 in what was destined to become the south eastern corner of Wilts & Dorset territory. In addition to Sussex Motor Road Car excursions and tours offices he'd opened at Hastings, Eastbourne, Newhaven and Seaford, was another at the George Inn Yard beside the Bargate, Southampton (Hants), whence an unlicensed vehicle had been run back and forth to Lyndhurst – part of an unsuccessful attempt to gain a foothold in Southampton.

Such a plan was still in his mind at the time of the formation of Wilts & Dorset and of Southdown Motor Services Ltd. The registered name of the latter company had to be changed at the last minute from the preferred 'South Coast Motor Services Ltd' (in June 1915; see Morris 1985) because officers at Companies House found the name to be too similar to another company in that field, recently incorporated. The intended area for 'South Coast Motor Services Ltd' was to range from Hastings in the east – to Weymouth (Dorset) in the west.

For some time after the founding of Southdown, its declared territory was in the west 'bounded by a line drawn from and including Weymouth, Salisbury (Wilts) to Winchester (Hants) – until, at length, Mackenzie and

Percy Lephard: although described as an 'agriculturalist', it is clear that his link with Mackenzie and Cannon came through social connections initially, not least by becoming an eager participant in that duo's early motor tours of Britain. A sufficient amount of a family fortune, made in the paper manufacturing industry, came his way to enable him to make a strong contribution to the setting up of Wilts & Dorset. He became its first chairman. COLIN MORRIS COLLECTION

Cannon reluctantly came to terms with the fact that William Wells Graham had, together with another important 'mover and shaker' of the emergent motor omnibus industry, Walter Flexman French, formed Bournemouth & District Motor Services Ltd (Hants & Dorset) in 1916, thus putting the territory between Poole and Southampton, at the very least, beyond their reach.

And the bitter pill to be swallowed with that was that the founding chairman of Southdown, he who'd actually come up with that substitute name at the last minute, was – Walter Flexman French. It is clear from the intermittent attempts thereafter to forge physical links between Wilts & Dorset and Southdown operations, that Mackenzie and Cannon's initial interest in taking over and expanding what Maurice Coombes had started was part and parcel of their wider plans for what would have been 'South Coast Motor Services Ltd' (and the name for that ironically came from Walter Flexman French's 'London & South Coast Haulage Co. Ltd – also incorporated into Southdown). Such attempts gained some momentum after the somewhat premature death, following an accident, of French at the age of 69, in 1925.

The enigmatic figure of the trio from Worthing was Percy Edwin Lephard – earmarked to become the first chairman of Wilts & Dorset. He appears in a photograph, together with Mackenzie and Cannon, beside a Daimler of Worthing Motor Services' 'Sussex Tourist Coaches' tour to the Lake District in 1914. Alan Lambert's records show that he was not a director of Worthing Motor Services Ltd, but it is highly likely that his shareholding in that company was considerable. Charles F. Klapper and Charles E. Lee (1978), founders of the Omnibus Society in 1929, variously describe him as a 'member of the Lephard family; the Brighton paper merchants' – and that Cannon and Mackenzie 'relied on finance' from that source to set up Wilts & Dorset. Klapper was in fairly regular correspondence with Mackenzie, so that must have come from the horse's mouth. How much? The nominal capital at registration, on 4 January 1915, of £5,000 proved, as was usual in such matters, a shade optimistic, and by 5 June 1915 1,000 £1 shares remained unissued. A total of 501 shares had been taken up by Percy Lephard – an 'agriculturalist' of 'Highfield', West Tarring, Worthing; 125 by his wife Mabell; 50 by his widowed mother Elizabeth of The Manor House, West Worthing. So was the rest of the Lephard family contribution within the 1,125 shares in Wilts & Dorset taken up by Worthing Motor Services Ltd? Well, yes: 125; 60; 20 respectively – making an £881 family contribution toward the initial target. By the same date – and by comparison – Douglas Mackenzie had by both routes taken up 456 shares; Alfred Cannon 650.

Other shareholders hailed from Worthing – among them William Wenban Smith, whose family still trade as builders' merchants in the resort, and Salisbury – John Hart the butcher, of Butcher Row, weighing in with £100, to become the first local subscriber.

In its early years Wilts & Dorset depended heavily on vehicles hired from other operators. IB708 was a Daimler B that belonged to Worthing Motor Services, which sought to avoid sounding too parochial by using the 'Sussex Tourist Coaches' title on some of its buses. It is believed to have come to Wiltshire in November or December 1914, possibly only for a brief spell. During that time it carried a Hora 30-seat body new earlier that year. ALAN LAMBERT COLLECTION

46 High Street, Amesbury; his Scout bus; Ford taxi; garage business; and the goodwill of his stage carriage service between Amesbury and Salisbury.

Shortly before Christmas 1914, whilst the details were still being formalised, a Daimler B (IB708) with Silent Knight sleeve-valve engine and a 30-seat Hora body built to Mackenzie's own tiered-slipper design, was sent up from Worthing to operate from Amesbury to Larkhill Camp, and the Amesbury–Woodford Valley–Salisbury routes, in support of Coombes' original (still yellow) 40 hp 22-seater Scout. The 'borrowed' Daimler was painted in WMS' green and cream livery and labelled 'Sussex Tourist Coaches'.

The formal agreement with Maurice Coombes was signed on 16 March 1915. In return for 100 £1 shares and employment as Wilts & Dorset's Amesbury manager, Coombes handed over title to his leasehold premises at

It is difficult to take too seriously Klapper's claim that Mackenzie and Cannon 'frankly formed (Wilts & Dorset) to cash in on the wartime stationing of troops on Salisbury Plain'. For although that may have seemed a potential banker, other than going to Larkhill and Bulford, they did not initially fan outward to serve the various camps, save a brief extension to Sling in December 1914. Instead, they reinforced the route southward to Salisbury to establish what every new bus company needs – a reasonably well-populated town or city at the centre of things. In Salisbury they opened an office, at 16 Queen Street.

And when they laid hands upon some additional vehicles the military did not wish to requisition – some more locally built Scouts – they sent Coombes' original

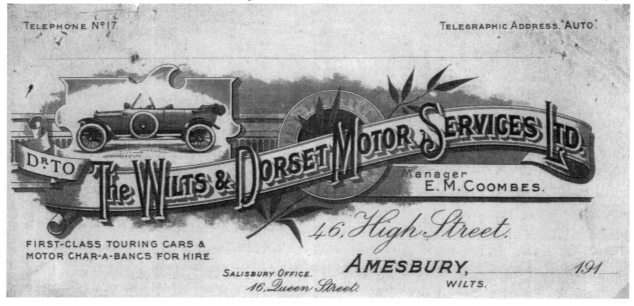

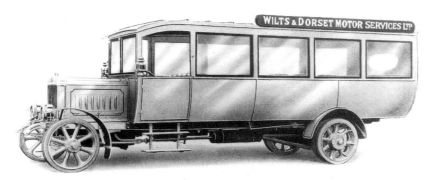

Maurice Coombes said his 1914 saloon had the first Scout chassis to be fitted with a worm-driven rear axle, 'which was not very satisfactory'. Previous chassis from the Bemerton works of Alfred and William Burden were chain-driven. Coombes said his vehicle was painted yellow and had about 22 seats along the sides and at the rear. The lack of chain-case in front of the rear wheels suggests that this picture is of Coombes' first bus, but this cannot be confirmed. DAVID PENNELS COLLECTION

one south to Cranborne in Dorset to 'mark that gatepost' as quickly as possible, under the care of driver/manager Vatter.

In a letter to David Pennels in 1963, R. Maskell, who had worked for both Coombes and Wilts & Dorset, recorded the Scout's weekly schedule whilst at Cranborne in 1915:

Mon: reserved for its maintenance
Tues, Thurs, Sat: Salisbury via Damerham, Rockbourne,
      Coombe Bissett
Wed: Ringwood via Edmondsham, Woodlands, Verwood
Fri: Poole via Edmondsham, Woodlands, Horton, Holt,
      Wimborne
Sun: no service from Cranborne (see below

This record is invaluable, because it illustrates a classic piece of Mackenzie 'suck it and see' – a probing for traffic potential, as he was to do so successfully at Southdown. It also lends great weight to the view that the direction in which the probing was taking place marked a determined attempt to 'infill' as soon as possible towards Weymouth – as marked on a map kept somewhere in a drawer at Mackenzie's 'Counting House', the WMS office at 23 Marine Parade, Worthing. Coombes recalled (1961) that the vehicle went back up to Amesbury to help out on the Salisbury run

when the troops from Larkhill and Bulford Camps had Sunday leave – always a busy day.

The probing to Wimborne and Poole proved premature (by several decades), but the Wednesday journeys to Ringwood brought Wilts & Dorset into contact with A.A. Brewer's one-Scout-bus operation in that Hampshire town and, in March 1915, his 25-seat Pullman saloon, plus its one-per-day runs from Ringwood to Southampton or to Salisbury, became the second acquisition by Wilts & Dorset. So far as Mackenzie was concerned, a route into Southampton from the west would 'do very nicely, thank you', and driver/manager Keats was placed in charge at Ringwood.

above] In March 1915 Wilts & Dorset made its first acquisition of another bus operator, A.A. Brewer of Ringwood, who ran to Salisbury and to Southampton. His Scout bus was described as having a 26-seat Pullman body built by Acton, whose premises were in Greencroft Street, Salisbury. It was painted French grey with a contrasting green line, and the interior had walnut woodwork and decorative gold stars on the roof panels. This manufacturer's illustration is believed to show the Brewer vehicle. DAVID PENNELS COLLECTION

left] A Wilts & Dorset Scout charabanc poses for the camera before setting out from Salisbury Market Square in 1915 or 1916. At the wheel of IB802 (2), the company's first charabanc, is Cyril Adams, later proprietor of Victory Tours, Sixpenny Handley. Inspector Bean stands by the bonnet. Scout Motors Ltd of Bemerton built the chassis. Marks of Wilton may have built the body. DAVID PENNELS COLLECTION

The destination board on Scout bus IB804 (4) shows the company's first route, Amesbury-Woodford-Salisbury. Driver Leonard is at the wheel. Inspector Bean wears the boater and Norfolk jacket. The body, nicknamed 'The Greenhouse' was transferred from a Worthing Motor Services vehicle. Douglas Mackenzie, director of both Wilts & Dorset and the Worthing firm, apparently chose to register vehicles in County Armagh because it was the only authority that agreed to assign consecutive numbers to vehicles entering service at widely separated intervals. DAVID PENNELS COLLECTION

And that, until after World War I, marked the limit of stage carriage operations. Four new Scout chassis, plus the one from Brewer, had entered the fleet during the conflict. They were joined in August 1916 by a McCurd, built at Hayes in Middlesex, and fitted with a second-hand Brush saloon body. It was destined to become something of a star performer in the post-war fleet, far outlasting the Scouts.

The two Napier cabs sent to operate at the beck and call of the Larkhill officers' mess were replaced in the summer of 1915 by three touring cars – all 20 hp models: a Hupmobile and two Fords. Mackenzie got to work on the registration numbers of these as well, including Coombes' original Ford which, with help from across the Irish Sea (County Mayo), became IZ406 – until it was lost by collision early in 1917. At one stage in the war the four Scout buses operating were IB801/2/3/4 and the four touring cars BP405, IZ406, CD2413 which became 'something or other' 407 and CD408. All eight vehicles were registered to Wilts & Dorset Motor Services Ltd, 23 Marine Parade, Worthing – probably as a result of the number changes.

On 16 March 1915, Coombes' 'old friend' Frederick Sutton, the confectioner, purchased 100 shares in Wilts & Dorset and was promptly made a director. So too did George Henry Davis, the auctioneer of St. Thomas's Square, Salisbury – with the same result. The first annual

general meeting of the company took place on Friday 31 March 1916 at Davis's offices. Mackenzie and Cannon had become joint managing directors. Because of the war, the board had adopted the principle of setting aside a large sum for depreciation. In addition, to 'meet the heavy taxation now imposed', they recommended a dividend of five per cent, less income tax – which would absorb £170, and that £59.1s.4d. should be carried forward. A new garage had been completed at Amesbury: thus Wilts & Dorset marched forward into its second year.

At the beginning of 1916, the over two million volunteers who had joined the army found new, and less willing, comrades in arms, as the compulsory military recruitment of single men – and, later, married men – between 19 and 41 years was enforced. The camps now took them in, trained them as quickly as possible, and got them out to the trenches in France at the double. For those on the Plain, the Somme became a more likely destination than a weekend trip into Salisbury. It seems inappropriately unfeeling to claim that Wilts & Dorset suffered accordingly. The loss of traffic, plus difficulties in obtaining spares, and new equipment in particular –

The McCurd Lorry Mfg. Co. Ltd, of Hayes, Middlesex, advertised its chassis with the slogan 'Thought out first – Not found out afterwards.' Wilts & Dorset must have agreed; it kept its McCurd, IB806 (6), for 10 years until 1926. It was the company's first bus to be painted red. The Brush body, with perimeter seating for 26 passengers, was originally on a Southend-on-Sea Corporation Tilling-Stevens. DAVID PENNELS COLLECTION

led to the imposition of a larger allowance for depreciation – and no dividend for the shareholders.

The close of the year saw Alfred Cannon called up for service with the Royal Engineers. Much of his time, until his release in 1919, was spent as a lieutenant near Arras with the army's Railway Operating Division – a reversion to his apprenticeship days' experience with the GWR. He was followed into the military by Wilts & Dorset's Amesbury manager, Maurice Coombes, who became a captain in the Army Service Corps (RASC from 1918), concerned in his case with military road transport. He has put it on record that he left with assurances that, if he survived the conflict, he would, upon his return, be reinstated in post.

Back in Wiltshire, things went from bad to worse. In October 1917 Wilts & Dorset possessed three buses – just one of which was in service; and four taxicabs – none of which was in paying service. Twelve months later, it had two buses in stock – one of which, a Southdown Straker-Squire, was hired – and the two remaining taxis had earned absolutely nothing throughout that whole year of 1918. In contrast the garage sales and repair business, and the letting of the cars, had earned £1,319 in 1917 and £668 in 1918 – as against £2,510 and £2,133 respectively in bus traffic receipts. By such a thread hung the fortunes of Wilts & Dorset at that time.

At Amesbury, the absent Maurice Coombes had been replaced as local manager by a trusted driver from Worthing, George Wallis – 'as he has had many years experience of the *motor omnibus* (Mackenzie was also secretary at this stage) industry, the directors feel that he will do his best for the company's interests under the present difficult conditions'. A McCurd hired from Southdown was probably its no. 21 (CD3327) – a 28-seat coach, which was on loan in 1919, because it turned up again in Sussex the following year, after a year's absence.

Immediately after the Armistice (the cessation of hostilities) in November 1918, orders were placed for up-to-date rolling stock. But the manufacturers, still geared to the production of military vehicles, were not in a position to respond. The 1919 season was well advanced before even the mass refurbishment, for public service use, of ex-military chassis – particularly of AEC and Daimler manufacture – got under way; a large clearing centre at Slough becoming the main source of supply. Thus it was that the first post-war bus to arrive at Wilts & Dorset – an AEC YC charabanc – did not enter service until June 1919.

In the meantime, Maurice Coombes – happy to have survived (750,000 had not) – reported back for his promised re-engagement with Wilts & Dorset, to be informed that the company was unable to fulfil what he reasonably considered was its obligation. Cannon survived also, but had not returned in time to become involved in such an outcome, although, as a joint managing director his position was, of course, secure.

Mackenzie? He has been described as one of the nicest, most fair-minded employers one could have wished to work for – and most of his time was spent, head down, in his 'Counting House' at Worthing. Lephard was seldom in Wiltshire as well. Fred Sutton? Years afterwards Coombes still referred to him as his 'old friend'. Mackenzie, however, 'owing to pressure of business' had resigned the position of secretary (although he remained a director of Wilts & Dorset) and he had been replaced in that post by George Davis. Coombes had no word for *him*.

There are, of course, two sides to every dispute. Here was a company which had suffered trading losses in the two previous years; one which also felt that it ought to protect the position of George Wallis, the trusted employee brought in from Worthing, since he was too old for military service. Personalities aside, however, it was a shabby episode which, curiously, was to be repeated somewhat in another which took place 53 years later, as the story of *this* Wilts & Dorset came to a close (see Chapter 9).

Whatever, Maurice Coombes, who now set up home in Winchester Street, Salisbury, used his military gratuity to purchase a yellow Thornycroft charabanc – bodied by his brother-in-law's Salisbury Carriage Works – and which he defiantly called *The Victory*, thus setting down his marker. His 100 shares in Wilts & Dorset were sold on 10 October 1919 – to George Davis.

The registered office of Wilts & Dorset had been removed from 46 High Street, Amesbury, to Davis's office at 2 St Thomas's Square, Salisbury on 5 February 1917 – just after Coombes had left to join the army. On 13 June of that year, land and premises in Salisbury Street, Amesbury, were acquired and a replacement garage was built upon the site.

Although compulsory military recruitment did not cease until 30 April 1920, troops and airmen from Europe and Mesopotamia began returning to local camps and depots in 1919, boosting custom in the process. The arrival of two open-topped double deckers that year, one an AEC, the other a Leyland, saw the opening of a route between Salisbury and Wilton in September, with a single fare of 8d (about 3.3 pence). The departures were at half-hourly intervals from Harnham Bridge, City Centre, and Wilton Market. A garage for one vehicle was rented from John White in Wilton, and in November 1920 two houses and a 'motor garage' in Castle Street, Salisbury, were purchased. George Wallis was transferred to the latter as 'garage manager'.

On 24 October 1919 the nominal capital of the company was raised to £15,000 to meet the cost of planned expansion. In order to make this target realistic, it became necessary, on 7 August 1920, for Wilts & Dorset to become a public company.

Having reached Ringwood in 1915, it was not until April 1920 that Mackenzie and Cannon managed to get a stage-carriage service extended to the coast at Christchurch

Buses delivered from 1919 up to mid-1920 were all registered in Brighton. CD3177 (10), an AEC YC, heads south through woodland towards Bournemouth. Wilts & Dorset reached the Hampshire (as it then was) seaside resort in 1920. This was soon to become a joint service with Hants & Dorset. No. 10 kept its Dodson CD19 body with its characteristic clerestory roof for most of its working life, but some time before it was withdrawn in 1929 this was replaced by an ex-Southdown dual-purpose body. COLIN MORRIS COLLECTION

By mid-1920 seven AEC and Leyland buses had been delivered, enabling Wilts & Dorset to overcome the severe shortage of vehicles that had afflicted it between 1918 and mid-1919. CD5247 (11), one of the Leylands, had a 33-seat Harrington charabanc body. It had police plates permitting it to operate in Salisbury and Southampton. The Brighton registration reflected the close links with South-down Motor Services Ltd. DAVID PENNELS COLLECTION

Two Wilts & Dorset charabancs wait to set off from the White Horse Inn with around 60 happy trippers from Quidhampton, probably in the summer of 1920. Both vehicles had Harrington bodies, like most of the company's coaches up to the end of the 'thirties. Leyland CD5247 (11) was delivered complete in May 1920. The AEC behind it, CD3330 (7), was a year older and had a body intended for a longer chassis. Marks of Wilton are believed to have adapted it to fit. DAVID PENNELS COLLECTION

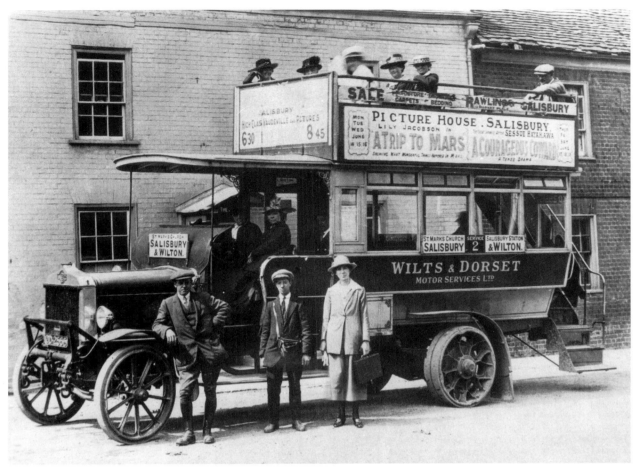

The company's first double deck was Brush-bodied AEC YC CD2555 (8). Driver Bert Cooper went to Sussex to collect it in July 1919. The seat alongside the driver was a prime place to pose for photographs, but dusty in dry weather and damp when it rained. How many of the passengers who rode to Wilton in this bone-shaking 45-seater would have imagined that within 80 years unmanned spacecraft would indeed have been making a trip to Mars? DAVID PENNELS COLLECTION

and Bournemouth. To do that, they had to put up with the fact that, initially, Bournemouth Council would only permit Wilts & Dorset through to the Lansdowne (rather than Bournemouth Square); and grant reciprocal running arrangements to Salisbury for William Wells Graham's *Bournemouth & District*. This joint operation became very popular and the Wilts & Dorset board discovered that citizens of Warminster and Trowbridge were coming to Salisbury by train, and using the buses to continue the journey to the seaside; information acted upon in the obvious way the following year.

As the troops returned to the Plain for demobilisation – a process which by its very nature eventually diminished passenger numbers – there was a comparatively short flurry of traffic for the coaching side of Wilts & Dorset's business. Added to the euphoric response to the restoration of peace evident among the local civilian populace, this briefly created a situation where 'advance orders for the coming season are so good that no advertised public tours will be undertaken'. It would be harsh to suggest that this was just as well, because at that stage Wilts & Dorset didn't have sufficient specialised vehicles to cope.

This upward trend in the figures for 'passengers carried' was then put into reverse gear by events in Ireland. During and after the 1916 Easter Rising in Dublin it had been considered necessary to reinforce the loyalist Irish regiments in situ with units drawn from British county regiments. In the midst of World War I, and expecting to fight in France, many of these newly trained recruits thought that was where they had landed. After the Armistice, the build-up of troops in Ireland increased apace, until, by 1920, their numbers had increased to somewhere in the region of 40,000. Many of them seem to have been sent from camps on Salisbury Plain, for an article on Wilts & Dorset published as late as April 1921 noted that 'with so many troops now in Ireland [traffic] is not so marked as it has been'.

As if things were not bad enough from that quarter, Wilts & Dorset's fortunes received another set-back from the carefully planned retaliatory action now brought to bear by Maurice Coombes. On 10 March 1920, together with James Street and Thomas Kerr as fellow directors, and C. Kenelm Hubert as secretary, Coombes launched Salisbury & District Motor Services Ltd – the title surely inspired by William Graham's firm at Bournemouth. It

right] S. & E. Collett, the Salisbury agents for the Canadian Maxwell chassis had this 16-seat charabanc painted in Wilts & Dorset red in 1920 and displayed it in their showroom. Salisbury Carriage Works built the body. The company bought HR3186 (14) so none of its rivals could run it in competition. It proved unreliable and was sold after less than three years to a buyer at the other end of Wiltshire. DAVID PENNELS COLLECTION

below] Wilts & Dorset made a short-lived foray in 1921 from Salisbury to Trowbridge, where Dodson-bodied AEC YC CD5248 (12) stands ready for the return journey. Another bus used on this 30-mile route was the solitary McCurd, no. 6. The route ran parallel to the Salisbury-Bath railway line and the service was cut short at Warminster at the end of the year. The company did not reach Trowbridge again for nearly 10 years. DAVID PENNELS COLLECTION

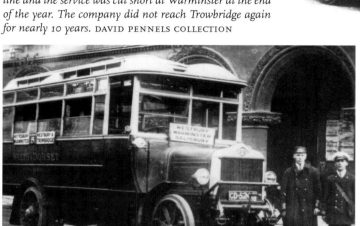

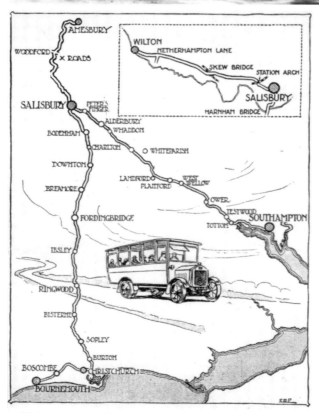

Published in Motor Transport *4 April 1921*

was incorporated as a private company with the capital divided into 10,000 shares of £1 each. Eventually, every employee was listed among the shareholders.

No doubt with some glee, this firm's registered office was established at 14 Queen Street, Salisbury, right next to what had been Wilts & Dorset's original Salisbury office at no. 16. Salisbury & District acquired the lease of the Angel Garage in Fisherton Street, rented premises in Wilton, and based Kerr's Thornycroft saloon contribution to the fleet at its original Fordingbridge lair. It then set out to cross swords with Wilts & Dorset along all three of its established routes, with a fleet which quickly grew to nine vehicles: seven Thornycroft Js and two ex-War Department 14-seat Crossley 8J tenders – not far short of the number of buses that a struggling Wilts & Dorset could muster.

In combating the competition put up by Coombes and his colleagues, Wilts & Dorset incurred expenses which materially affected its efforts to make a profit, in the first six months of 1921 in particular, as the Salisbury & District fleet was brought up to its full complement. Some 14 months after the launch of what became known locally as 'The Yellow Victory', Wilts & Dorset's directors emerged waving a flag of truce. That probably came rather too quickly for Maurice Coombes, who was most likely enjoying the turn of events considerably. If nothing else, his spell of military service had taught him how to put up a good fight.

On 30 June 1921, the two companies reached an accommodation, whereby Wilts & Dorset prepared to take over the whole of the assets and liabilities of Salisbury & District. As the annual general meeting of Wilts & Dorset was told in April 1922 . . . Salisbury & District was 'wound up voluntarily. This procedure necessitated the provision of a considerable capital sum which was readily forthcoming, mostly from the old shareholders . . .' Although this was achieved without increasing the capital of Wilts & Dorset beyond £15,000,

above left] A Wilts & Dorset conductor sets the time in Salisbury: 'Next bus for Wilton 11.37'. Unfortunately some well-meaning dear old ladies thought such departure-time devices were real clocks, and told toe-tapping conductors: 'Young man, your clocks are always fast'. COLIN MORRIS COLLECTION

above] Wilts & Dorset's first all-Leyland bus arrived in 1921 at the height of the battle for traffic with E.M. Coombes' Salisbury & District. HR4483 (16) was a G3-type with 45 seats. The company put double decks on the Harnham-Wilton service in 1919. Coombes responded with two Thornycroft double decks of his own in 1920. COLIN MORRIS COLLECTION

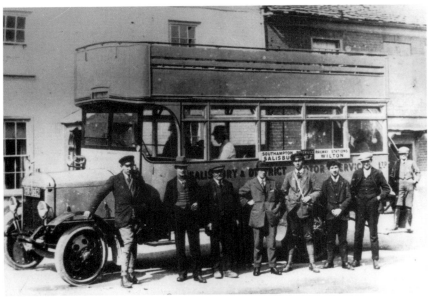

left] E.M. Coombes, in the hat, stands defiantly among the crew of his Salisbury & District bus and workers at Salisbury Carriage Works, who built the body. The driver on the left of the picture is Cyril Adams, who was soon to set up Victory Tours, of Sixpenny Handley, together with his father. Sitting inside the vehicle is Joe Gilbert, who worked for the coachbuilder. The Thornycroft J bus, HR1952, became Wilts & Dorset's no. 22 in 1921. DAVID PENNELS COLLECTION

there can be little doubt that the purchase price of Salisbury & District was exceeded only by what the company was to spend upon the acquisition of Sparrow & Vincent's *Victory Motor Services* and Shergold & White's *Silver Star Motor Services Ltd*, many years later.

Because the negotiations proved to be a lengthy process, involving Lloyds Bank in Salisbury, the actual cost of the purchase did not emerge on the 'purchase date' – 2 August 1921 – and is therefore not mentioned in the formal agreement or the directors' minutes. It could not have been far short of £10,000, for the formula seems to have been '£1 each for 10,000 shares the holders were prepared to sell, plus 35 £1 shares in Wilts & Dorset for E.M. Coombes'. One S&D driver

and four conductors carried their shares over into a W&D holding. In Maurice Coombes' own words (1961), the whole S&D fleet was taken over 'at a very substantial amount above its value, to the satisfaction of everyone concerned'.

To have achieved so much in such a short space of time, during a period when local traffic was not at its best, speaks volumes for the three S&D directors. Rather than adopt the policy of appointing to the board – 1980s fashion – tradesmen from outside the field of transport, it does suggest that Wilts & Dorset missed out big-time by not offering a directorship to Coombes at the outset. An interesting adjunct to all this is that one of Coombes' drivers, Cyril Adams, returned to Sixpenny Handley and

right] Acton & Co, of 2 Greencroft Street, Salisbury, built this imposing 42-seat body for Salisbury & District in 1920. Painted yellow, it must have cut quite a dash on the city's streets. Like most of E.M. Coombes' 'Yellow Victory fleet it was on a Thornycroft J chassis. Supplied by S. & E. Collett, of Catherine Street, it was registered HR3037. When Wilts & Dorset bought Coombes out in August 1921 this bus became its number 23.
COLIN MORRIS COLLECTION

below] The lady wins on style in this study of contemporary headgear. She stands beside one of Salisbury & Districts two ex-War Department Crossley tenders. The happy trippers were photographed outside Sydenham's shop at Bournemouth Pier. The Crossleys were nicknamed 'the soapbox' and 'the sardine can'. This is probably HR2275, to which Salisbury Carriage Works fitted perimeter seating. DAVID PENNELS COLLECTION

helped his father Albert set up the Handley-based *Victory Motor Service*. Although this operation was not acquired by Wilts & Dorset, the name *Victory* was set to turn up to haunt the company from time to time before World War II.

In the meantime, prime minister Lloyd George's best efforts (or, rather, the best he could achieve – and which pleased hardly anyone), led to parliament recognising an 'Irish Free State' with dominion status. Civil war promptly broke out in the Emerald Isle between those revolutionaries who approved the concessionary treaty – and those who did not.

It seemed an appropriate time to withdraw some British troops; and gradually the camps on Salisbury Plain became once again an economic prospect in the fortunes of Wilts & Dorset. The company started running to Old Sarum Aerodrome in February 1921, and to Blandford the following June. Services to

left] One of the three Thornycroft J charabancs that Wilts & Dorset inherited from Salisbury & District, HR1887 became Wilts & Dorset's no. 18. It was later rebodied as a saloon. Salisbury & District did not use fleet numbers so the number 5 on the bonnet presents a mystery. The most likely explanation is that when Wilts & Dorset took over in August 1921 it used the vehicle before repainting it, and assigned it a temporary number.
DAVID PENNELS COLLECTION

right] HR5605 (25), the second of the two Crossleys that Wilts & Dorset took over from Salisbury & District in 1921. Salisbury Carriage Works, Wilton Road, built the 14-seat charabanc body. The young man wearing a dark suit at the front is Raymond Longman, who became secretary of the company in 1924. Just visible, behind the passengers' heads, is the top of Edward Locke's Landford Motor Service bus. DAVID PENNELS COLLECTION

below right] HR4559 (17) outlasted the other six Thornycrofts that Wilts & Dorset took over from Salisbury & District in 1921. Acquired as a charabanc, it was rebodied first as a saloon and in 1925 by Dodson as a 45-seat double deck. The pneumatic tyres were fitted in about 1927. The driver's uniform still included breeches. DAVID PENNELS COLLECTION

If the gentleman wishing the trippers a good day out needed an overcoat, they certainly had to wrap up well for a journey in an open charabanc. Could scenes such as this have prompted unkind comparison of an ill-favoured face to 'the back end of a bus'? HR5605 and the other ex-Salisbury & District Crossley were sent to Larkhill Camp as 'chasers' in August 1926, when the company was competing for traffic there. DAVID PENNELS COLLECTION

Porton (January 1922), Fargo – where a military hospital encampment had been established – (June 1922) followed, and Larkhill, which had gone without a Wilts & Dorset service for some considerable time, had that facility restored in September 1922. A route from Salisbury to the Tidworth camps commenced in January 1923.

Additionally, throughout this period, a considerable number of 'first journeys' are to be found in the company records. Many appear to be further cases of Mackenzie and Cannon probing for custom, whilst some may represent local tours, private hire or contract work – no differentiation is made. Three in the first category are of particular note, however: one return journey on Fridays only began in March 1921 between Salisbury and Southampton; bearing in mind where some of the early Bournemouth-route passengers had hailed from, a logical step of a connecting service (August 1921) between Salisbury, Warminster, Westbury and Trowbridge; Salisbury and Blandford Forum (June 1921) then went on to Dorchester (October 1921) – thus drawing that symbolic line towards Weymouth as originally planned as a boundary marker for South Coast Motor Services. In similar vein, on 31 August 1921, Wilts & Dorset wrote to Hants & Dorset proposing a joint service from Southampton to Winchester via Romsey – and claimed the right to 'run into Winchester via any road north of Romsey'. A surely foreseeable curt reply was received; 'since these roads were distinctly within Hants & Dorset territory, it could not agree to Wilts & Dorset running such a service'. Clearly alarmed, Hants & Dorset promptly started its own Romsey-Winchester service; found that it didn't pay – and withdrew it in March 1922.

The first note of what became a popular charabanc excursion from Salisbury was made in October 1921, that to Larmer Tree – once the site of an ancient elm tree which marked the boundary on Cranborne Chase between Dorset and Wilts. The Larmer Grounds were stocked by General Augustus Pitt-Rivers in the late 19th century with 'Greek temples' and archaeological curiosities.

The returns for that month also include £1.10s.0d (£1.50) earned for one round trip from Bournemouth to Sandbanks – Hants & Dorset territory. The likely scenario is that Hants & Dorset's scheduled vehicle refused to start, and Wilts & Dorset's crew on lay-over from Salisbury were asked to make that one journey in their own vehicle (probably McCurd IB806) – and promptly took the fares earned back to Salisbury to be cashed in. Such initiatives taken by employees on the spot were not likely to have been frowned upon by the management of either company. Licence-issuing Bournemouth Council would not have approved, but they probably never found out.

An odd spin-off from the thrust toward the south-west was the temporary testing for potential traffic on sparsely populated Cranborne Chase. Once past the Dorset boundary – a lonely former stage-coach inn, the Shaftesbury Arms – at Woodyates, the road becomes very wild and solitary, at Handley Cross particularly. Yet Wilts & Dorset based a bus at Sixpenny Handley, less than a windswept mile to the west of that point whence, from November 1921, it undertook journeys, on a limited schedule probably, to Shaftesbury and Farnham – the

latter just a mile away. In January 1922, trips to Ringwood and to Blandford were tried – it appears with little success. Perhaps Coombes was involved in that attempt, for he was at least 'offered' re-employment in a managerial role as part of the 1921 agreement – and both location and timing seem appropriate, possibly in conjunction with Adams. The latter purchased the abandoned Wilts & Dorset garage at Handley soon afterward.

However, on Wednesdays from December 1921 the Handley vehicle was switched to Codford in the Wylye Valley. That day it ran to Warminster and Frome (Somerset), where it spent some four hours before returning to Codford St Mary.

After the abandonment of Handley, in April 1922, a Thursdays only run started to Chitterne, Lavington and Devizes (at the time the eastern extremity of the Bath Tramways Motor Co Ltd network). Since it did not appear to go via Tilshead, it may have served the doomed little community at Imber en route. Harold Couchman's *Wylye Valley Motor Services* certainly served that village (from Warminster) until it was compulsorily evacuated for military training purposes in World War II – and remains thus to this day. Codford to Wishford that same April was extended to Salisbury on Tuesdays, whilst a journey to Wylye went on to Dinton in January 1923 – day unrecorded. April 1922 saw short journeys to Warminster run on Mondays. Codford to Hindon (June 1922) was extended to Wincanton (Somerset) in April 1923 – one month after the first journey from Codford to Tilshead is listed.

During this near-desperate search for custom, there came the first indication that a closer relationship with the 'interloping' Hants & Dorset company – rather than Southdown – was seriously considered. In May 1922, Lephard and Cannon called upon Walter Flexman French at his Putney home, where it was suggested that Hants & Dorset should take a financial interest in the Wilts & Dorset company. As a result, Albert Webster, Hants & Dorset's secretary, was instructed to obtain particulars of Wilts & Dorset's affairs, together with a copy of its latest balance sheet. Unfortunately, the first volume (1915-26) of the Wilts & Dorset directors' minutes has not survived, so we have no record of the outcome from a Wilts & Dorset perspective. Nor indeed from Hants & Dorset's, for the matter is not mentioned again – save the comment in the latter's minutes that 'until such an agreement might be reached, each company should continue to take their own receipts

In the three years after it won the battle with Salisbury & District in 1921, Wilts & Dorset bought only four new vehicles. HR9541 (27) was the only double deck among them. A Leyland G7 with body by Harrington, it was put to work on Salisbury city services. 'Stations' on the destination board referred to the adjacent Great Western and Southern Railway stations. The company fitted it with pneumatic tyres in about 1927. DAVID PENNELS COLLECTION

Raymond Longman: originally an assistant to George Davis, a Salisbury auctioneer and estate agent, who was secretary of Wilts & Dorset from 1919 to 1924. Longman himself became W&D secretary from 1924 to 1942, a director from 1927 to 1962, and chairman 1949-1962. Whilst Alfred Cannon retained control over the make and type of buses to be purchased, all other aspects of Wilts & Dorset's well-being fell increasingly into Longman's capable hands. DAVID PENNELS COLLECTION

upon the Southampton and Salisbury route'. No such financial interest was taken, either then or upon a later occasion.

No help there then; yet, curiously – in the very lean 'twenties for Wilts & Dorset – the company's publicity material took on a Hants & Dorset, rather than a Southdown flavour. In particular, instead of resembling the latter's timetable booklets (by the Southern Publishing Co Ltd), Wilts & Dorset's were printed in Hants & Dorset style and layout by H&D's chosen local philanthropist Edward Pearce, at the Boscombe Printing Company's works, Bournemouth – with red cover, of course, rather than Hants & Dorset's green.

Back in the military sphere, Netheravon finally got a Wilts & Dorset service from Salisbury in September 1923. A glance at Pennels' fleet history (1963) shows that all this activity must have been undertaken with Wilts & Dorset's AECs and Leylands and the ex-Salisbury & District Thornycrofts. A one-off Maxwell and two 14-seat Crossleys would have picked up the cricket and skittles matches, Sunday-school outings and pub crawls. The McCurd's stamping ground was, in the main, the Bournemouth run. Until October 1923, Wilts & Dorset

possessed just 21 vehicles. Light maintenance work was carried out in Castle Street garage in Salisbury, but all heavy docking was undertaken during this period by Southdown Motor Services Ltd at Brighton. In addition to the garage at Castle Street, extended in 1923, Wilts & Dorset had taken up the lease of the Fisherton Street garage, whilst accommodation for vehicles was provided at Amesbury, Fordingbridge, Larkhill Camp and Wilton. In 1924 a garage at Netheravon was added to the list.

Alfred Cannon resigned his post as joint managing director in 1924, but retained his directorship of the company. That September, George Davis, joint managing director and secretary, died in office. His post as secretary (only) was taken up by Raymond Longman, Davis's assistant in the estate agency business. Since Davis's office was also the registered office of Wilts & Dorset, Longman had familiarised himself with the running of that company also. His signature first appeared on a Wilts & Dorset document on 22 July 1920, when he witnessed the signing of a contract. He was at the time living in Coombe Road, Salisbury!

In this humble way, the man who was to become the most influential figure in the conduct of the company's affairs entered the motor omnibus industry. Raymond Ilfred Henry Longman was the son of a Winfrith, Dorset, farmer. Called to the colours in World War I, by the age of 21 he was based at the Central Flying School, Upavon, where, in addition to the training of pilots for the Royal Flying Corps, the testing of modifications to production aircraft was undertaken for such firms as Armstrong Whitworth Aircraft Ltd. Perhaps it was there that he also rubbed shoulders with personnel from the Royal Naval Air Service for, in addition to acquiring a lifelong interest in flying, he was to take to the sea in some style when sufficient funds became available. Upon demobilisation in July 1919, he had re-joined Davis's firm at 2 St Thomas's Square, Salisbury – eventually becoming a partner.

Frederick Sutton, by then a justice of the peace, had been elected vice chairman of Wilts & Dorset in 1919. Sadly, he died on 6 March 1926, to be replaced as a director by William Fielden, a gas engineer of Harnham House, Salisbury, since it was felt that 'his experience as a manager in commercial undertakings will be of considerable benefit to the company'. It was a benefit which was to last until his retirement, aged 76, on 31 December 1952. A shareholder in Wilts & Dorset since 24 September 1923 (with just 25 shares initially) by 25 February 1934, 4,102 shares in the company had been allocated to him at one time or another.

In the middle 'twenties, routes going north of Salisbury were, for the first time, dubbed 'the Northern Services' – an in-house identity destined to last many years. By 1925, they were by and large in trouble. Following the relative calm in Ireland and, with the French and Belgian armies taking a larger share in the occupation of the Rhineland, there were – once again –

fewer troops in training on Salisbury Plain. A map in a surviving timetable of that year shows (upon an office-only copy – red ink and pencil amendments respectively telling the tale) that services to Warminster, Westbury and Trowbridge had been withdrawn and replaced by vehicles operated by the Lavington & Devizes Motor Services Ltd.

The 'Northern Services' continued to produce 'poor returns' in 1926 and Bertram Wells, W&D's first traffic manager, was given the task of monitoring their loadings. The Amesbury to Enford service was reduced as a result, then curtailed at Netheravon and, in short order, cut back to Durrington – for Larkhill and Bulford.

In contrast, Wells liaised with Sidney Horsey of Fordingbridge, for him to construct a garage there, built to the W&D board's specification, and which the company was to rent from him at £33 per annum. Sited in Salisbury Street, it opened in August 1926, and replaced the one previously rented in that Hampshire town from H.T. Parker. This reinforcement upon the road south from Salisbury was accompanied by the inauguration of a new service to Downton, Redlynch and Woodfalls, where a small garage was rented – on the northern fringes of the New Forest.

That year there was another shift of accommodation along similar lines, this time at Wilton. John White was told that his garage was to be vacated and replaced by custom-built premises to be constructed by A.M. and A.F. Marks (Marks & Son). This deal included the rent of standing accommodation for five years at £22 10s.0d (£22.50) per annum. An arrangement was also agreed with H.N. Pitt for the rent of a garage at Larkhill.

On 19 April 1926, as the Baldwin government faced the approaching climax of several months of industrial strife nationwide, Raymond Longman met with Frank Wort of Wort & Way, Salisbury, to discuss the 'scheduling of certain Wilts & Dorset vehicles for hire (by that firm) for carrying troops in the event of a national emergency arising before 30 September 1926'. It came much

earlier than that. The General Strike was called on 4 May by the Trades Union Congress which, to the dismay of trade unionists, quickly recognised the effectiveness of just such preparations nationwide, and put an end to the strike a mere nine days after it had begun. Unlike municipal transport operators Wilts & Dorset, in concert with practically all territorial bus companies at that time, only employed non-union men, and would have been ideally placed to support a protracted remedial effort. Indeed, with its finances far from healthy and in dire need of an injection of funds, Wilts & Dorset's dismay probably matched that of the 'betrayed' trade unionists.

So it was that the company was obliged to seek a £5,000 overdraft from Lloyds Bank in order to keep up to date with a national trend of a different kind. The numerous private bus operators throughout the country were challenging territorial companies on profitable routes with nimble vehicles running on pneumatic tyres. Wilts & Dorset's treasured army camps had attracted just such attention. In August 1926 two single deck Wilts & Dorset buses were fitted with pneumatics for use on the Larkhill service. It was the beginning of a year-long reshodding process which was to cost the company in excess of £10,000 – all surviving single deck buses and charabancs in the fleet being converted piecemeal, the cost to be written off within three years and three months.

above] CD2555 (8), new in 1919 as a double deck, was rebodied as a saloon only four years later by Christopher Dodson. In the mid-1920s Wilts & Dorset fitted new wheels and pneumatic tyres to its older vehicles. In this form it was used from Salisbury on country routes like this one serving army camps on the Plain, such as Larkhill. Driver Harold Weekes stands to the right of the radiator. DAVID PENNELS COLLECTION

left] In the 1920s Wilts & Dorset frequently swapped bodies around among its buses. CD3330 (7), an AEC YC, began life in 1919 as a solid-tyred charabanc, then acquired a double deck body. In its final form, with pneumatic tyres in place of solids, it carried this curvaceous Harrington saloon body, which had been removed from an elderly Thornycroft chassis. The registration number previously belonged to a Southdown Straker-Squire which was loaned to Wilts & Dorset in 1918. DAVID PENNELS COLLECTION

At least eight charabancs and a saloon lined up for a private hire contract in Salisbury Market Square in about 1927. The ice cream vendor and the umbrellas tell of a hot summer's day, but many of the passengers have yet to turn up. Astride the motorbike is Wilts & Dorset inspector George West, later depot superintendent at Andover. In the front row the charabancs, from left to right, are Leylands CD5247, MR6636 and HR6404 (11, 34 and 26), AEC CD5249 (13), two more Leylands and TP4769, a Thornycroft of Don Motor Coach Co, Southsea. Why the Thornycroft was there is a mystery, but by coincidence it was later sold to Venture, Basingstoke. DAVID PENNELS COLLECTION

Meanwhile, it was decided to send the two ex-Coombes Crossley 14-seaters to Larkhill and despatch all suitable spare vehicles to that camp for 'chasing' purposes – so that every time a rival operator's bus was leaving for Salisbury, a Wilts & Dorset 'chaser' was sent to the city direct 'and every effort made to get the Saturday military traffic'.

Alfred Cannon was authorised to order three Dennis 30 cwt chassis, fitted with lightweight duralumin bodies by Short Brothers of Rochester. Unfortunately the latter could not deliver such ideal 'chasers' within the necessary time-frame, so W&D ordered wooden-framed bodies instead – the equivalent of handicapping a thoroughbred racehorse. They were delivered in February 1927, and were followed by other examples of the type that arrived in pairs over the next twelve months. Nevertheless, the company prepared to set out to serve the camps at Tidworth, as part of a concerted move toward Andover. A new garage at the Ram Hotel, Tidworth, was leased from Portsmouth United Breweries, in March 1927, at £18 per annum. The road eastward from Tidworth to Andover had been served by Mobility Ltd. In December 1923, whilst that firm underwent a change of ownership, Hants & Dorset had been requested to operate a bus upon the Ludgershall–Andover section of the route. In the event, Anna Valley Motor Co Ltd of Andover purchased the operation and ran it under its original

name until, on 18 May 1927, it sold part of the bus side of the business (including a route to Winchester) to Hants & Dorset. The latter promptly offered the Ludgershall–Andover and Anna Valley–Andover routes, plus one old Dennis bus, to Wilts & Dorset for £400. Wilts & Dorset declined – but the board changed its mind and took both routes, if not the old bus, on 1 November 1927 (See Chapter 6).

The best part of six years had elapsed since the purchase of Maurice Coombes' *Salisbury & District*, in August 1921, when at last Wilts & Dorset felt able to acquire the operations of another competitor. Apparently as a result of a hint dropped by garage manager George Wallis, Arthur J. Corp, the proprietor of B&C Motor Services based at Bulford (previously Thomas C. Bannister and A.J. Corp) approached Wilts & Dorset with an offer of sale. The deal was agreed on 8 April 1927: £400 for B&C's goodwill, two saloon buses and Bulford garage, subject to Corp's engagement as traffic superintendent at £4 per week plus 2½ per cent commission upon new private hire business obtained by him.

Although he was replaced by another traffic manager, S.J. Hall of Bristol, Bertram Wells departed that summer of 1927 to become instead traffic manager of Hants & Dorset at the Royal Mews, Bournemouth – where he was remembered as a highly efficient martinet.

On 30 June 1927, with Sparrow & Vincent's *Victory Motor Services* raising the competition levels to a new high – particularly en route to Wilton – Douglas Mackenzie presumably recognised that the 'grand design' of 'Southdown/Wilts & Dorset/South Coast Motor Services' was at an end – and resigned his directorship of Wilts & Dorset, giving 'pressure of business' as his reason. One thousand of his shares in the company were divided equally between Lephard, Cannon, Fielden and Raymond Longman. The last-named now became a director to replace Mackenzie – a considerable honour!

The one bright spot towards the close of the difficult year of 1927 came in October when the new traffic manager was given authority to start a geographically bold service from Salisbury to Marlborough with effect from 1 November 'provided that no additional rolling stock is necessitated thereby'. A garage for one vehicle was rented in that town.

In contrast, that September conversations had taken place between Alfred Cannon and Thomas Wolsey, chairman of Hants & Dorset since 1925, reference the purchase by the latter of Wilts & Dorset Motor Services Ltd. The negotiations continued on the basis of the purchase price being in shares of Hants & Dorset for the amount of the Wilts & Dorset capital – and cash for Wilts & Dorset's liabilities in respect of loans and mortgages. All that the Wilts & Dorset minutes disclose (on 13 October 1927) is that there had been 'correspondence with Hants & Dorset', and (on 11 November) 'no progress could be made with Hants & Dorset'. What had happened was that on 1 November Wilts & Dorset had indicated by letter the minimum terms upon which they were prepared to sell the undertaking – and Hants & Dorset had declined those terms; which in both firms' minutes go unrecorded. Thus the second attempt to get Hants & Dorset to take control of what was then a lame duck proved unsuccessful.

Instead, it was resolved that the nominal capital of the company would be increased to £25,000 by the creation of an additional 10,000 shares of £1 each – enough to cover the cost of putting the single deck fleet upon pneumatic tyres. The depth of the financial difficulty is disclosed by the resolution of 19 December 1927: the seven double deck buses in the fleet (three Leylands and four Thornycrofts) with seating capacities ranging from 45 to 54, were to have those seats reduced to 40 apiece, and each was to be licensed for the year 1928 on that basis.

The year 1927 ended with authorisation for new services from Salisbury to Romsey and to Shaftesbury via the Chalke Valley. Three charabancs with covered tops helped out upon these new routes pending the purchase of two more Dennis 18-seat saloons and three modern Leyland PLSC3 Lion 36-seaters – to be purchased from Leyland upon deferred terms. Presumably not too many of the 10,000 new shares had been called up.

February 1928 saw the regularisation of the company's leasehold premises at Bulford Camp, and an agreement with the War Department's land agent for the use of a parking lot at Porton Camp for a rental of £13 per annum. Conversely, relations with Wilton Town Council (in particular over the running of buses to

Ditchampton) became somewhat strained at this time, as the corporation planned to reduce Wilts & Dorset's standing space in Wilton Marketplace, to make room for Sparrow & Vincent's vehicles, now running in competition. Unable to buy sufficient new equipment to cope with this, Alfred Cannon was obliged to purchase written-down second-hand Daimler chassis and saloon bodywork from Southdown. He also attempted to buy the Leyland Lion saloon bus running as a demonstrator on the Salisbury–Andover service in June 1928, but was unable to raise funds. The company did manage to purchase some 70ft x 110ft of land at the corner of Castle Street with Mill Stream for a new garage, but was obliged to send representatives to the RAF's Stonehenge

left] In 1927 Wilts & Dorset received the first of its 14 Leyland PLSC3 Lions, MW567 (52). It was already some eight years old when photographed in Chipper Lane, Salisbury before the bus station was built; the vehicle parked in front is a 1935 Leyland Titan. The PLSC Lions broke new ground for comfort and performance. Their chassis were designed specifically for bus use, and were delivered new with pneumatic tyres. Leyland built the bodies too, which were Wilts & Dorset's first to have roller blinds to show the destination. THE OMNIBUS SOCIETY

below] This Leyland PLSC3 Lion, MW1852 (56), displays the detail of the red and grey livery with white roof that was current when it was new in 1928. After Wilts & Dorset sent the chassis to John C. Beadle, of Dartford, to be rebodied in 1946, it lasted another four years, only being withdrawn when new Bristol saloons arrived in July 1950. DAVID PENNELS COLLECTION

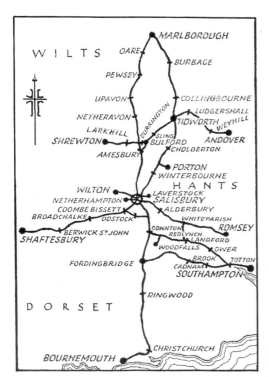

above] The expansion and contraction of Wilts & Dorset's route network in the 'twenties could be likened unto an octopus swimming in deep water. This February 1929 map discloses the temporary loss of services to Codford, Warminster, Westbury, Trowbridge, Devizes etc, and the road to Blandford and Dorchester south of Coombe Bissett. This skeletal framework began to fill out again after a cash input from T&BAT and the Southern Railway.

below] Sparrow & Vincent's Victory Motor Services posed a growing threat to Wilts & Dorset in 1928, but the company did not have sufficient new buses to cope with it. The short-term solution was to take in seven well-used Daimlers from Southdown; none of them stayed beyond the end of 1929, apparently too short a time to be caught on camera in Wiltshire. Dodson-bodied CD5215, photographed whilst still with Southdown, became W&D's no. 22 for just a month at the end of 1928. DAVID PENNELS COLLECTION

Aerodrome site to seek out second-hand constructional materials to make the project viable. Design work was carried out by Michael Harding of J. Harding & Sons, architects, and the tender of C. Collins & Sons for the construction work was accepted. On 26 January 1929, Wilts & Dorset took out 'a debenture of £2,500 with Barclays Bank in respect of 143 Castle Street and the garage adjoining'. The new premises were built in 1931, by which time the financial difficulties of Wilts & Dorset were well on the way to being considerably eased as a result of two separate but interrelated pieces of national legislation.

As Ronald E. Lephard, claims officer for Southdown before World War II, and its area manager Worthing afterward, told Alan Lambert (in 1985), 'Wilts & Dorset's very existence was saved by the financial interest taken in the firm by the Southern Railway Company' – and considerable credence may be attached to that statement, for Ronald Lephard was the son of Percy Lephard. The details are, however, rather more complicated than that.

First, the four mainline railway companies' desire to give some legal clout to their operation of bus services here and there in Great Britain led to each gaining appropriate Parliamentary powers to do so, when four separate Railway (Road Transport) Acts became law on 3 August 1928. Instead the railway companies opted to buy their way into the existing bus industry by purchasing a holding in each operating company equal to that already held by Tilling & British Automobile Traction (a marriage of Thomas Tilling and BAT interests which lasted from 1928 to 1942).

However, despite the early financial interest of Tilling and BAT (separately) in both Hants & Dorset and the all-important Southdown company, for some reason never formally disclosed, no such investment in Wilts &

The solitary 18-seat Dennis G coach that Wilts & Dorset bought in 1928 had an 'all-weather' canvas-hooded body by Thomas Harrington, of Hove, who bodied most of the company's coaches, and those of Southdown, in the 1930s. The complete vehicle, MW1854 (47), cost around £675. The company bought no further coaches with less than 20 seats. DAVID PENNELS COLLECTION

Dorset Motor Services Ltd had been made by either of those holding companies. The chairman of Southdown was now Sidney Garcke, and he became a member of the negotiating committee set up by T&BAT and the railway companies to iron out the foreseeable problems associated with the forthcoming arrangements. On 26 June 1929 Garcke, in his capacity as chairman of the British Electrical Federation (a BAT in-house group) kindly offered to conduct the preliminary negotiations with the Southern Railway on Wilts & Dorset's behalf. The Southern Railway, whose main line to the West Country went right across the middle of Wilts & Dorset's territory, *had* shown an immediate interest in the firm. Garcke's offer was accepted by the Wilts & Dorset board without a second thought!

The second seminal piece of legislation is outlined in the next chapter.

Three 'all-weather' coaches, with Harrington bodies, line up in St Thomas' Square advertising the company's excursions. Stonehenge and Lyndhurst are among the day's attractions. Other destinations on offer include Bournemouth, Highcliffe, Sandbanks, Southampton, Beaulieu Abbey and Bognor Regis. The 1928 Dennis on the right, MW1854 (47), is the youngest of the trio. The two Leylands, MR6636 and MR6437 (34 and 33), date from 1926. DAVID PENNELS COLLECTION

3
Tilling & BAT and Southern Railway's
Wilts & Dorset

T H E P R O C E S S by which the Tilling & British
Automobile Traction Co Ltd and the Southern
Railway Company conjointly rescued Wilts & Dorset
from extinction proved to be a rather lengthy one, not
least because an additional company attempted to
become a party to the arrangement.

One of Wilts & Dorset's first official contacts with
the Southern Railway actually came several months
before the Railway (Road Transport) Acts became law.
In May 1928, Wilts & Dorset had been asked to co-
operate with the SR in the issue of combined road and
rail tickets. Probably because the board was initially
unsure of its ability to enter into such an agreement, it
was not until the following January that the directors
were 'pleased to consider any proposals for coordination
of through . . . booking facilities in our territory'.

On 1 May 1929, Lephard and Longman had been to
London for a meeting with the Southern Railway's Lt
Col Gilbert Szlumper and that company's chief
accountant. These preliminary discussions took place
before the involvement of T&BAT, when it was thought
that up to 50 per cent of any future capital issue would
be taken up by the railway company – and that three SR
directors might join the board. In the event, the only
item to remain as discussed at that meeting was that the
price to be paid for each share should be 25 shillings
(£1.25).

Lephard and Longman again visited London, on 7
October, and met with Ralph Davidson and Herbert
Short of the SR; as a result of which Davidson and Short,
together with T&BAT's Sidney Garcke, made a tour of
Wilts & Dorset's premises and operating area in the

Canvas hoods were all up on a dank day in the winter of 1929/30, when a dozen Wilts & Dorset coaches and buses lined up by the tall trees that still grew in Salisbury Cathedral Close. The pride of the fleet at the time, Leyland TS1 Tiger MW4594 (66) heads the convoy. New in June 1929, the style of its Harrington body, with folding top, soon grew out of fashion, so it was sent back to the coachbuilders at Hove to receive more up-to-date coachwork in 1936. DAVID PENNELS COLLECTION

The Leyland TD1 Titan, launched at the Commercial Motor Show in November 1927, laid the ground for the extensive use of double decks on bus services across the United Kingdom. This was made possible by the availability of reliable pneumatic tyres capable of sustaining the weight of such vehicles; the lowbridge version averaged about 6.5 tons unladen. MW6050 (74) was Wilts & Dorset's first of the type, delivered in December 1929. Parked in Chipper Lane, Salisbury, it shows off well the red and French grey livery of the early 1930s.
THE OMNIBUS SOCIETY

company of Cannon, Longman and Fielden. Davidson submitted amended terms – Wilts & Dorset rejected them. Following another meeting in London, on 25 November, a draft agreement along the lines already accepted as standard by omnibus companies throughout the country, in such road/rail co-operation, was adopted as the basis for a similar arrangement with Wilts & Dorset – and a map of the company's operating territory was to be sent to the Southern Railway Company.

On 21 February 1930, the SR 'could not view with favour the [proposed] issue of an additional 5,000 £1 shares' to Wilts & Dorset's existing shareholders, and instead offered to loan W&D £5,000 at 6 per cent interest. Wilts & Dorset politely declined that offer. In May, the chairman and secretary announced that they would be pleased to attend another meeting in London. They were not invited.

It was not until October 1930 that the company learned the reason for the hold-up. By virtue of its branch line into Salisbury from Warminster and Wilton (along the Wylye Valley) and its participation in another which came south-east via Ludgershall and joined the SR at Andover Junction (and its supporting but temporary bus services to the latter), the Great Western Railway Company wanted to participate in the running of Wilts & Dorset. Lephard had received no communication to the effect that such 'negotiations' rail-to-rail were going on but he 'understood' that this was the case. Eventually, that December, it was decided

Leyland's chief engineer, John Rackham, ensured that the firm's body and chassis engineers worked closely together to make the TD1 Titan a lightweight double deck with low overall height, about 13 feet. The lowbridge design, with sunken top deck gangway along the offside and rows of four seats abreast, became the standard for many operators. Wilts & Dorset's use of double decks like MW7048 (87) on the Wilton route played an important role in the battle with Sparrow & Vincent. DAVID PENNELLS COLLECTION

that 'no immediate meeting between Wilts & Dorset, the Southern Railway and the Great Western Railway' would take place 'as no useful purpose would be served'.

Meanwhile, Longman had twice met with the general manager of a bus company in which there was to be a joint GWR/SR participation – Theodore Graham Homer of the Thames Valley Traction Co Ltd – concerning operations between Newbury and Marlborough. Wilts & Dorset was 'pleased to consider the main [A4] road west of Newbury to be Thames Valley's – and that the country to the south of this road should be considered Wilts & Dorset territory, with running rights to Marlborough, Hungerford and Newbury'. The 'territorial map' to be submitted to the Southern Railway was clearly still being redrafted to advantage around the edges.

The boundary with Hants & Dorset had already been inked in, and a remarkable feature of that was the earmarking as Hants & Dorset territory of the entire A36 road from Southampton, right up to the south-eastern city limits of Salisbury. Indeed, in the event, it was Hants & Dorset which provided the bus stops and its characteristic rustic waiting rooms along that route. The Wilts & Dorset map was ready for submission in March 1931.

The Southern Railway Company having fought off the GWR designs upon Wilts & Dorset, the board of the latter was now in a position to approve, on 10 April 1931, a preliminary agreement between (1) Tilling & BAT, (2)

Salisbury's Blue Boar Row was decorated for the coronation of King George VI, when the camera caught MW8754 (97) as it was about to leave for West Harnham. Altogether Wilts & Dorset bought 17 Leyland TD1s between the end of 1929 and mid-1931. DAVID PENNELS COLLECTION

Wilts & Dorset, (3) Percy Lephard, (4) Alfred Cannon, (5) William Fielden and (6) Raymond Longman, whereby Tilling & BAT and two of its directors would take up shares in Wilts & Dorset equal to those to be acquired by the SR and two of its nominated directors. Thus, with effect from 1 July 1931, ordinary shares were taken up as follows:

Tilling & British AutomobileTraction Co Ltd		9,800
George Cardwell	(Tilling)	100
Charles Stanley	(BAT)	100
The Southern Railway		9,800
Ralph Davidson	(SR)	100
Lt Col Gilbert Szlumper	(SR)	100

To give a clear idea of where Wilts & Dorset, with its fleet size at just over 50 vehicles, featured in the scale of things at that time, Tilling & BAT and the Southern Railway conjointly paid the following amounts per £1 share in each of the southern territorial bus companies listed below:

Southdown	£3 5s 0d	(£3.25)
Maidstone & District	£2 8s 0d	(£2.42½)
Hants & Dorset	£2 5s 0d	(£2.25)
East Kent	£2 3s 0d	(£2.17½)
Aldershot & District	£1 6s 6d	(£1.32½)
Wilts & Dorset	£1 5s 0d	(£1.25)

The Southern Railway, of course, also took up shares in Southern National (Exeter) and Southern Vectis (Isle of Wight), but there was no such arrangement in the case of the 'Brighton & Hove Omnibus Section' of Thomas Tilling Ltd – or its successor, the Brighton Hove & District Omnibus Co Ltd – whose entire share capital was the straightforward property of Tilling. The SR holding in the Thames Valley Traction Co Ltd was less than half that of the GWR.

The new era was marked by a more rigorous approach to the company's choice of vehicles. The highly successful Leyland TD1 Titan was to become the first of Wilts & Dorset's 'modern' generation of double deckers: not too many of them to start with – just two. But when the board discovered that the delivery period for this highly popular model was 22 months, it took the bold step of reserving an additional two, for delivery by May 1931 – the new influx of money had not yet reached the bank. When it had, a further four arrived.

Two Leyland TS1 Tigers with 'sunsaloon coachwork' were ordered for tours and excursions use – joining the three canvas-roofed 'allweather' coaches of the type delivered in 1929-30; and the board considered standardising upon 32-seaters for single deck bus work. It then decided that these would prove far too expensive to operate and, until such time as the increased funds emboldened them, resolved instead to cover the country routes with smaller vehicles. Six Morris Viceroy chassis were chosen for that role, fitted with 24-seat bodywork by Heaver of Durrington – an unusual purchase, but the patronage of a local coachbuilder is reminiscent of the company's earliest days.

Burrowing rabbits gave Leyland TD1 MW9396 (102) an inauspicious start in July 1931. The driver of the brand new bus had just descended White Railings Hill on its way from Amesbury to Salisbury, and pulled on to the verge to let a car pass. The nearside wheels sank into the soft ground, and the bus crashed through the iron railings, toppled over, and slid down a steep bank into a corn field. Seven people were injured but none seriously. The Salisbury Times said 'it is thought that the undermining of the road by rabbits and rain caused it to subside under the weight of the bus.' Subsequently, until the road was improved many years later, the company made northbound buses wait at the top of the opposite gradient until the southbound bus had made its way up. DAVID PENNELS COLLECTION

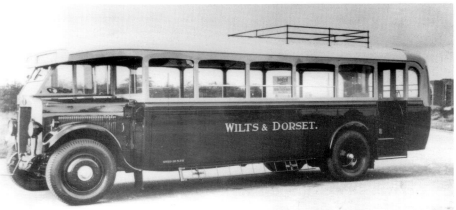

below] The company had half a dozen Leyland LT2 Lions. Two of them had 35-seat bus bodies by Leyland – the others were coaches. New in August 1930, the buses had a more rounded profile to roof, canopy and windows than the LT1s delivered earlier in the year. The first of the pair, MW7052 (91), was used in 1939 to try out producer gas propulsion. With the French Gohin-Poulenc gas plant installed in place of the rear seats, it ran as far afield as Ringwood and Trowbridge. It was restored to normal petrol propulsion three years later. ANDREW WALLER COLLECTION

above] A pair of Leyland TS1 Tiger coaches was delivered in 1930 with locally built bodies by Heaver, of Durrington. The interior view gives an idea of the level of comfort expected at the time. The seats were covered in what was then the company's standard moquette. The two Tigers, MW6293/4 (85/86), received new Harrington bodies in 1938. DAVID PENNELS COLLECTION

left] The Leyland Tiger, with varying styles of Harrington body, was the mainstay of Wilts & Dorset's well-respected coaching fleet in the 1930s. All 16 of these coaches remained in service at least until the first underfloor-engined Bristols arrived at the end of 1952. WV650 (107), a TS3 Tiger, stands in its original form in Salisbury Market Square. THE OMNIBUS SOCIETY

A further example of where Wilts & Dorset stood in the territorial pecking order came in March 1931. Wilts & Dorset agreed to pay Hants & Dorset £150 per annum for the privilege of running into that firm's impressive new Bournemouth Bus Station – but accepted £50 per annum from H&D in respect of reciprocal facilities offered at 6 Endless Street, Salisbury – a traffic office, booking office and waiting room (the Wilts & Dorset bus station on a site next door did not come into operation until 1939). The appropriate licences were exchanged accordingly.

The second piece of legislation which benefited Wilts & Dorset at this time, and brought it into a more stable position in relation to competition, was the Road Traffic Act 1930. As Hibbs (1968) explained, 'the road service licence, without which it is illegal to run a regular bus service or to advertise an excursion of any kind or a tour . . . set out the route to be followed, the time- and fare-tables and, for most express services and excursions, the number of vehicles that may be run at any one time or upon any one day. . . It is a licence that confers upon its holder the privileges and the responsibilities of a state-controlled monopoly'.

In effect, the Act made it difficult for small independent operators with meagre funds to compete with territorial companies in process of being reinforced with cash from railway sources. Vehicles now required an annual certificate of fitness, drivers and conductors were obliged to hold licences indicating good character and health – and wear badges with numbered identification similar to those issued by municipalities since the 1880s. There was conversely no need for the buses to display licence plates previously issued by each authority through whose territory they passed. Area traffic commissioners were appointed to preside over 'traffic courts' to decide which operator should prevail in the aftermath of 'objections' from his rivals.

It was a procedure which weighed heavily in favour of the territorial companies, who employed their own traffic staff capable of preparing each case. Until 1930, Wilts & Dorset had acquired the businesses of seven rival operators (including two members of the 'romantic' Gulliver family of Bowerchalke and Bishopstone), five of which involved the employment of the vendors by Wilts & Dorset, mostly as drivers. Thereafter, competing operators, or some of their stage-carriage services, were acquired at an average

left] The company management must have been well enough pleased with their 1931 Morris Commercial Viceroy saloons to order two coaches of the same type in 1932. WV652 (127) was the first of the pair. The Leyland Cub was already available as a small-capacity coach by this time, but Wilts & Dorset waited until 1935 to take delivery of its first two of this type. Another pair followed the next year. Viceroy and Cub coaches alike had Harrington 20-seat bodies. DAVID PENNELS COLLECTION

above] At least 17 Wilts & Dorset vehicles lined up before Salisbury Market Place hostelries for a private hire contract in about 1932. Almost all of them were Leylands. On the left is a pair of smart new TS3 Tigers, WV647/8 (104/5), and alongside are canvas-roofed Leyland G7s dating from the 1920s - HR9541, MR6437, MR6636 (27, 33, 34) – and five Lion saloons. DAVID PENNELS COLLECTION

right] The shining glass of Amesbury bus station reflects a Morris Commercial bus waiting to leave for Larkhill. Wilts & Dorset, whose head office was in Amesbury until February 1917, took out a £1,000 mortgage later that year to secure premises in Salisbury Street. In 1932 the company bought an additional plot of land there, and opened its waiting room and local office the following year. DAVID PENNELS COLLECTION

rate – save 1932 and 1936 – of three per year until World War II (1939). During 1932, no fewer than 13 local operators in 'Wilts & Dorset territory' gave up what had become a thoroughly unequal contest, and sold the goodwill of their services to the company. Gilbert Haines of Downton did relatively well by relinquishing his service to Southampton, together with his excursions and tours work; whilst P.C.J. (Charlie) Sawyer of Netheravon became a company driver and, post-World War II, depot inspector at Pewsey, until his retirement in 1963.

The potential cost of updating their vehicles, as technology rapidly improved in the 'thirties, no doubt contributed to a further eight operators giving up at least a part of their operations in favour of Wilts & Dorset during 1936, (for details of all such acquisitions by the company, see Appendix C).

Pre-World War II, the biggest and most expensive purchase was that of Sparrow & Vincent's *Victory Motor Services*, on 22 November 1933, thus bringing to an end a series of protracted negotiations and a contest of some seven years' duration: this also involved heated exchanges with Salisbury City Council which at one point tried to impose an 'adjusted timetable'

on the company. Until the injection of T&BAT and SR funds, that contest had thrown up the biggest threat – among the many – to the future of Wilts & Dorset Motor Services Ltd. Apart from cosying up successfully with Wilton Town Council, proprietors Charles A. Sparrow, Sidney A. Sparrow and Charles G. Vincent of 79 Fisherton Street, Salisbury, had run rival routes in the city and upon a rural route, acquired from a smaller operator, to Whaddon and the Grimsteads. At the same time, Victory Motor Services hoovered up a considerable portion of the Salisbury-based excursions and tours traffic at a time when Wilts & Dorset had begun to invest in new and expensive vehicles for just such work. Samuel Dennis, Wilts & Dorset's somewhat anachronistically named 'charabanc superintendent' had a difficult time keeping the excursions and tours side of the company's business up and running.

right] Leyland built the bodies for a half dozen TD2 Titans that it supplied to Wilts & Dorset in 1933. The smoother upper deck front profile gave a more modern appearance than the piano fronts of the TD1s delivered in 1929-1931. WV2382 (112) was photographed on 26 January 1933, before it left the town of Leyland. COLIN MORRIS COLLECTION

left] Salisbury City Council's decision in June 1927 to license Sparrow & Vincent to run a bus service to Wilton signalled the start of intense competition between the local independent and Wilts & Dorset. Sparrow & Vincent's big guns in the battle for traffic were a pair of Leyland PLSC3 Lions. The crew of MW2955, later Wilts & Dorset's no. 133, relax on Wilton Market Square before taking it across the city to Laverstock. DAVID PENNELS COLLECTION

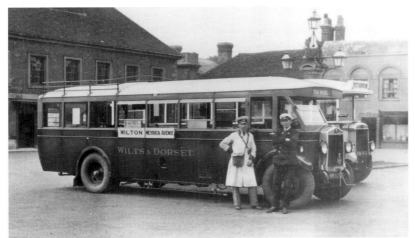

left] Rivals line up on Wilton Market Square. From 1927 until Wilts & Dorset took over Sparrow & Vincent's Victory Motor Services in December 1933, competition between them on Salisbury city services was fierce. Wilts & Dorset bought three 35-seat Leyland LT1 Lions in 1930 to help meet the challenge. MW6284 (76) stands next to Sparrow & Vincent's MW912, a PLSC3 Lion that was later to become the company's no. 131. The driver is Oliver Blake, who was later in charge at Blandford, and subsequently at Amesbury depot. DAVID PENNELS COLLECTION

right] Archie Curtis of West Grimstead bought this REO bus, MW4352, in April 1929. It was known as the Blue Belle. He had registered a Dodge two years before, and previously ran a Ford. By early 1930 he had sold out to Sparrow & Vincent's Victory Motor Services, which was already giving Wilts & Dorset a run for its money in the city. The company can hardly have welcomed its appearance on a country route as well. After the traffic commissioners became involved the timetable and fare chart were coordinated with Wilts & Dorset, and most of the fares went up by a penny or so. DAVID PENNELS COLLECTION

below right] The 16 vehicles that Wilts & Dorset took over with Sparrow & Vincent's Victory Motor Services in 1933 included vehicles of no less than six different makes, including four Albions. MR9964, which the company numbered 129, was one of a pair of PM28 Vikings with bodies by Northern Counties of Wigan. It is parked next to the competition on Wilton Market Square. DAVID PENNELS COLLECTION

The involvement of railway companies in the operation of bus services proved, from time to time, to be a constraint rather than an advantage. The territorial bus maps requested prior to the investment of funds from the appropriate railway company primarily proved to be bargaining chips for inter-railway company negotiations as to 'who would become involved in which bus company'. As such, each map remained elastic around the edges when the 'territorials' vied for further tracts of land occupied by medium-sized independents which seemed open to offers.

On the other hand, bus company plans for long-ranging joint operations with neighbouring concerns quickly set the alarm bells ringing at the relative railway headquarters. Cash never comes without strings attached – and those expected to pull them when it mattered proved to be those politely smiling directors representing, in Wilts & Dorset's case, the Southern Railway. Three examples serve to illustrate the point.

As early as September 1928, well before serious discussions with the Southern Railway had commenced, Southdown had approached Hants & Dorset with a view to running a joint express service between Brighton and Bournemouth. That must have been a 'clear the decks' paper exercise, because it was an open secret that Hants & Dorset had just four years previously promised Elliott Bros (Bournemouth) Ltd that it would not operate such a service. Indeed, when Hants & Dorset predictably declined to participate, Southdown turned to Wilts &

right] Sparrow & Vincent's Dennis Arrow MW9860 stands before Salisbury Guildhall. When it was new in 1931, with its Duple body and six-cylinder Dennis engine, it seemed an advanced vehicle for its time. It became Wilts & Dorset's no. 137 until the Air Ministry requisitioned it in 1941. DAVID PENNELS COLLECTION

below] This Albion PV70 Valiant coach, WV3371, was Sparrow & Vincent's last new vehicle. It was only six months old when they sold out to Wilts & Dorset, and it survived with the company until 1946, as no. 139. The seat backs in its unusual Osborne & Hassell body were found to be too high, obstructing passengers' vision, and had to be cut down within months of its delivery. DAVID PENNELS COLLECTION

already provided by the SR. In the interim, Elliott Brothers (*Royal Blue*), by reason of an agreement they believed current with Southdown, also served notice of an objection. On this occasion the most proficient chess player in these mind games was Hants & Dorset, which turned the tables by simply doing nothing, safe in the knowledge that Royal Blue and the SR would do the objecting, thus leaving the bus company in the middle smelling of roses. On 31 May 1932, the Southern Area Traffic Commissioners considered the opposing points of view – and rejected the application.

A concurrent application for a Wilts & Dorset-operated Newbury-Andover-Salisbury-Bournemouth express service again called for no overt action on the part of Hants & Dorset, since the notion was also opposed by the directors representing the SR on the grounds that the railway service adequately provided for passengers between these points. Although still being eagerly discussed by William Fielden and the Tilling & BAT directors upon the board as late as January 1933, the railway representatives remained aloof, and that service did not come to fruition either.

Dorset to anchor the western leg of the proposed service. In the event, that did not come to fruition but, in March 1931, Hants & Dorset learned that Wilts & Dorset and Southdown planned to run a Salisbury-Southampton-Portsmouth & Southsea service. Hants & Dorset promptly objected. Exactly 12 months later a 'new' service between Salisbury and Southsea was still being discussed by all three bus companies – Cannon and Mackenzie no doubt the main proponents of this variation on a well-worn theme.

On 7 April 1932, the Southern Railway representatives on the Wilts & Dorset board, Ralph Davidson and Herbert Short, put the lid on this latest attempt by declaring that the Southern Railway company would oppose the applications at the public sitting (if the subject came up) and ask the traffic commissioners to decide the necessity for such a service in view of the facilities

The ex-War Department Daimler CB chassis of HR6408 was the oldest in the Sparrow & Vincent fleet that Wilts & Dorset took over in 1933. By then its Salisbury Carriage Works charabanc body had been replaced by new Harrington coachwork. The company numbered it 142, but kept the vehicle less than a year. Jethro Crabb, who later worked for Wilts & Dorset, stands by the wheel in white summer uniform coat. DAVID PENNELS COLLECTION

To a considerable extent Wilts & Dorset's attempts to launch express services were hampered in part by Tilling & BAT's agreement with the railways, which provided for Standing Joint Committees to be set up; two bus directors, two railway representatives. In Wilts & Dorset's case, it was a lion's den situation – the meetings were held in the Southern Railway's divisional superintendent's office at Southampton.

In similar vein, the Southern Railway, and a degree of vacillation on the part of the Southern National Omnibus Co Ltd, scuppered a 1932 attempt by Wilts & Dorset to extend a stage carriage service beyond Shaftesbury westward along the A30 to Sherborne and Yeovil (in Somerset). Southern National 'could not see our way to join in the operation'. Four months later (8 July), Southern National had 'reconsidered', but the Southern Railway, whose main line to the west was in sight of that section of road along almost its entire length, said 'No'. Thus Drummond's T9 class locomotives, with their 'clump-clump' corridorless stopping trains went unopposed along this section for a further 16 years. Southern National and Wilts & Dorset were to start their joint Salisbury–Yeovil service on 5 December 1948 (until 1959); and added another which went via Mere, Wincanton and Queen Camel (between 1949 and 1952).

Another proposed joint service which seemed more likely to go unopposed was, in 1932, that between Salisbury and Winchester. Charles Emmence had been operating stage carriage services from King's Somborne to Salisbury and to Winchester, and agreed that April to sell the goodwill of these to Wilts & Dorset for £250. The latter and Hants & Dorset were soon well on the way to devising an increased timetable between the two cities, via King's Somborne. This time there was no objection from the Southern Railway, but the traffic commissioners had other ideas. They refused licences to run (a) such a joint service with Hants & Dorset, (b) to operate the King's Somborne section to Winchester and (c) to replace Emmence on the existing service from King's Somborne to Salisbury. Both territorial companies appealed in vain – and, in a not-too-common gesture toward an independent, the commissioners rubbed salt into the wound by granting a licence to Robert Chisnell (*King Alfred*) to run from Winchester to Stockbridge – via King's Somborne.

All was not gloom in 1932, however. Some reinforcement of territory once vacated in earlier times occurred when Harold Couchman (the first five letters of that surname to rhyme with 'couch'-grass) of Codford St Mary, sold the goodwill of his Salisbury-A36 main road-Warminster service to Wilts & Dorset for £500. The agreement permitted Couchman's *Wylye Valley Motor Services* to continue running shorter services from Codford to Warminster via Boyton and Sutton Veny; and from Codford to Salisbury via Wylye, Hanging Langford and Wishford – both along the somewhat lucrative 'back-road'.

There was at that time an opportunity to purchase the goodwill for such of the services of the Lavington & Devizes Motor Services Ltd considered to be in Wilts & Dorset's territory. Western National was likewise expressing an interest in acquiring those of its services

left] What appears to be a local football team setting out for an away match poses for the camera at the New Canal, Salisbury, in Sparrow & Vincent's REO charabanc, with its locally built body, by Heaver of Durrington. By the time MR3214 became Wilts & Dorset's no. 144 in 1933, it was already eight years old. It lasted less than a year with the company. Ransom Eli Olds established the REO marque in 1908, after being ousted from his Oldsmobile concern. DAVID PENNELS COLLECTION

right] By the time Wilts & Dorset's two Leyland TS6 Tiger coaches were built in 1934, the Harrington coach design had moved on somewhat from the previous examples two years earlier, with fewer windows and a more streamlined roof profile. WV5527 (118) stands in Amesbury, where it was based for most of its working life. DAVID PENNELS COLLECTION

which operated to the west of Devizes. As early as June 1931, a meeting between Longman and Alfred Chivers, an L&D director, had taken place, but the decision to purchase had been deferred. In the event, both Wilts & Dorset and the National company 'missed the bus'. The Lavington & Devizes concern – founded before World War I by Fred Sayer, a former Bath Tramways Motor Co driver – was sold to his former employers, and it was not until December 1937 that the latter sold the ex-L&D Hindon-Salisbury and Easterton-Devizes services (only) to Wilts & Dorset.

This gives an idea of the difficulties attached to ordering priorities which faced a Wilts & Dorset board without an endless supply of money to spend. At best Wilts & Dorset's 'compensatory' acquisition of the Hindon and Easterton services came only after an application by Bath Tramways Motor Co Ltd – by then a Bristol Tramways & Carriage Co Ltd subsidiary – to run a new stage carriage service (without reciprocal arrangements for Wilts & Dorset) from Bath to Salisbury via Devizes, was granted despite an objection, at a sitting of the traffic commissioners on 4 November 1937 – at Bristol!

The decision was always a thorn thereafter in the western side of Wilts & Dorset, and it was not until more than twenty years later that the Bath service was allowed to terminate at the company's bus station in Salisbury; instead it had to use the New Canal bus stand, together with the rural independents' market-day buses. However, back in 1932, the Western National Omnibus Co Ltd had not been too dismayed at the turn of events – at that time it owned the Bristol Tramways & Carriage Co Ltd; wheels within wheels!

The £5,000 that Wilts & Dorset had been looking for since 1931 (to help upgrade and extend existing buildings primarily) came at last in January 1933, when Tilling & BAT Ltd and the Southern Railway subscribed for a further 5,000 £1 ordinary shares, in the following proportions:

The Southern Railway	2,500
Tilling & British Automobile Traction Co Ltd	2,200
E. Garcke T&BAT	100
E. Bennett T&BAT	100
I.M. Smith T&BAT	100

Plans for a waiting room and local office at Amesbury were put in train immediately. That work was complete within five months and further land was purchased suitable for a garage extension.

The acquisition of Sparrow & Vincent's *Victory Motor Services* saw Wilts & Dorset take over the following

Wilts & Dorset broke with its normal practice in 1934. Instead of having Leyland build the bodies for two TD3 Titans, the chassis were sent to Brush, which offered favourable terms for them, along with ten very similar bodies on Hants & Dorset TD3s. WV4922 (115) was photographed in May of that year before leaving Brush at Loughborough. COLIN MORRIS COLLECTION

Toward the end of his period of office as Wilts & Dorset's garage manager-cum-chief engineer, George Wallis appears to have toyed with the idea of clearly labelling each bus with its chassis number. Titans nos. 115/6 bore them in large numerals at platform level upon the rear panelling. COLIN MORRIS COLLECTION

agreements previously held by Sparrow & Vincent: the tenancy of the garage at Old Wessex Works, Southampton Road, Salisbury; the tenancy of Sparrow & Vincent's offices at 79 Fisherton Street; an advertising contract with J. Abrahams & Sons Ltd; and a contract with H.G. Pinner, the booking agent, of Queen Street, Salisbury.

The stalwart efforts of Samuel Dennis, Wilts & Dorset's 'charabanc superintendent' in keeping the company's tours and excursions up and running in the face of the competition put up by *Victory*, was rewarded in time-honoured fashion. That firm's Charles Sparrow was appointed 'charabanc superintendent' and 'since the volume of business to be handled is anticipated to be more than a man of Mr Dennis' age could manage' he was promptly retired – and given £50 in January 1934 and another £50 the following September, on the condition that he didn't do any similar work in the company's area.

Ordinary members of the board were spared from making such hard-nosed decisions, by the setting up of an Executive Sub-Committee, in operation between 1931 and 1940. Its minutes were recorded in a separate book and throughout the major part of its life the sub-committee comprised:

P.E. Lephard (Chairman)
William Fielden
R.I.H. Longman (Secretary)
Charles D. Stanley (T&BAT)

Their separate minutes were circulated and submitted to the full board of directors – whether for information or discussion depended upon the gravity of the subject.

In March 1929 Wilts & Dorset had informed the National Omnibus and Transport Co Ltd that it was to extend its Salisbury-Dorchester service to the coast at Weymouth – that age-old plan fulfilled, after a fashion. The National company replied that it did not wish to participate. In February 1930 Wilts & Dorset had increased its timetable and again invited National to join in. Having seen that the receipts varied from 15.1 pence per mile in August to 6.9 pence in January, the now Southern National company again declared that it did not wish to take part.

Exactly four years later, Percival Stone-Clark of Southern National felt that it was now time for his company to come in on a 50/50 basis of vehicles, mileage and cash receipts. Raymond Longman's reply was relatively short and to the point: 'National on two occasions had been given the offer to join...as this company [Wilts & Dorset] had pioneered the service and built it up over nearly five years, during which time they had spent money on development, vehicles, obtaining

Leyland introduced the TD4 Titan early in 1935. Until then Wilts & Dorset had always opted for petrol engines, even though diesel units had been available for three years. Leyland only offered a diesel version of the new type, so WV7474/ 5 (140/1), delivered in 1935, were the company's first diesel units. But their metal-framed Leyland bodies harked back to an earlier design, with a pronounced vee to the front of the upper deck. COLIN MORRIS COLLECTION

licences and fighting objections...No!' Southern National was thus prevented from running through from Weymouth to Salisbury until 1 January 1949, by which time both companies had been 'nationalised' under the control of the British Transport Commission, (see Chapter 5).

Another link with the early days of Wilts & Dorset was severed in November 1935 when George Wallis – the 'trusted employee' from Worthing – the 'garage manager' (in effect the chief engineer) who was 'approaching 65', was retired early. If that wasn't bad enough, he was replaced – as chief engineer – by his son, George R.E. Wallis; pride and pain in one package.

It is possible that the enforced retirement of Wallis the elder had been hastened by a perceived technological breakthrough; the introduction to the Wilts & Dorset fleet of its first buses fitted with diesel engines. Alfred Cannon had undertaken to supply details upon the operation of diesel-engined buses by an 'associated company' (most likely Southdown) for perusal by directors and relevant staff accordingly. A programme of replacing the petrol engines of earlier vehicles with specially purchased diesel units commenced soon after, and new diesel-engined stage carriage vehicles became the norm.

A noteworthy example of the negotiations designed to consolidate the company's territory in the expansive year of 1936 was initiated by George Cardwell. Figures for the earnings for seven weeks in the year 1935 were received from Newbury & District Motor Services; they related to that company's services to the south and south-west of Newbury. Whilst the directors considered a report on the estimated mileage and traffic earnings if these services were to be operated by Wilts & Dorset buses, discussion with the Thames Valley Traction Co Ltd took place upon the possibility of a joint purchase of the goodwill of Newbury & District. Raymond Longman duly visited Reading on 13 May 1936 and met with Theodore Homer, the general manager of Thames Valley. Homer was in favour of a shared purchase of Newbury & District as a whole, but was still awaiting his copy of the balance sheet. Instead, Thames Valley turned to the east and, that same month purchased the Chiltern Bus Co Ltd. Newbury and District was acquired instead by the Red & White group (see Chapter 7), but was absorbed in that favoured 'whole' by Thames Valley after nationalisation in 1950.

Three successful take-overs of 1936 concerned much smaller operators, but serve to illustrate the bargaining processes involved in such acquisitions. It took some 16 months to close a deal with Walter O. Swadling for his Tisbury-based *Victor Bus Service* on 5 March of that year. Three stage-carriage services from Salisbury to villages in and around the Nadder

Walter Swadling's Victor Bus Service of Tisbury ran to Salisbury four days a week until Wilts & Dorset took over in March 1936. It paid £3,300 for the business, which included tours and excursions from Tisbury. No vehicles were involved, but driver Reg Lyons transferred and stayed with the company for many years. Swadling had used Bedford WLB GW9092 for four years in the early 1930s. He sold it to an operator near Lymington who, in turn, passed it on to Hants & Dorset. DAVID PENNELS COLLECTION

concerned Wilts & Dorset, the section from Totton to Southampton. Plied with appropriately good white wine and suitably beguiled, Graham paid £2,200 and, probably tongue in cheek, suggested that Wilts & Dorset should contribute £800. Raymond Longman wrote him a cheque for £300 – in February 1937.

On the northern fringe of the New Forest, at Nomansland, Wilts & Dorset took the lead in negotiations with Joseph C. Rose who, under the fleetname Nomansland Motor Services, ran a stage carriage service from that village, which always seemed home to more ponies than humans, to Salisbury and another to Southampton – together with contract carriage work. Of the total purchase price of £275, Hants & Dorset contributed £165 for the Nomansland–Brook–Southampton service. Presumably this Rose was not as fragrant as Sybil.

The benefits to Wilts & Dorset coming from Raymond Longman's additional talent as an estate agent were well illustrated in October 1936. Through the local grapevine he heard that certain of the Salisbury freeholds of W. Rowland & Sons, including the goodwill of the firm's motor engineering business had been sold. Stepping in quickly, he obtained the offer of Rowland's contract carriage and tours business, together with seven public service vehicles. Thus, for the very reasonable sum of £2,250 Wilts & Dorset gained a near-monopoly of the excursions and tours trade in Salisbury together with five Leyland 32-seat coaches – which joined the W&D fleet – an elderly all-Leyland charabanc and even older 'stretched' Rolls Royce Silver Ghost 14-seater charabanc, which Longman promptly sold for £15.

Provisions for the increase in garage and parking space at Amesbury were now to prove most timely. In 1935, public opinion, formed primarily and understandably by memories of World War I and its horrors, began to turn away from a groundswell call for disarmament. A National Government headed by Ramsay MacDonald – a pacifist if ever there was one – at last recognised the threat developing in central Europe and opted for 'the security of armed force'.

The practical result upon Salisbury Plain was an immediate refocusing of priorities for the War Department's land agent. In 1933 there had been plans for rearranging Bulford Camp which included a relocation of facilities for Wilts & Dorset, specifically the letting of a site for a 'bus station' on the corner of the Bulford and Marlborough Roads. Wilts & Dorset's proposal to erect a waiting room was approved in November 1934, but not a replacement garage upon 'Barnes Encroachment' at Bulford. Following MacDonald's White Paper of March 1935, a further expansion of military accommodation upon Salisbury Plain put paid to Wilts & Dorset's premises upon the camps involved.

In May 1936 the Wilts & Dorset board decided to relinquish the leasehold garages at Larkhill and Bulford Camps, and concentrate upon building a garage at Amesbury big enough to house a dozen buses, thus, as

Valley, contract carriage and excursions work came into the Wilts & Dorset fold. Swadling had originally quoted £10,000 for his goodwill and £2,000 for his 14- and 32-seat Thornycrofts, two 25-seat Gilfords and one 20-seat Bedford. This figure was whittled away by eliminating the vehicles from the equation at an early stage, and playing a 'your turn next' waiting game (see Appendix C).

Wilts & Dorset left it to William Graham of Hants & Dorset to go to Minstead in the New Forest to undertake personally the far from unpleasant task of negotiating with the beautiful Sybil White, proprietress of White Brothers' *Forest Queen* stage-carriage service from Minstead to Southampton, together with one Guy Vixen saloon bus. Only the eastern half of her route

W. Rowland & Sons set up in business before World War I. By the mid-1920s they had a thriving tours and excursions concern. Private hire was also important. They ran everything from Sunday school trips to the seaside, requiring one charabanc, to village football club annual outings, like this one from Barford St Martin in 1923. All six charabancs used on this occasion, a Sunbeam, a Dennis and four Leylands, were withdrawn well before Wilts & Dorset took over Rowland's business in 1936. DAVID PENNELS COLLECTION

left] W. Rowland & Sons' no. 3, Lancashire-registered Leyland B5517, stands ready to leave the Castle Street premises of Salisbury ironmongers Woodrow & Co. Its passengers were all men, probably a staff outing. Previously it had a charabanc body, with a door to each row of five seats. In the mid-1920s Rowland had it rebodied as an 'all-weather' coach, with doors at front and back and a fold-back canvas roof, but it had been withdrawn by 1936. DAVID PENNELS COLLECTION

right] Wilts & Dorset took over six Leylands and a Rolls Royce when it bought out the well-established Salisbury coaching firm of W. Rowland & Sons at the end of the 1936 season. WV8166 (148), a Leyland LT7 Lion, was the youngest in the Rowland fleet. Its Duple body made it non-standard to Wilts & Dorset, and it was one of a pair of ex-Rowland Lions hired to the Southern Vectis Omnibus Co Ltd, on the Isle of Wight, for about four years from 1943. DAVID PENNELS

it was put, 'facilitating working and saving dead mileage'. In the autumn of that year, Wilts & Dorset bought six cottages adjoining the Amesbury property. Longman visited all six of the company's new tenants and arranged appropriate reductions in the rent in return for sufficient of their gardens to make room for the new garage. The Larkhill and Bulford garages were then demolished. In addition to this, the War Department rebuilt the Army's Southern Command offices, and rented Wilts & Dorset's house and garden at 141 Castle Street, Salisbury, which became Southern Command Headquarters until the rebuilding was complete. At the same time, Longman attempted to negotiate for the whole of Edward Shergold and Bernard White's *Silver Star Motor Services*. They relinquished their Sling Camp–Bulford Barracks–Salisbury service, plus excursions from Bulford Camp, in favour of Wilts & Dorset with effect from midnight on Saturday 7 August 1937, but held on to the remainder of their business for another 26 years (see Chapter 8).

'Please lower your head when leaving your seat': that's what you were advised to do if you sat on the right hand side of the lower saloon of a lowbridge double deck. If you paid no attention you banged your head on the underside of the sunken upper deck gangway, which ran along that side of the bus. The inside view of 1936 Leyland Titan AHR400 (145) also shows the fluorescent light fittings that Wilts & Dorset tried out briefly in 1949. DAVID PENNELS

In the midst of indications that there were to be greatly increased numbers of potential passengers within the Wilts & Dorset area, economies were still looked for. Announcing a programme of oil-engine conversions for the company's fleet (in October 1937) Alfred Cannon decided that, in addition to the fitment of five 6-cylinder Leyland diesel engines into Leyland TD2 Titans, some shuffling of the pack was to take place. He proposed to take the oil engines from two new Tiger chassis and fit one into a TD2 Titan chassis and the other into a TD3, both originally with petrol engines, thus making a total of seven conversions. The two new Tiger chassis, meanwhile, would be equipped with petrol engines taken from the Titan buses. The remaining five petrol engines were to be stored as spares. Although it was another year before a five-cylinder Gardner oil engine for fitment into a Titan chassis was considered, things seemed to have moved on since George Wallis' days (at this time diesel, rather than petrol, engines were also referred to in the trade as 'oil engines' or 'C.I.' – compression ignition – engines. It really did come down to which official, engineer or fitter one was speaking with). The Wilts & Dorset works at Salisbury gained a good reputation in this field, and in the forthcoming World War II service personnel were taught about the idiosyncrasies of diesel engines under the tutelage of the company's engineering staff. One, Mrs Porter, became so proficient that she remained in the company's employ and, by 1950, was in charge of the injection equipment testing and servicing section of the main workshops.

In January 1937, Percy Lephard was declared to be unwell; Alfred Cannon was appointed temporary chairman in his place – an arrangement that lasted rather longer than expected. In March 1938 Lephard was granted further leave of absence and was kept informed of the company's business by periodical visits from Cannon. Lephard, a director since the founding of Wilts & Dorset Motor Services Ltd in 1915 and chairman 1915-1919 and 1926-1937, died on 27 November 1938.

AHR400 (145) was Wilts & Dorset's last Leyland Titan bus to remain in service. New in July 1936, it was not withdrawn until 24 March 1957, ending its days on Salisbury city services. It was substantially still in original condition, although new destination equipment and sliding window vents were fitted in 1948. DAVID PENNELS

Meanwhile, among its many achievements, Wilts & Dorset did something which must remain unique among the annals of bus company history. It moved a pub.

In order to secure a sufficient number of joined-up properties in Endless Street, Salisbury, so that the construction of what was at first to be a 'coach station', but in the event became its famous 'Endless Street Bus Station', could go ahead, Wilts & Dorset came to an agreement with the brewers Gibbs, Mew & Co Ltd. Their 'Woolpack Inn' was no. 8 and adjoined no. 10 which was to become part of the new station. However, Wilts & Dorset's existing traffic offices were at no. 6. Surprisingly, in response to Longman's request, Gibbs, Mew & Co not only agreed to move the Woolpack Inn lock, stock and many barrels into no. 6 for somewhere in the region of £1,500, but urged Wilts & Dorset to get on with their part of the paperwork, because the licensing justices were due to meet in February (1938). The latter approved, the contract was concluded and – in 1940 – the registered office of Wilts & Dorset Motor Services Ltd moved from 2 St Thomas's Square, Salisbury, to take up residence on the site of the old Woolpack Inn.

The capital of Wilts & Dorset Motor Services Ltd was increased in June 1937 by the creation of 50,000 new ordinary shares of £1 each. Alfred Cannon came to the conclusion that the time had arrived when the company should provide additional workshop and garage accommodation in Castle Street, Salisbury. At the time the company owned some 90 buses and it was clear that the increase in military traffic within its area would necessitate a larger fleet. No-one at this stage, however, guessed that this figure would be doubled some two years later (see Chapter 4). The planned expansion and updating of the facilities at Castle Street were put in train and came into use early in World War II.

A rather expensive acquisition in 1938 was made jointly with Hants & Dorset. This was the goodwill only of Austin William Alner and K.J. Hayward's *Victory Motor Service* (that name again) based upon Fordingbridge in Hampshire. The purchase price of £4,750 was shared equally between the companies. Victory had operated local services and market day journeys to Salisbury and to Southampton. Wilts & Dorset did not do too well from its part of the deal, particularly because the five-mile journey from Fordingbridge to Whitsbury, taken over together with a service to Hyde, in July produced about 1.8 pence per mile for some 64 miles per week. It transpired that the Whitsbury service had always been unremunerative since Victory introduced it at the request of the traffic commissioners. So as to keep in the good books of those officials, Wilts & Dorset found another local operator, Douglas Jerrard of Whitsbury, who, that December, proved willing to pay the nominal sum of £10 for the goodwill over this route. This episode is reminiscent of the 'suck it and see' period of Wilts & Dorset's search for custom way back in the 'twenties, but the Bournemouth route was protected thereby.

After the purchase of W. Rowland & Sons' tours and excursions business, the only rival – and a small one at that – left in the field in Salisbury was the Gem Coaches operation of Cyril Joseph Adolphus Cully. In addition Cully had licences for a service of express carriages, upon race days, from Salisbury Railway Station to the Race Plain. On 27 September 1938 Cully sold the goodwill of his operations to Wilts & Dorset for £350. The company was now without competition in the Salisbury tours and excursions field.

As 1938 drew to a close, the plans for the new Salisbury bus station, drawn up by Messrs Michael Harding & Elgar were approved by H.J. Starkey, the

Tilling architect. The latter also seems to have been responsible for selecting the properties to be demolished to make way for the new station. The construction contract, worth £13,686, went to H. & J. Taylor (Contractors) Ltd of London, which firm was also chosen to build the garage extension in Castle Street, Salisbury. In yet another example of the cost-saving culture maintained as of necessity at Wilts & Dorset, the board agreed to do without an attractive clock tower featured in the plans for the Endless Street bus station. The station was completed and opened in August 1939, in the last weeks of peace.

In March 1939, upon the proposition of Alfred Cannon, George Cardwell was unanimously elected chairman of the Wilts & Dorset board of directors: Cannon, relinquishing his seat as acting chairman became instead deputy chairman. Although Cardwell at the outset of his managerial career had been a British Electric Traction Company employee, at one stage serving with the Aldershot & District Traction Co Ltd, he had changed horses in 1930 and joined Thomas Tilling Ltd. Thus, when in 1931 he had become a director of Wilts & Dorset at the time of the involvement of the company's affairs in the Tilling & British Automobile Traction Co Ltd, he was very much the Tilling nominee, (just as Charles Stanley was BAT's). Although the marriage of Tilling and BAT interests was to survive until divorce in 1942, the elevation of Cardwell to the chairmanship seems to have led, as it did in other companies, to a distinct shift in vehicle purchase policy away from what might be described as a distinctly BET flavour (Leylands and Brush bodywork for instance) towards the products of two distinctly Tilling-style manufacturers, Bristol and Eastern Coach Works.

The crew of a 1937 Leyland LT7 Lion pose with a colleague beside their new bus at Tidworth. AMW481 (153) was Wilts & Dorset's first diesel-engined single deck; it had a Harrington 32-seat dual purpose body. It was waiting to take the Bourne Valley route to Salisbury, with Cholderton and Winterbourne squeezed above Salisbury in the narrow destination display. After 12 years in service a more powerful Gardner 5LW engine replaced its original the four-cylinder Leyland unit. Arthur Blake, DAVID PENNELS COLLECTION

Wilts & Dorset's new chairman not only referred the board to a pooling scheme promoted by the Tilling Association to provide for the supply of vehicles to associated companies in the event of 'disaster by fire', he oversaw the placement of an order for twelve new Bristol K5G double deckers to be fitted with ECW bodywork. When these arrived (in 1940), they were painted in Tilling red and cream, the latter replacing the previously applied French grey in the appropriate places. Although the coach fleet's livery was to retain a distinctly Southdown arrangement in its rufous version of the latter's green (which survived briefly beyond World War II), the stage carriage fleet had taken its first step toward becoming a recognisably Tilling-oriented stable.

This pattern was only halted by a very large influx of second-hand vehicles – a fleet of many colours – whose purpose is explained in the following chapter.

To mark his coronation King George VI reviewed the fleet at Spithead on 20 May 1937. Coachloads converged on Southsea to see the ships. One of them travelled on Wilts & Dorset's first Leyland Tiger, MW4594 (66), which Harrington had rebodied in 1936. It waits beside one of the pair of Leyland Cubs new that year in Salisbury Market Square, which the company used as the starting point for excursions until the bus station opened in August 1939. DAVID PENNELS COLLECTION

4
Wilts & Dorset's War

THE GREAT WAR of 1914-1918 slowed the development of the infant motor bus industry. By contrast World War II, despite all the restrictions that it brought with it, placed such demands on the business that it expanded greatly. This can hardly be more true of any operator than Wilts & Dorset; it had to more than double its fleet, almost overnight, by finding an extra 115 buses, enough to carry well over 5,000 seated passengers.

Since 1934 UK defence spending had gone mostly to the navy and the air force, and Britain was to have what the historian A.J.P. Taylor called a 'limited liability' army, fit only for colonial defence. In the aftermath of the September 1938 Munich Agreement, Germany's dismemberment of Czechoslovakia changed minds in the British government. 'The great jump was made in February 1939. Limited liability was abandoned,' wrote Taylor, and it was the army's turn to spend money.

This led to a vast and rapid expansion of army facilities on and around Salisbury Plain. Fleets of buses were needed to convey construction workers to sites at some distance from the towns where they lived. One of the biggest was

Blandford Camp, a few miles across the county boundary in Dorset. Used by both the navy and the air force between 1914 and 1919, the site had since been returned to farming. Now it was to be a mobilisation and training centre for reservists called up to meet the threat of war.

Raymond Longman, secretary of Wilts & Dorset, put

Among the quaintest buses that spent a brief time with Wilts & Dorset in 1939 were three AEC Regents from Brighton Hove & District. They had been with Thomas Tilling's Brighton fleet until November 1935. None of them stayed with the Salisbury company beyond the end of 1939. GP6237 (136) ended its days as a showman's vehicle. THE OMNIBUS SOCIETY

Hants & Dorset was the first to help out when Wilts & Dorset had to find an extra 115 buses in 1939. It provided a dozen Leyland TD1s, all with open staircases, and four Leyland PLSC3 Lions. RU9495, its original owner's E288, is parked at Gosport. It became Wilts & Dorset's no. 47, received a diesel engine in 1942 and a new body by Duple in 1943. Painted in wartime all-grey it re-entered service at Amesbury depot. THE OMNIBUS SOCIETY

London dealer W.R. Wintour supplied eight ex-Ribble Motor Services Leyland TD1s in 1939. CK4208, seen in its original condition, stayed long enough with Wilts & Dorset to be numbered 215, but by March 1940 it had gone back north to Ribble's neighbour, Cumberland Motor Services Ltd. DAVID PENNELS COLLECTION

above] When Wilts & Dorset bought Leyland TD1 Titans in 1929 it opted for the enclosed-staircase version, but some of those that it obtained in a hurry in 1939 had open staircases. Four of these came from Tyneside Tramways & Tramroads, via W.R. Wintour, including TY6972, photographed for Leyland publicity when it was brand new in 1930. It became Wilts & Dorset's no. 224, received a diesel engine in 1942 and a new Duple body in 1943, and remained in service until 1952. DAVID PENNELS COLLECTION

above right] Seven of the 115 extra buses that Wilts & Dorset assembled in a hurry in 1939 came from Maidstone & District and its subsidiary, Chatham & District. Only two of them remained beyond the end of the year, including TD1 Titan KR6530 (204), caught by the camera at the back of Endless Street bus station, still with its original Leyland body. The surviving pair of ex-Chatham vehicles was sent to Loughborough in the last months of the war to be rebodied by Willowbrook. ALAN CROSS

left] Wilts & Dorset took whatever buses it could lay its hands on in 1939 when it was confronted with the demand for 119 buses a day to Blandford Camp alone, more than its entire prewar fleet. A motley collection of elderly machines was pressed into service right away, without repainting. It included four AEC Regents that Nottingham Corporation had withdrawn and sold to a London dealer. One of these was its no. 39, registered TV1639, with camel-hump roof. For a few months it became Wilts & Dorset's no. 228. ANDREW WALLER COLLECTION

in a bid for the contract to convey the workers to Blandford Camp. Donald Bealing, who worked in the company's machine shop for many years and knew him well, said Longman himself had told him the story. 'He had no idea how he was going to do it, because he didn't have enough buses to do it. And much to his surprise, and I doubt very much if that was correct, he was awarded the contract,' Bealing explained.

At the end of the war the Tilling Organisation hailed the group's achievements in a booklet called *The War that Went on Wheels*, which contained a contribution from each member company. Wilts & Dorset, which became part of the Tilling group in 1942, described how

Aerodromes, transit camps, shadow factories grew up rapidly, and first the men who built them and then those that manned them had to be given transport to and from their scattered billets or into the towns for

Ex-Tyneside TY6974 (225) was one of the huge fleet of buses that conveyed workers to Blandford Camp in 1939. There it came to grief in a ditch. The driver must have climbed out through the window over the bonnet, but the bus does not seem to have sustained serious damage. Wilts & Dorset had engineers on site, because some of the second-hand vehicles bought in haste needed urgent mechanical attention to ensure they could complete the journey back to Salisbury. DAVID PENNELS COLLECTION

The fourteen aged Tilling-Stevens that came from Southdown to swell Wilts & Dorset's numbers in 1939 stayed so short a time that they seem to have eluded the camera, but Short-bodied UF4659, which carried the number 6 for just three months, passed to Shergold & White and soldiered on in regular service until 1946. After that they used it for several years as crew quarters, in which guise it is seen parked beside Silver Star's garage on Ministry of Defence land at Porton Down.
MICHAEL PLUNKETT

Southdown provided by far the biggest contingent of second-hand buses in 1939. There were 41 Leyland TD1s and 17 assorted single decks. The Short-bodied Titans were Wilts & Dorset's first highbridge double decks, and looked massive beside the company's lowbridge vehicles. UF7078, which became no. 19, was photographed whilst still with Southdown, at Pool Valley in Brighton. SOUTHDOWN ENTHUSIASTS CLUB

Thirty-one Wilts & Dorset men pose for the camera at Blandford Camp in 1939. Most had driven busloads of workmen constructing the new army camp; two had their driver's badges but were apparently not yet issued with uniforms. Some of the men were no doubt engineers sent out to make sure that every bus, however road-weary, could make the run back to Salisbury at the end of the workers' shift. The man with goggles perched on his cap must have come by motorcycle. DAVID PENNELS COLLECTION

recreation. At one time we were running 119 buses each day to Blandford Camp alone; more than our entire pre-war fleet, for in April 1939 we were managing very nicely with a total of 108 vehicles.

Longman 'had to go all over the country to buy second-hand buses,' Bealing recalled. 'A lot of them were not roadworthy. In fact they were towed into Salisbury.' Fitters worked overnight in the Castle Street engineering shop so the buses could drive to Blandford Camp in the morning. 'I was in the machine shop. We used to make the parts, or recondition the parts for the fitters to use. They used to take the buses that were in reasonable roadworthy condition down to Blandford and engineers would work on them during the day so that they could bring the workers back home at night.' David Pennels described the situation in mid-1939 as 'so acute . . . that recently acquired vehicles were pressed into service

Of Wilts & Dorset's 650 peace-time employees, almost all men, nearly 300 joined the armed forces in World War II. Many women took their places, as conductresses and as work-shop mechanics. Blandford driver Stan Jay, who was later in charge of the depot, poses with his conductress before one of the 115 second-hand buses acquired in 1939. The photograph dates from some time between 1941, when Blandford garage was built, and 1943, when ex-Hants & Dorset Leyland TD1 TK2591 was rebodied. DAVID PENNELS COLLECTION

immediately, most of them still wearing the liveries of their former owners. Very often vehicles were hurriedly refuelled and made ready for Blandford Camp contract work within a few hours of their arrival in Salisbury.'

Bealing said Longman told him that 'he made so much profit from this contract that he handed some of it back to the government, because he felt that the amount of money that they made was inappropriate at that time for the sake of the country. It wasn't fair to take that amount of profit, so he handed it back to the government.'

Two of the company's near neighbours were among the first to make withdrawn buses available to Wilts & Dorset. Sixteen came from Hants & Dorset in April and June 1939, and Southdown provided 58 between June and October. Most of the remainder came from dealers in second-hand buses in London and Leeds. Elderly buses from Brighton, Kent and Essex, from Nottingham and Huddersfield, and from Birkenhead, Bolton, Preston and Tyneside, all joined the daily convoys to Blandford and construction sites on Salisbury Plain.

For the passengers, whether military or civilian, it was no fun travelling by bus during World War II. Few people had cars, many needed to travel, and there weren't enough buses. When a bus did turn up it might already be full of standing passengers packed in like sardines. In 1941 the government changed the rules about standing passengers in single decks. If the seats were rearranged around the periphery of the bus, it could carry as many standing passengers as there were seats, up to a maximum of 30. The pre-war limit was eight. *The Salisbury Journal* described a trial run in an adapted saloon:

> The seats now run along each side of the bus, after the manner of the old tramcar seats, and down the centre of the vehicle is a spacious well in which two rows of passengers may stand. The conductress has sufficient room in which to pass up and down collecting fares.

The paper's reference to a conductress makes it clear that by then it was perfectly normal for women to have taken the place of male bus conductors who had been called up, but in fact it was a big social change for so many women to be working on the buses. In April 1939 the Government had ordered six months' conscription for all men of 20 plus. This was automatically extended when Britain declared war on Germany on 3 September that year.

The Salisbury-Andover route, no. 8 via Amesbury, Tidworth and Ludgershall, was one of Wilts & Dorset's most frequent and heavily used country services. Before the war it was hourly most of the day, half-hourly at peak times. By 1942 there was a bus every 15 minutes at peak times. Tidworth, a busy British garrison in peacetime, was given over to the American military that year. There were plenty of people in Amesbury and Ludgershall too, who needed to go to town to work or shop.

With British troops fighting the battle of el-Alamein in the Egyptian desert, the *Andover Advertiser* captured something of the atmosphere at home with an item headed 'Ludgershall bus queuing question' on 3 July 1942. It read:

It must have seemed that every bus in sight would be needed to clear wartime queues like this at Salisbury bus station. UF7383 (4), still with its original Short highbridge body, heads a line up of four double decks, another ex-Southdown Titan bringing up the rear. The second bus is a Park Royal-bodied Titan. On the right is a Tiger TS8, with Harrington body, working the Woodford Valley service to Amesbury. THE OMNIBUS SOCIETY

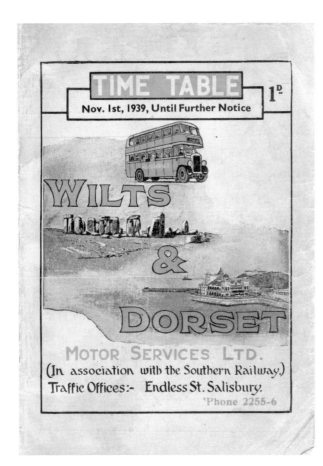

Recently 'Bus Stop' notices were installed at two main shopping points in the village and last weekend the queuing order was seen under the new conditions for the first time at the height of the rush hour. It proved far more satisfactory than the state of affairs at this time of day for weeks past. The presence in the vicinity of a Senior Police Officer may have had something to do with this; nevertheless, for once physique was not of more importance in getting on a bus than patience.

All too regrettable though it was in the past, on Saturday afternoons particularly, when the bus pulled up at recognized – but in the past unmarked – stopping places at the height of the busiest period, there would be a concerted rush towards the conductor's platform, hardly giving the alighting passengers room to leave the vehicle. The prospective fares would swarm round in undignified fashion.

Let us hope this state of affairs has gone for ever. On each side of the main street there are stopping notices. The head of the queue should start beneath them and face the oncoming bus. The entrance of the bus will be level with the head of the queue. If there are a couple of seats available, then the pair at the head will take them, if more, then likewise.

For many in recent months the possibility of getting on a bus for Andover on a Saturday afternoon, even though its purpose may be of vital importance, has been a dread. Queue orderliness and obedience should cause this to

disappear, for it is unlikely that the company, in these days of petrol and labour shortage, not forgetting the rubber question, could, even if they were allowed to do so, put on more buses on the Salisbury to Andover route.

To add to passengers' discomfort lighting had to be dimmed for fear of air raids. Conductors were issued with little torches that shone blue so they could see to collect fares. The buses themselves had their headlamps masked so that drivers had to find their way at night with only a thin strip of light before them. To reduce the danger of collisions at night the leading edge of the front mudguards, the rear skirt and the lifeguard rails along the side were painted white.

Six months before prime minister Neville Chamberlain declared 'this country is at war with

Delivered just months before Britain declared war in 1939, Leyland TD5 Titan BWV663 (166) was photographed whilst still in prewar livery, but with masked headlamps and white-lined mudguards – to assist night-time visibility in reduced lighting. The conductor, cap jauntily tilted to the left, sports a Setright ticket machine, which stamped pre-printed tickets with the fare, date and the stage number at which the passenger boarded. DAVID PENNELS COLLECTION

UF7407 was a Wilts & Dorset bus (no. 243) for no more than six months, but as a company breakdown wagon it lasted another 21 years to become the company's last TD1 Titan. Southdown's Portslade works had carried out the conversion to its new role. Its price for scrap in 1961 was £88, but years later preservationists took an interest and a Taunton auctioneer sold it for £700 in 1990. DAVID PENNELS

In the late 1930s Wilts & Dorset began to paint the window surrounds of its buses cream, instead of French grey. By the time WV4923 (116) was repainted the wide cream band above the lower deck windows was omitted. This Leyland TD3 Titan was photographed in Marlborough early in World War II, with masked headlamps and white tips to its mudguards. A taller destination box had replaced the original single-line display, although in this case it offers no extra information. THE OMNIBUS SOCIETY

Wartime austerity was still over the horizon when Wilts & Dorset's first Bristol double decks arrived in January 1940. The livery style, and even the position of the fleet number, followed the Southdown practice that pervaded the company in the 1920s and 1930s. Eastern Coach Works built the body but, with its flared skirt and the D-window behind the stairway, it mimicked the design of Park Royal bodies on Wilts & Dorset's last Leyland Titans, the type that the company chose until it was obliged to opt for Bristol chassis. COLIN MORRIS COLLECTION

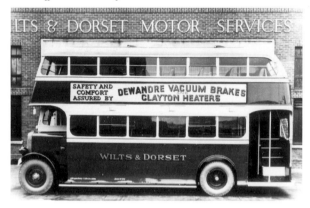

UF7411 (16), one of the 41 ex-Southdown Leyland Titans acquired in 1939, shows off its shiny new Wilts & Dorset body outside the Castle Street works in 1941. Eastern Coach Works rebodied seven other Titans in the same year, and 16's new bodywork was to a similar design. After it was withdrawn in April 1952 no. 16 went to Crosville Motor Services Ltd, Chester. Later in the 1950s it frequently came back to Salisbury as a showman's vehicle. DAVID PENNELS COLLECTION

Germany' the Wilts & Dorset board was forewarned that new vehicles were urgently needed because of the extra traffic on Salisbury Plain. In the event the order for three new Leyland Titans that was recorded at the time was woefully inadequate. They arrived in June 1939, two months after the company had begun to absorb the 115 second-hand buses.

More than half of these vehicles stayed only months with the company, for as the building contracts were completed they were no longer needed. Fortunately for Wilts & Dorset another two dozen new vehicles were delivered by the end of March 1940. The 12 dual-purpose Leyland Tiger saloons and 12 double decks were all built to pre-war standards. The double decks were the company's first Bristols, which became the standard chassis until Hants & Dorset finally absorbed the

With its Castle Street depot given over to assembling Spitfire parts, Wilts & Dorset still found space to build new bodies for five of its aged Leyland Titans between 1941 and 1944. The new body on TK2592 (38), originally Hants & Dorset's E52, resembled the Eastern Coach Works design on the Bristols that arrived in 1940, except for the rake on the front of the top deck. The grey paint, a wartime economy measure, also made the bus less visible to hostile aircraft. DAVID PENNELS COLLECTION

company 32 years later. The single decks were all converted to the standee layout described above between 1941 and 1943 and only returned to normal after the end of the war. The arrival of the Bristols foreshadowed a change in the company's ownership in 1942.

Fifty-three of the second-hand buses, all Leyland Titans dating from 1929-1931, remained with Wilts & Dorset. Of these, 33 came from Southdown and had the highbridge bodies which were standard to the Brighton company. These buses, with a central gangway on the upper deck, were a foot higher than Wilts & Dorset's lowbridge vehicles, which had a sunken upper deck gangway along the offside, giving access to four-abreast seats. This restricted the higher vehicles' use on routes with low railway bridges.

Once the government took control of production in 1940 there was little prospect of new buses being delivered, so Wilts & Dorset embarked upon a major programme to prolong the useful lives of the 53 acquired Titans and its own older buses. By the end of the war the company's Castle Street workshops had built new bodies for five of them. Between 1941 and 1945 another 44 double decks were rebodied by six different coachbuilders around the country, most of them to austere and somewhat basic specifications laid down by the Ministry of Supply. In time, apart from four vehicles given Leyland diesel units before the war, all the TD1 Titans received Gardner diesel engines. The last one in passenger service ran until 1955.

In mid-1940 the War Department requisitioned 12 of Wilts & Dorset's older vehicles 'by mutual agreement'. The following April the Royal Air Force took another nine single decks. At the time these 21 vehicles' book value averaged a mere £10 apiece. However, when compensation became available in December 1947 the company received £3,910 for them in toto. Also requisitioned, by the Royal Navy, and later returned with handsome compensation, was Raymond Longman's private yacht *Dulcibella*.

A much greater sacrifice for the war effort was demanded soon after the first dozen buses were called up by the War Department. In September 1940 the Luftwaffe successfully bombed the Vickers Supermarine aircraft factories at Woolston on the Itchen estuary in Southampton. Fearing just such an event, Lord Beaverbrook, the Minister of Aircraft Production, had already ordered that production of the Spitfire fighter be dispersed, among other places to Trowbridge, Newbury, Salisbury and Reading. The Castle Street depot was one of a half dozen sites in the Salisbury area commandeered to work on Spitfires. According to local legend Supermarine representatives, accompanied by the police, turned up unannounced to take over the Salisbury premises. These were right next to Wilts & Dorset's new workshops, into which company engineers had hastily moved their equipment from the old workshops on the other side of Castle Street.

Using equipment salvaged from the wrecked Southampton factory, Spitfire wings were built in the Wilts & Dorset depot, whilst the fuselages and other parts of the planes were assembled in different premises nearby. Articulated transporters, known as *Queen Marys*, then ferried the completed aircraft parts to High Post Aerodrome, on the Amesbury Road, or the Chattis Hill training gallops, near Stockbridge, for final assembly and flight testing.

This left Wilts & Dorset with only about half of its Castle Street site. In this confined space the company overcame the shortage of spare parts by reconditioning items that would otherwise have been scrapped. Worn parts, like axles and ball-bearing housings, were built up with welded metal and machined to standard dimensions. In the interests of economy reconditioning worn parts remained an important part of the works' activities after the war.

Wilts & Dorset's engineers stayed at their workbenches because they were in what the government classified as a 'reserved occupation'. Being next to the temporary Spitfire works they were able to make their own informal contribution to the war effort. Don Bealing recounted that 'When the Spitfires were in there, if they had any sort of minor engineering trouble, they used to come into our workshop.'

One day they came in and they said: 'Can you check this, because our wings are so much out.' . . . They brought it into the machine shop, and we had a laying-out table . . . and we set it up and checked it. I think it was five-and-a-half thou[sandths of an inch] out from the central boss to the end of the wing. Now five-and-a-half thou on that sort of distance makes a lot of difference when you get down there at the end of a wing.

So we said: 'There we are. There's your problem.' So we turned it over, and where it had been ill-treated,

Donald Bealing, who joined the engineering department before World War II as a teenage apprentice, at work in the Castle Street machine shop. DONALD BEALING

Early in October 1940 Wilts & Dorset's new 'Retreat' garage – so called because of the property that stood there before – was requisitioned for wartime use as an aircraft factory. Vickers Supermarine, whose Southampton premises were a ready target for German bombers, had already moved in with lorry-loads of jigs for building Spitfire wings when these photographs were taken. A few buses were still in residence, including (upper picture) an ex-Southdown Leyland Titan and MW2750, the ex-Rowland Leyland PLSC3 Lion that Wilts & Dorset rebodied in 1937. In the lower picture the line-up includes three buses from other operators requisitioned for war service. Two, both with their engines missing, can be identified as a Southern National Dennis Ace coach, and a Hants & Dorset Leyland Cub. Captain Parker, Chief Inspector Supplementary Transport, Southern Command, was based in Salisbury; he called up a number of Southern National Aces in July 1940, and may have asked Wilts & Dorset to provide mechanical backup. VICKERS SUPERMARINE, NORMAN PARKER COLLECTION

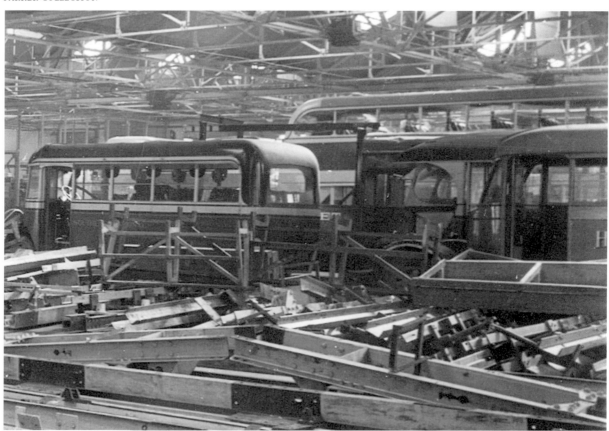

Vickers Supermarine apparently had these photographs taken in order to gain an impression of the size of the premises they were taking over. They found a handful of newly washed buses still parked in the depot as Spitfire-building material was being moved in and taking up space. The five vehicles in the top picture, all Leylands, show how bus design developed in the 1930s. From left to right they are an unidentified PLSC Lion, WV2379 (109) - a 1933 TD2 Titan, MW4596 (68) - a 1929 LT1 Lion, TS8 Tiger CHR476 (177) – newest of them all, showing off well the curved rear corner windows of its Harrington body, and BWV667 (170) – a 1939 LT8 Lion. The lower picture looks across to the Castle Street exit where a Park Royal–bodied Titan TD5 seems to be standing guard over the premises it was being obliged to hand over. VICKERS SUPERMARINE, NORMAN PARKER COLLECTION

The German U-boat threat to Britain's fuel supplies began to diminish in 1943, but the war effort still had a prior call on scarce supplies. To save fuel, the government required bus companies to convert a small proportion of their vehicles to producer gas propulsion. The eight Leyland TD1s and a TD2 that Wilts & Dorset selected for conversion pulled Tilling T2 trailers containing an anthracite furnace and gas production unit. All-grey TD1 MW9397 (103), pictured in March 1944, stands at the bus stop for Wilton in Blue Boar Row, a two-way street in those days. By the lamp post lurks a 'Wilts & Dorset' watering can, thirsty buses for the use of – as the army would have put it; the gas filtration tank, as well as the radiator, needed topping up. Everybody's was a popular weekly illustrated magazine. Another gas bus was UF7409 (235), with its trailer receiving the attention these units frequently required from the mechanics. DAVID PENNELS COLLECTION

unfortunately, there was a burr on one edge. So we carefully filed that off, and made it absolutely accurate. And that made all the difference.

Another problem they had; they wanted to drill a hole with a flat bottom. Nobody seemed to know how to do this. To us it was pretty obvious. You did one of two things. You want an end-milling machine, or you could do it by hand, or you could use a flat-bottomed drill. So, we said 'well, what you want is a flat-bottomed drill then.' 'Ah, where do we get one of those then? What's a flat-bottomed drill?' So we just made one. It's only an ordinary drill; instead of having a point like that, you just round it off, and make it flat on the end. They thought that was wonderful, that was. We gave them two or three of those and away they went.

With the temporary loss of its depot, as well as its much increased fleet, the company was seriously short of parking space. Buses had to be dispersed around car parks in different parts of Salisbury. One site that was extensively used was the old swimming pool car park, which lay across the river Avon from the back of the Castle Street works. With hard-worked vehicles spending cold winter nights out of doors there was often a problem starting them in the morning. Don Bealing said the workshop devised a kind of canopy on wheels, which directed hot air from an oil heater at the radiator to warm it up gradually so the bus would start.

Faced with the threat of night-time air raids the government imposed a strict blackout to prevent enemy pilots being able to pick out their targets; instrument-

based targeting was at best rudimentary by modern standards. All vehicles had to mask their headlights. David Pennels recalls a journey from Figheldean to Salisbury being interrupted at Amesbury while a fitter was called out from the depot to screw masks on to the interior lights. With severe restrictions on paint supplies, newly bodied vehicles were delivered in all-over grey livery.

In 1943, as part of a national drive to save fuel, bus companies had to convert a small proportion of their

No, this is not Walmington-on-Sea. These doughty warriors are somewhere in landlocked Wiltshire. Wilts & Dorset's directors decided to sell off their six Morris Commercial Viceroy saloons in 1940, because they took up space that could be put to better use in wartime, but MW8984 (125) stayed on to serve the war effort until 1943. The 24-seat Viceroys, with bodies by Heaver, of Durrington, cost around £800 apiece in 1931. DAVID PENNELS COLLECTION

Compared to many operators Wilts & Dorset did not suffer badly from enemy action during World War II, but Leyland Lion MW4596 (68) was a casualty at Trowbridge in July 1942. It was sent to Eastern Coach Works for a replacement body, which was partially to Ministry of Supply austerity specification, but of pleasing if somewhat utilitarian appearance. Though photographed at Salisbury in August 1949, 68 spent most of its rebodied life at Blandford depot. J.H. ASTON

Wilts & Dorset bought six new Leyland coaches in 1930. Four of them were LT2 Lions like MW6290 (82). A few years later their four-cylinder engines were found to be not powerful enough and six-cylinder units replaced them. They went to Eastern Coach Works in 1943 to have their Harrington bodies rebuilt. When photographed in Salt Lane car park in June 1952, 82 had long since been relegated to stage bus duties. The slots above the fleet number plate were fitted in anticipation of a car running number system that was never fully implemented. DAVID PENNELS

CWV779 (261) was one of four utility Daimler buses that arrived in 1943. They were painted grey all over, except for patches of white for night-time visibility. The wartime Ministry of Supply restricted opening windows to one per side on each deck and stipulated that panel-beating be kept to a minimum, hence the 'lobster-back' rear roof panels. Initially used on Salisbury city services, the Daimlers spent some of their early years at Blandford depot. S.L. POOLE, LONDON BUS PRESERVATION GROUP

Wilts & Dorset rebuilt its 1943 Daimlers just after the war to bring them in line with its standards of appearance, ventilation and destination display. In this guise CWV 781 (263) and the other three Brush-bodied CWG5s were frequently used on the longer routes to Bournemouth and Southampton, but they returned to Salisbury city services at the end of their working lives in the mid-1950s. DAVID PENNELS

The demand for bus travel grew dramatically during World War II. However, there were constraints on the output of new vehicles and on manpower to run them, so in September 1941 the government raised the maximum number of standing passengers allowed from eight to 30. All 16 Leyland TS8 Tigers, new in 1939/40, were converted to perimeter seating for 28, plus (officially) 20 standing passengers. Like the rest of the batch, CHR485 (186) returned to its normal seating for 32 in 1946. Portsmouth Aviation rebuilt it three years later. ALAN CROSS

vehicles to producer gas propulsion. Wilts & Dorset was one of several companies that had experimented in 1939 with the French Gohin-Poulenc system, using a Leyland Lion saloon. In a similar test on a Hants & Dorset saloon the system was installed in the boot and a gas filtration unit, filled with water, replaced the fuel tank. The engine suffered excessive cylinder wear and bad weather made the system temperamental.

British operators eschewed the Gohin-Poulenc system. Perhaps they were persuaded by the fate of a Brighton Hove & District double deck, on which the boiler exploded and blew the staircase off. Instead they adopted the solution proposed by W.J. Morison, Chief Engineer at the Eastern National Omnibus Co Ltd in Chelmsford, to use producer gas trailers. He had remedied problems of filtration and cylinder wear, made

Trouble starting! One man to wrestle with the starting handle and another to tease the engine into action once the spark plugs showed signs of life: it was a serious business, with the side panel of the bonnet propped up beside the bus. MW3852 (65) was the last of the Leyland PLSC3 Lions, new in 1929. Looking much more modern with its 1945 Beadle body, its 5.1 litre engine must have been a bit tired on a July day in 1946. THE OMNIBUS SOCIETY

As World War II drew to a close Wilts & Dorset set about rebodying four of its elderly Leyland Lions. MW7052 (91) was the first of the four, emerging from the bodyshop in July 1945 with the outswept skirt and two-aperture destination display then favoured by the company. By the time the other three bodies were built a three-aperture destination display was the new standard. DAVID PENNELS

right] The notice on the Castle Street frontage of the company's main workshops, completed in 1939, reads: 'Parking for Wilts & Dorset cars only'. In this case it meant what most people understand by the word 'car', not Douglas Mackenzie's preferred term for what is generally referred to as a 'bus'. Donald Bealing collection

below] The Weymouth bus already has a full load, mostly of soldiers, as it waits in Salisbury bus station on a grey day in March 1944. In the background is one of the ST-type AEC Regents that London Transport loaned to Wilts & Dorset for 18 months in December 1942. Apart from its grey paint and masked headlamps Bristol K5G CHR497 (198) is still as it was when new in 1940. The Weymouth service retained the number 20 from when it started in 1929 until it became a joint operation with Southern National in December 1948, when both companies numbered it 34. DAVID PENNELS COLLECTION

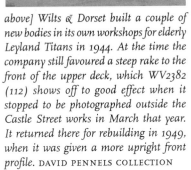

above] In 1941 the company slipped in an order with Eastern Coach Works for seven new bodies for old Leyland Titans it had bought from Southdown. Wartime restrictions demanded that the Western Regional Transport Commissioner license the use of timber and steel, and the plywood for their roofs. One of the seven was UF7410 (23), which still looked in solid condition when it worked the Bournemouth service on 12 June 1948. Wilts & Dorset wanted another six ECW bodies in 1942, but that year it was out of luck. However, ECW did rebody another six in 1943-44. ALAN CROSS

above] Wilts & Dorset built a couple of new bodies in its own workshops for elderly Leyland Titans in 1944. At the time the company still favoured a steep rake to the front of the upper deck, which WV2382 (112) shows off to good effect when it stopped to be photographed outside the Castle Street works in March that year. It returned there for rebuilding in 1949, when it was given a more upright front profile. DAVID PENNELS COLLECTION

left] Northern Coachbuilders, of New-castle-upon-Tyne, rebodied seven of Wilts & Dorset's ex-Southdown Leyland Titans in 1944. Built to the Ministry of Supply's specification, they were among the most austere and angular of the wartime bodies that the company received. UF7387 (232) rests in Salt Lane car park, a stone's throw from Endless Street bus station. Wilts & Dorset used this park for many years after World War II to accommodate vehicles not immediately required for service. JOHN SANTER

hopper and firebox doors airtight and used anthracite treated with soda to stop clinker forming in the firebox.

The Bristol Tramways & Carriage Co Ltd built the two-wheeled trailers for bus companies around the country. Painted black, they looked like corrugated iron cylinders with a furnace beneath. The trailers hooked on in such a way that buses could reverse with them. The vehicles' engines tended to tar up, so had to be serviced frequently, and mechanics had to wear respirator masks when cleaning and testing the gas units. Despite the problems Wilts & Dorset ran at least four of its gas buses on the Salisbury-Bournemouth road, a joint service with Hants & Dorset. Though a relatively long route it had the advantage of having very few hills. One of these vehicles was an ex-Hants & Dorset bus that Wilts & Dorset had rebodied.

From the latter part of 1940 the supply of new buses was strictly regulated. Wilts & Dorset had ordered eight small-capacity Bedford-Duple saloons, but they never materialised. This was probably just as well, because the directors decided to sell off six ageing Morris-Commercial 24-seaters on the ground that parking space was at such a premium that it could be better used. In July 1942 the board authorised Raymond Longman, who had been appointed general manager on 19 March that year, to apply for a dozen Guy Arab double deck chassis with six-cylinder engines, and to negotiate for 12 bodies for them. The Ministry of Supply ordered 500 of these chassis from Guy's Wolverhampton factory in 1942, but none were allocated to Wilts & Dorset.

The only new vehicles delivered once restrictions were imposed were four Daimler double decks that arrived in 1943, painted all-over grey. During the war operators took whatever vehicles came their way. In the event this foursome did well. After starting on Salisbury city services, they were transferred to Blandford to run the lengthy Salisbury-Weymouth route. Later they worked Salisbury to Southampton, before spending their last years in the mid-1950s back on city services.

Wartime restrictions inevitably led to what in today's jargon would be called rationalisation, in other words service cuts. But where there was heavy demand, as on the Salisbury-Andover run, extra journeys were added to the timetable, and relief buses were frequently required.

Food rationing, unsocial hours, crowded and hard-driven buses, all combined to make heavy demands on those who worked on them through the war. To provide for its staff Wilts & Dorset ran two canteens in Salisbury, one at the bus station and one at the Castle Street works.

left] Eastern Coach Works rebuilt 19 of the Leyland bodies on the company's TD1 Titans between 1944 and 1946, including half a dozen that it had acquired from Ribble Motor Services Ltd. ECW modernised their appearance, fitted them with sliding vents in place of half-drop windows and equipped them with new destination displays. MW7050 (89) was painted in the pre-war livery when it was rebuilt in 1945 and still wore it, like the ex-Ribble ECW-rebuild alongside, when photographed at Salisbury Bus Station in July 1946. THE OMNIBUS SOCIETY

right] Few homes had washing machines in 1946, so the New Forest Laundry must have believed it worthwhile to advertise on the side of BWV663 (166), photographed at Endless Street bus station in July of that year. New in 1939, it was one of the last of nine Park Royal-bodied Leyland TD5 Titans delivered to Wilts & Dorset before war broke out. THE OMNIBUS SOCIETY

left] Leyland TD1 RU9493 (40) emerges from Endless Street bus station in the late 1940s. Nine days before Christmas 1944 it caught fire whilst in service at Longhedge, Salisbury, and its two-year-old Duple utility body was destroyed. It had to be rebodied a second time, this time by Northern Coachbuilders, whose 1946 offering was slightly less austere than those that the Newcastle firm turned out in 1944. BILL CANNINGS

above] One of Wilts & Dorset's two Leyland TD3 Titans, WV4923 (116), was rebodied in 1946 by Willowbrook. It is on the stand for the Larkhill direct service at Endless Street in August 1949, a typical working, for most of the rebodied TD2s and TD3s were allocated to the northern depots, Amesbury and Pewsey. J.H. ASTON

above] New vehicles were still hard to come by in early post-war times. This kept the company's workforce busy making wartime bodies look less austere and replacing unseasoned timber that did not stand the test of time. As rebodied by Duple in 1942, UF7423 (252) had a metal panel instead of glass at the rear of the top deck, and a limited number of half drop windows. When Wilts & Dorset extensively rebuilt the body in 1948 it was pleased enough with the result to pose it with Salisbury Cathedral as a backdrop. DAVID PENNELS COLLECTION

above] In 1942 Wilts & Dorset turned to Duple for utility bodies for six of its second-hand Leyland Titans, after Eastern Coach Works said it could not provide them. One of the six was TY6972 (224), ex-Tyneside. Wilts & Dorset fitted sliding vents and new destination displays in 1947. It is heading south from Amesbury in March 1950. Rebodied TD1s worked the 30-mile services from Marlborough and Devizes to Salisbury for the best part of 10 years. JOHN SANTER

above] Eastern Coach Works, its bus bodying works relocated from Lowestoft to Northamptonshire because of the war, rebodied six of Wilts & Dorset's second-hand Leyland TD1s in 1943-1944. They were to a new, more austere design that foreshadowed the style of ECW products for many years to come. The first to emerge from the works at Irthlingborough was RU9490 (39). ECW had just rebuilt the Harrington bodies on four Leyland Lions and evidently had a supply of coach-style fleetname transfers left over. DAVID PENNELS COLLECTION

left] Like bus companies everywhere, Wilts & Dorset was still desperately short of new vehicles in 1946, when the first post-war buses arrived – five Bristol K5Gs. Their Eastern Coach Works bodies were standard to Tilling group companies, but the destination display, which is being used to good effect on DMR839 (267), was probably unique to Wilts & Dorset. When photographed at Salisbury bus station it still bore the company's pre-war style fleetname. BRISTOL VINTAGE BUS GROUP

When winters were colder and snow drifted deep on Salisbury Plain a serious snowplough was an essential piece of kit for a serious bus company. But you could be forgiven for wondering whether this monster plough might not prove too much for the ex-military Ford Canada V8 (EHR183) hiding behind it, which Wilts & Dorset added to its auxiliary fleet in 1947. DAVID PENNELS COLLECTION

W.H. Tryhorn, the chief engineer, thought highly of Willowbrook as a coachbuilder, so when elderly Leyland Titans needed rebodying after World War II five chassis were sent to the Loughborough concern in 1946. Four of them were of the TD2 type, like Pewsey-based WV2380 (110), seen here in Marlborough High Street in September 1953. JOHN SANTER

Don Bealing recalled: 'We used to have lunch in the canteen. A shilling (5p) we used to pay I think. It was a cooked lunch and of course it was ration-free.' People found other ways to boost their rations too. 'Someone in the machine shop used to catch rabbits at the weekend. One of the drivers used to fish. Some used to go sea-fishing at Hengistbury Head. Bellevue (House, which the company bought early in the war) had a chicken run. So we used to get our eggs from there.'

Raymond Longman, who – as secretary – had run the company since 1924 and became a full-time paid director in February 1940, technically moved on from its employment in 1942, even though he stayed with the company until 1962. It happened like this: Wilts & Dorset was one of the companies affected when, in September 1942, the Tilling & British Automobile Traction Ltd was wound up and the Tilling and British Electric Traction interests in it were severed. The newly formed Tilling Motor Services Ltd acquired Wilts & Dorset, along with Hants & Dorset and a number of other companies. Longman accepted an executive job with Thomas Tilling Ltd, which Wilts & Dorset paid for his services as general manager until 1 October 1946, when he became managing director at a salary of £2,250, also payable to Thomas Tilling.

The change of ownership imposed Tilling vehicle policy, which called for group companies to buy Bristol chassis bodied by Eastern Coach Works of

This service is liable to alteration during June, 1944

Service No. 20.   SALISBURY—WEYMOUTH.   DAILY

(All buses on this service pass Dorchester (Rail) Station)

	N.S.	N.S.	N.S.					Sun.	
	a.m.	a.m.	a.m.	p.m.	p.m.	p.m.	p.m.	p.m.	p.m.
SALISBURY (Bus Stn.)		9- 0	11–40		1–45	4–25	6–30	8–15	9–10
Coombe Bissett	..		9–10	11–50		1–55	4–35	6–40	8–25	9–20
Coote Arms	..		9–25	12- 5		2–10	4–50	6–55	8–40	9–35
Woodyates	..		9–30	12–10		2–15	4–55	7- 0	8–45	9–40
Handley Cross	..		9–35	12–15		2–20	5- 0	7- 5	8–50	9–45
Cashmore Inn	..		9–42	12–22		2–27	5- 7	7–12	8–57	9–52
Tarrant Hinton	..		9–50	12–30		2–35	5–15	7–20	9- 5	10- 0
Pimperne	..		9–57	12–37		2–42	5–22	7–27	9–12	10- 7
Blandford	..	8- 0	10- 5	12–45	2–50	5–30	7–35	9–20	10–15
Winterbourne Whit.	..	8–15	10–20		1- 0	3- 5	5–45	7–50		
Milborne St. Andrew	..	8–25	10–30		1–10	3–15	5–55	8- 0		
Puddletown	..	8–37	10–42		1–22	3–27	6- 7	8–12		
Dorchester (Antelope)	..	8–50	10–55		1–35	3–40	6–20	8–25		
Upwey	..	9- 1	11- 6		1–46	3–51	6–31	8–36		
WEYMOUTH	..	9–12	11–17		1–57	4- 2	6–42	8–47		
(King's Statue)										

This service is liable to alteration during June, 1944

WEYMOUTH—SALISBURY.   DAILY

(All buses on this service pass Dorchester (Rail) Station)

	N.S.	N.S.	N.S.					Sun.	
	a.m.	a.m.	a.m.	p.m.	p.m.	p.m.	p.m.	p.m.	p.m.
WEYMOUTH										
(King's Statue)	..		9–15	11–20		2- 0	4- 5		6–45	9- 0
Upwey	..		9–27	11–32		2–12	4–17		6–57	9–12
Dorchester (Museum)	..		9–40	11–45		2–25	4–30		7–10	9–25
Puddletown	..		9–55	11–58		2–38	4–43		7–23	9–38
Milborne St. Andrew	..		10- 5	12–10		2–50	4–55		7–30	9–50
Winterbourne Whitchurch	..		10–15	12–20		3- 0	5- 5		7–45	10- 0
Blandford	..	7–40	10–30	12–35	12–35	3–15	5–20	7- 0	8- 0	10–15
Pimperne	..	7–45	10–35		12–40	3–20	5–25	7- 5	8- 5	
Tarrant Hinton	..	7–52	10–42		12–47	3–27	5–32	7- 7	8–12	
Cashmore Inn	..	8- 0	10–50		12–55	3–35	5–40	7–15	8–20	
Handley Cross	..	8- 7	10–57		1- 2	3–42	5–47	7–22	8–27	
Woodyates	..	8–15	11- 5		1–10	3–50	5–55	7–30	8–35	
Coote Arms	..	8–20	11–10		1–15	3–55	6- 0	7–35	8–40	
Coombe Bissett	..	8–35	11–25		1–30	4–10	6–15	7–55	8–55	
SALISBURY (Bus Station)	8–45	11–35		1–40	4–20	6–25	8- 5	9- 5	

N.S.—Not on Sundays.   Sun.—Sundays only.   See notice on page 57

WHEN YOU ARRIVE BUY SOME SAVINGS CERTIFICATES

53

During the run-up to D-Day 6 June 1944 the utmost secrecy was enforced upon the proceedings. Thus Military Intelligence rushed round to the offices of a leading national newspaper when, as the fateful day for the invasion of Normandy approached, one of its crossword puzzles considerably alarmed them. Three of the answers happened to be the secret codewords Overlord, Juno and Sword. If they'd seen page 53 of the Wilts & Dorset timetable, they'd have rushed to Salisbury too. 'The road to the coast may be crowded in June!'
DAVID PENNELS COLLECTION

Lowestoft, both of which were also Tilling-owned. Wilts & Dorset's directors still kept up the pressure to acquire new vehicles. They decided in February 1944 to apply for six Bristol double decks to be delivered by the end of the year, and another dozen in 1945. But production was still strictly controlled and they had to wait until 1946 for the first five to arrive. Seven more trickled in by ones and twos the next year.

In *The War that Went on Wheels*, Wilts & Dorset recalled:

> In 1938 we carried 10 million passengers; in 1944 it was nearly 25 million. Our actual running did not change very much from around our normal four or five million miles per annum, but instead of the pleasant country trips with elbow room for all, and a timetable based on convenience, they were a tightly-packed strictly essential five million miles.

> Between 1942 and 1944 we covered 400,000 miles on producer-gas and saved 81,000 gallons of petrol.

> Of our 650 peace-time employees, nearly 300 joined the Forces.

Wilts & Dorset added that its National Savings effort was 'one of the most flourishing in the Tilling Group, and on several occasions headed the list in the monthly table.' Longman himself was especially keen to promote National Savings, and even the company's tickets reflected this. Other bus companies opted for paid advertisements or wartime slogans on the backs of their tickets, like 'Careless talk costs lives' or 'Beat the paperhanger, be a paper saver' – a derogatory propaganda reference to Adolf Hitler. But Wilts & Dorset's tickets bore the legend: 'Change! Put it into savings.'

The stars of Salisbury Arts Theatre Company's first Shakespeare production took their act out into the snow in March 1946, but this was not quite Two Gentlemen of Verona. The troupe hired Wilts & Dorset Leyland Cub WV7333 (119) to take them to Southampton. Standing by the radiator is their regular driver, Bert Cooper. Maybe they asked him to pull over for a photo opportunity. Silvia - beloved of Valentine, (Maxine Audley) aims a snowball at Thurio - foolish rival to Valentine, (George Cormack), as he strikes an actorly pose. Oliver Hunter, who played Valentine, stayed out of the picture. LES COOPER COLLECTION

5
Nationalised Wilts & Dorset

F OR THE BENEFIT of younger readers, the first thing to make clear about this chapter is that 'nationalised' does not refer to some predatory take-over by the National Omnibus and Transport Co Ltd or its rampant subsidiaries in the West Country, the Western and Southern National Omnibus companies – but to a major plank of Socialist policy, the so-called 'public' ownership of selected large industries.

Victory in Europe was celebrated on 8 May 1945. Once again, troops trained upon Salisbury Plain (and of course elsewhere) had reason to feel proud of themselves. Not unreasonably expecting electoral success, prime minister Winston Churchill called a general election. It took place on 1 July but, in order to permit the widespread members of the armed forces to participate, the result was not declared until the 26th of that month. Concerned above all else with postwar social security, the latter are largely credited with the unexpected result. The Labour Party had won 180 seats more than the Conservatives – and Clement Attlee became prime minister.

With victory over Japan (2 September 1945) still to be achieved, Attlee's government pressed ahead with the major objectives of its manifesto. The nationalisation of various forms of transport featured large in that programme. It had called for public ownership of the mainline railways, of airlines and road haulage firms.

MW6293 (85), a 19-year-old Leyland TS1 Tiger coach, was still doing yeoman service when photographed on excursion work in June 1949 and had four more years of working life. Wilts & Dorset had it rebodied by Harrington in time for the 1938 season, and gave it a more modern appearance in 1945 by fitting a Cov-Rad conversion radiator. THE OMNIBUS SOCIETY

Skylark Motor Services sold its stage licences to Wilts & Dorset in 1951. The siting of military camps on the northern fringes of the New Forest had boosted its passenger numbers, so that in the late 1940s it needed double decks to maintain its Woodfalls-Salisbury service, including this rare Thornycroft Daring OW4257, with body by Park Royal. It hid its real identity behind the AEC radiator fitted after Skylark bought it from Southampton Corporation. ALAN CROSS

As Hibbs (1968) opines 'possibly as a result of the absence of a considered plan', the road passenger industry was at first omitted from the forthcoming legislation.

However, all the subsidiary omnibus companies of both the British Electric Traction Co Ltd and Thomas Tilling Ltd were at least partially nationalised by the state take-over of the railways because, in the main, one third of the capital of each had been held by one or other of the former mainline railway companies. In Wilts & Dorset's case that had been, of course, the Southern Railway.

On 1 January 1948, the SR's representatives upon the Wilts & Dorset board, John Chambers and Herbert Short, found themselves representing instead British Railways (Southern Region) and the British Transport Commission, set up under the provisions of the Transport Act 1947.

Wilts & Dorset's first new coaches after World War II were Bristol L6Bs. A dozen of them arrived between 1948 and 1950. John C. Beadle of Dartford bodied the first eight, including EMW283 (278), which was photographed in the parking area behind Bellevue House, Salisbury, in September 1954. Southdown had 23 Leyland Tiger coaches. DAVID PENNELS

In February 1948, 'Uncle' George Cardwell, a director of Wilts & Dorset since May 1931, and its chairman from March 1939, submitted his letter of resignation in view of his appointment as a member of the Road Transport Executive of BTC. Two points of particular note arise therefrom: (1) that this important representative of Thomas Tilling Ltd was invited to join the British Transport Commission's RTE some eight months before Tilling agreed to sell up, and arrange for the formation of the Tilling Group management board of ex-Tilling officers, who would run the nationalised firms on behalf of BTC; and (2) Cardwell, having resigned simultaneously as director and chairman of Hants & Dorset Motor Services Ltd, was replaced as chairman of H&D by – Raymond Longman. That was a full year before Longman became chairman also of Wilts & Dorset (he'd become a director of Hants & Dorset in 1942, and its managing director in 1945 as a representative of Thomas Tilling Ltd).

This was an interesting foretaste of BTC's – and its successor's the Transport Holding Company and National Bus Company's – plans for the bringing together of Hants & Dorset and Wilts & Dorset, which were to unfold over the next 22 years.

In September 1948, and to the dismay of the British Electric Traction group (and Alfred Cannon, no doubt, as well) Thomas Tilling Ltd agreed to sell its transport interests to BTC. As obliged to do, the Wilts & Dorset officers declared their directorships of 'other companies'. Retrospectively it is no surprise that William Fielding was additionally a director of just the Salisbury Gas Co Ltd; but one might have expected that Alfred Cannon would have held a similar position with more than just London Coastal Coaches Ltd and Southdown Motor Services Ltd.

Stanley Kennedy of Thomas Tilling Ltd resigned his directorship and year-long reign as chairman of

Wilts & Dorset on 10 February 1949; and railway representative John Chambers departed upon the same date. His colleague Herbert Short's final act as a Wilts & Dorset director was to propose (and Alfred Cannon seconded) that Raymond Longman should be elected as chairman of the Wilts & Dorset board of directors. This was carried unanimously.

The honour was no more than Longman deserved. In his role as company secretary, and as the most senior officer actually based in Salisbury, he had held virtual control over the affairs of Wilts & Dorset from 1924 until the parting of the ways for Tilling & BAT in 1942. During this period, only the choice of vehicles had been left to Cannon. A director since he replaced Douglas Mackenzie in 1927 and destined to serve the company directly until 1962, if one man could be said to have been synonymous with Wilts & Dorset Motor Services Ltd over the longest number of years, he is surely Raymond Ilfred Henry Longman.

Longman's service with the Royal Flying Corps and the Royal Air Force had lasted from April 1915 until July 1919. His interest in aviation remained with him thereafter. From 1941 to 1945, during World War II, he set time aside from his Wilts & Dorset duties to undertake the role of officer commanding 1010 (City of Salisbury) Squadron of the Air Training Corps. Flight Lieutenant Longman's NCOs were largely Old Wordsworthians, having previously served in No. 28 Squadron ATC at Bishop Wordsworth School. During

Portsmouth Aviation bodied the last four of Wilts & Dorset's Bristol L6B coaches in 1949-50. The design was much the same as the Beadle bodies on the earlier post-war coaches, but for their first few seasons the Portsmouth bodies had maroon streamline flashes along the sides, instead of the narrower cream flashes on the waistline of the Beadle version. FAM3 (286), photographed before it left the works at Portsmouth in 1949, differed in detail from the three coaches bodied there in the spring of 1950. DAVID PENNELS COLLECTION

the war, such cadet units made substantial contributions to the rank and file of the Royal Air Force. In addition, he was the driving force behind a War Weapons Week fund-raising drive, which raised the record sum of £500,000.

Post-war his major relaxation was to drive from his home in Salisbury's Bouverie Avenue South to the Beaulieu River in Hampshire, where his spick and span yacht *Dulcibella* lay moored. In a fascinating interview with Andrew Waller (2006) Don Bealing recalled that this was Longman's pride and joy. It had been requisitioned during World War II for potential use as a medical evacuation auxiliary vessel, but came through the hostilities relatively unscathed. With appointed captain and crew, *Dulcibella* sailed the Solent and along the South Coast, frequently with Wilts & Dorset personnel, and occasionally their ladies, aboard as guests – or in the company of a fellow club (Parkstone) commodore, William Wells Graham of Hants & Dorset Motor Services Ltd.

Thus, at a personal level, beyond the Tilling connection, a closer relationship between Wilts & Dorset and Hants & Dorset was forged by Longman.

One of the first letters received by Roger Wigmore, in his new role as secretary of Wilts & Dorset, came from the secretary of the Tilling Association Ltd in November 1949:

> Revaluation of Assets of Road Passenger Companies formerly in the Tilling Group for the purpose of acquisition by the British Transport Commission:
>
> I hereby certify that I have had access to all relevant reports and certificates by surveyors, engineers and accountants in connection with the revaluation of the tangible assets of Wilts & Dorset Motor Services Ltd for the purpose of acquisition by the British Transport Commission which was effected by agreement dated 5 November 1948 between the British Transport Commission and Thomas Tilling Ltd, which was in respect of that company's interests in any such assets; and further certify that the total valuation of the company's assets upon which that acquisition was based, after taking into account subsequent transactions was, at 1 January 1949, in aggregate £1,201,865. Details of which amount have been supplied in separate schedules to the secretary of the said Wilts & Dorset Motor Services Ltd.

In November 1950, following the acquisition by BTC of the bus interests of the Red & White group of companies (see Chapter 7), Wilts & Dorset entered into a management agreement with that concern's Basingstoke-based subsidiary, Venture Ltd. On the vehicle front, this brought an influx of AEC Regents and Regals into the fleet, plus a pair of Bedford OB coaches.

Wilts & Dorset buses only went to Yeovil for 11 years. The company extended its route 27, Salisbury-Shaftesbury, westwards into Somerset in 1949, in a joint operation with Southern National. EAM614 (271), seen arriving in Yeovil, was a Bristol K6B. This type's powerful six-cylinder Bristol engine proved more suited to long hilly journeys than the K5Gs with their five-cylinder Gardner units. ANDREW WALLER COLLECTION

Leyland TD4 Titan AHR399 (144) leaves Amesbury bus station 'on the Via'. There were two Salisbury-Amesbury-Larkhill routes; number 3 ran to Bulford between Amesbury and Larkhill and was always known to staff and passengers alike as 'the Via'. (Service 2 was 'the Direct'). Wilts & Dorset rebuilt this bus in the Castle Street workshops in 1948, fitting three-aperture destination boxes and sliding vents in place of the original half-drop windows. DAVID PENNELS

From 1946 onwards, the Tilling group of companies had standardised upon Bristol chassis fitted with Eastern Coach Works series 2 bodywork for all new stage carriage vehicles, relieved in small batches by a limited number of Bristol L chassis whose coach bodies were built by other firms.

In Wilts & Dorset's case, new 32-seat coaches were provided by Beadle (of Dartford) and Portsmouth Aviation until, that is, the advent of underfloor-engined Bristol chassis, when coaches and dual purpose saloons also received Eastern Coach Works bodywork. This policy was to be reinforced following partial and then complete nationalisation until, between 1965 and 1971, overstretched production capacity at ECW's Lowestoft factory obliged the Transport Holding Company to switch orders for some saloon and coach chassis to Bedford (Vauxhall Motors Ltd of Luton). Wilts & Dorset received

The interior of post-1945 coaches was more austere than had been the custom in the 1930s, but the décor of the Beadle body on Bristol L6B EMW184 (275) retained something of the atmosphere that pre-war travellers would remember. When this coach was built in 1949 it was still quite normal to provide passengers with ashtrays set into the seat backs. DAVID PENNELS

The bulkhead heater, the overhead luggage racks and cigarette stubbers on the seat backs were regular features of a half-cab single deck bus when GHR867 (306) was built in 1950. It was one of six Bristol L6B saloons delivered that year, which had 35-seat rear-entrance bodies by Eastern Coach Works of Lowestoft. As one-man-saloons became the norm in the late 1950s, these six were delicensed in December 1957, but they returned to service after about a year. DAVID PENNELS

several Bedford chassis types bodied by Duple, Duple Northern, Strachans or Willowbrook, but the pattern was otherwise only relieved by the acquisition of Silver Star Motor Services Ltd of Porton Down (see Chapter 8) and second-hand purchases (see Appendix D – Fleet Summary).

In April 1952, Wilts & Dorset had the better of a deal with Crosville Motor Services Ltd (of Chester), whereby the latter received 10 rather tired Leyland TD1 Titan double deckers in exchange for a similar number of 1937-vintage Leyland TS7 Tiger saloons fitted with ECW bodywork, albeit of slightly odd frontal appearance.

This transfer was made as a sad event effectively erased the last link with Brighton, Southdown and the 'grand design' of 'South Coast Motor Services'. Alfred Cannon had attended his last Wilts & Dorset board meeting at 10 Fleet Street, London, on Wednesday 26 March 1952. He sent his apologies for absence from the meeting of 20 May – and died on 11 June. He was aged 69, and had survived Douglas Mackenzie, 13 years his senior, by just eight years.

Two events of particular note took place in 1953. First, plans were put in

above] In 1950 Wilts & Dorset painted six of its ex-Southdown Leyland TD1s green and loaned them to the Southern Vectis Omnibus Co Ltd on the Isle of Wight. They all had 1944 Brush bodies with the 'lobster-back' roof profile typical of many utility buses. They left the island in 1952 for yet further service with Potteries Motor Traction Ltd, of Stoke-on-Trent. Newly painted UF7417 (258) is parked in front of the Castle Street works before leaving Salisbury for the Lymington-Yarmouth ferry. JOHN SANTER

right] Upavon RAF, on the northern edge of Salisbury Plain, is barely two miles from Upavon village in the valley below. AHR522 (147), one of a pair of 1936 Leyland Cub coaches relegated to bus duties at Pewsey depot in 1950, waits there to pick up passengers. The company adapted the two Cubs for one-man operation, the first vehicles so equipped after World War II, when loadings were so heavy that every bus needed a conductor. R.C. CARPENTER

Horace L. Barber sold the stage service licences of Skylark Motor Services Ltd to Wilts & Dorset in 1951. He started as a driver with the Woodfalls-based firm and stands beside its 1927 REO saloon, MW208. Barber became manager in 1936, and registered Skylark as a limited company at the height of its success as a stage operator, in 1947. It continued in the coaching business until it merged with A. E. Budden & Sons in 1973. DAVID PENNELS COLLECTION

train for the demolition of part of the bus station at Endless Street, Salisbury, and the construction, for £7,459, of a two-storey extension of the building.

Secondly, the share capital of Wilts & Dorset Motor Services Ltd was increased from £150,000 – at which it had stood since 22 June 1937 – to £800,000 by the creation of 650,000 ordinary shares of £1 each. The sum of £469,916 was capitalised and distributed (!) among the holders of 120,000 shares registered in the company's books as held by the British Transport Commission – in the proportion: BTC, 119,998, and British Transport Commission Nominees, Sir Reginald Wilson and Sidney B. Taylor 2. In a fascinating example of nationalised finance, by such means each of the state-owned territorial bus operators remained, for all intents and purposes, separate limited liability companies – Wilts & Dorset included.

Meanwhile, throughout this period, directors appointed to the Wilts & Dorset board represented the Tilling Association Ltd and British Railways (Southern Region). In 1955, the latter disclosed that, as part of a railway modernisation scheme, the Salisbury-Southampton-Portsmouth line was to be operated by an accelerated service of diesel-electric multiple-unit trains. The elderly

One of the four Leyland LT8 Lions bought just before war broke out in 1939 - BWV667 (170), waits at Amesbury to serve the Woodford Valley villages. Wilts & Dorset rebuilt its Harrington body in 1951. In the process it raised the floor each side of the gangway so all seats faced forward, it fitted sliding vents in the windows and new destination equipment. At the same time it replaced its four-cylinder Leyland engine with a more powerful five-cylinder unit. DAVID PENNELS

Drummond T9 light-traffic steam locomotives were to be put out to grass.

The after-effects of the Finance Act 1950 already having raised the cost of fuel and much else, this was not good news for Wilts & Dorset, Hants & Dorset and, in the eastern section, Southdown as well. Already, increased bus fares and fewer passengers, as the travelling public turned to acquiring their own motorised means of transport, were beginning to signal the beginning of the end of what turned out to have been the 'heyday' of travel by bus.

Wilts & Dorset began to sell off 'surplus' properties and rent out others to such bodies as Wilts County Council and local businesses.

In addition, the British and French governments' Suez Campaign of 1956 led to a surcharge upon stage-carriage fares under the Hydrocarbon Oils Duties (Temporary Increase) Act 1956. That followed a further exodus of troops and airmen

In the early 1950s Wilts & Dorset's coaches were still painted in colours that echoed the albeit green scheme used by Southdown. Mainly red below the waistrail, they had maroon roof, window surrounds and wings, with narrow cream bands above and/or below the windows. Leyland TS6 Tiger WV5527 (118), on an excursion from Amesbury, was one of three Wilts & Dorset coaches that went to Brighton on August Bank Holiday 1952. The others were a Bristol from Salisbury and an AEC from Basingstoke. DAVID PENNELS

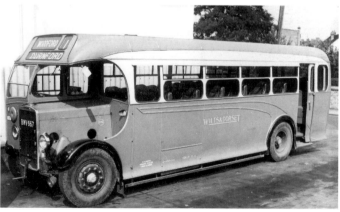

Wilts & Dorset and Hants & Dorset began a joint service between Salisbury and Poole in 1948, via Cranborne and Wimborne. GMR29 (308), a 35-seat Bristol L6B of 1950 with body by Eastern Coach Works, turns into Wimborne Square before wending its way along the Dorset lanes to Cranborne. Joint service 97 only lasted until May 1953, when Wilts & Dorset retained the Cranborne-Salisbury section as its service 42. THE OMNIBUS SOCIETY

A change in the regulations in 1950 affecting the length of buses allowed single decks to be 30 feet long. The three extra feet made room for four more seats. GMW913 (323) was one of a trio of Eastern Coach Works-bodied 39-seat Bristol LL6Bs that arrived by the following January. It is waiting in Salisbury 'on the dump', as company staff called it, having been washed and refuelled, ready for a Hindon-based driver to drive it back west to its home territory. DAVID PENNELS

CHR490 (191), a 1940 Bristol K5G still in its original form but in postwar livery, waits to run Wilts & Dorset's 'golden mile', the short working from Amesbury bus station up the hill to Boscombe Down RAF station. This route earned more revenue per mile than any other. DAVID PENNELS

In 1950 the government relaxed the rules on bus dimensions; double decks could be one foot longer and six inches wider – 27 x 8 feet. GWV305 (324), a Bristol KS5G, was Wilts & Dorset's last bus with the narrower chassis, but it received a wider body, hence the unusual gap between the wheels and the outer rims of the mudguards. Service 24, Salisbury-Trowbridge, was run jointly with Western National until that company's Wiltshire operations were transferred to the Bristol Omnibus Co. Ltd in 1970. DAVID PENNELS

Three elderly Hants & Dorset Leyland Tiger coaches found a temporary home with Wilts & Dorset to help cope with a shortage of vehicles in 1952. CEL226 (503) had a Beadle body of the type that was standard to its previous owner in the mid- to late 1930s. It only stayed just over a year with Wilts & Dorset but it made its small contribution to the weekend leave express services for soldiers stationed on the Plain. DAVID PENNELS

In the 1940s and early 1950s the company used to park a handful of waiting buses on Salt Lane car park, just a stone's throw from Endless Street bus station. BAM52 (156), a 1937 Leyland TD5 Titan, was waiting to return to its home base at Warminster when caught on camera there. It shows well the lines of its Park Royal body, unaltered but for the three-aperture destination boxes fitted by Portsmouth Aviation in 1947. DAVID PENNELS

Wilts & Dorset and Crosville Motor Services Ltd swapped some buses in 1952. Ten aged Leyland TD1 Titan double decks went to Crosville in Cheshire and North Wales in exchange for ten Leyland TS7 saloons dating from 1937, which stayed with the company until 1954. They had Eastern Coach Works bodies. BFM185 (515), previously Crosville's KA68, rests at the back of Endless Street bus station. In 1952 it was not unknown for these buses to be pressed into service on local excursions. DAVID PENNELS

The Harrington bodies on the sixteen Leyland TS8 Tigers delivered in 1939-40 had all seen heavy wear during World War II, and were in need of some tender care. All were rebuilt with new destination equipment and sliding window vents. The company itself did the work on four of them, but most of them were dealt with by Portsmouth Aviation, including BWV672 (175) – photographed whilst parked at Salt Lane car park in Salisbury. DAVID PENNELS

Wilts & Dorset took over a pair of 1947 Bedford OB-Duple Vista coaches from Venture, that company's first new vehicles after World War II. The type was a popular choice with small bus operators, and nearly 12,700 were built, but they were less common with the big companies. FOR634 (478) and its twin were transferred from Basingstoke to Pewsey depot, and became regular performers on the short run up to the RAF station at Upavon. On this occasion it is waiting to make the longer journey to Hungerford. DAVID PENNELS

Bus companies that rebuilt pre-war vehicles in the early 1950s tended to replace half-drop windows with sliding vents. The end-result was often as fussy as the phoney half-timbered row of shops on Wote Street, Basingstoke, where COT549 (436) is on the stand ready to run a relief working along the Alresford road. The AEC Regal was new to Venture as a coach in 1938. Wilts & Dorset rebuilt it as a bus in 1951. DAVID PENNELS

Four LT8 Lions delivered in 1939 were the last pre-war Leylands in passenger service with Wilts & Dorset until their withdrawal in 1957. Their Harrington dual-purpose bodies originally had curved glass corner windows at the rear, but these were found too vulnerable and were replaced by panelling. BWV665 (168), showing the rear destination display fitted by the company in 1952, stands in Devizes Market Square. THE OMNIBUS SOCIETY

(both regular and National Service) from the camps upon Salisbury Plain. The surcharge was removed on 23 April 1957 and the military personnel returned.

Throughout the best part of the 'fifties, Raymond Longman had been remunerated by BTC in respect of directorships he held under its jurisdiction. From 30 September 1959, he relinquished several of them. From 1 October he was paid by Wilts & Dorset for his services as chairman and managing director of the company. The latter seems to have celebrated this by purchasing a typewriter; the directors' minutes – about two decades after other companies – ceased to be handwritten thereafter. Parsimony was a habit difficult to break at Wilts & Dorset.

The departure of Roger Wigmore for Western and Southern National at Exeter saw his replacement as company secretary and accountant by Desmond G. Finley with effect from 1 February 1960. His appointment put into place the first of the management team which would, in the next decade, bring into being what eventually became the 'Hants & Dorset Group' of

companies. He was to act in that capacity for each one of them.

The engagement of George Carruthers as traffic manager of Wilts & Dorset, in December 1960, gave the company the services of an officer destined to play a leading role in the affairs of the National Bus Company a decade later. Another member of the future 'Hants & Dorset' team was slotted into place in September 1961, when W.L.F. Henderson became chief engineer of Wilts & Dorset.

Raymond Longman chaired his last meeting of the Wilts & Dorset board on 9 May 1962 – and announced his retirement. He went off in his typical sporting style to learn to qualify as a glider pilot. His place as managing director was filled, at general manager level, by David S. Deacon – an ex-Rugby schoolboy, bus enthusiast, photographer and, eventually, a director of so many state-controlled bus companies it would become difficult to fit them by name on one A4 sheet of paper. His diminutive size belied his dynamism. He was to occupy that post for just two years, becoming instead a Wilts &

above] Four-abreast seating on the top deck of a lowbridge bus was always a tight squeeze, especially if you had a bulky neighbour. In those days you could smoke on the top deck too. A slight change in the maximum permitted length of buses in 1950 enabled Eastern Coach Works to fit staggered seats on 1953 Bristol KSWs to achieve a little more comfort. DAVID GILLARD COLLECTION

above] CHR491 (192) heads northwards past Figheldean church en route to Netheravon. Wilts & Dorset rebuilt its twelve 1940 Bristol K5Gs in the early 1950s, giving the driver's cab a cleaner front profile and dispensing with the heavy waistrail moulding. At the same time most of them were equipped with three-aperture destination boxes. The last pair to be rebuilt showed only destination and route number. DAVID PENNELS

right] Wilts & Dorset urgently needed some additional saloons in 1952 as it awaited the new underfloor-engined Bristol LSs. To help plug the gap it bought two saloons and three coaches from Hants & Dorset, each different from the others. One of them was EEL800 (505), a 1938 Bristol L5G seen parked at Amesbury depot in August 1954. Its Beadle body was still in its original form, except for the rear skirt, cut short by its original owners so it could clear the ramps on the Sandbanks-Shell Bay ferry. DAVID PENNELS

Dorset director destined to be there (together with two others) until the company was wound up. George McKay of the Tilling Association Ltd was chairman during the period of Deacon's general managership.

In 1962, Harold Macmillan's Conservative government launched a new Transport Act which dismembered the British Transport Commission. Wilts & Dorset and other road passenger transport companies administered by the Tilling Association Ltd were placed under the control of the Transport Holding Company which had been set up under the provisions of the Act. Although financial links with the Railways Board were severed by this adjustment, British Railways officials H.E. Barber and Percy White retained their directorships of Wilts & Dorset Motor Services Ltd; and further British Railways and (from 1968) British Rail officers were to take their places upon the board.

In January 1963, Silver Star Motor Services Ltd approached Wilts & Dorset with a view to selling the undertaking, and on 4 June that year what was officially described as a 'merger' took effect (see Chapter 8). The deal added substantially to the company's network of weekend leave services for miltary personnel from units based at Salisbury Plain camps.

The year 1964 was a particularly important landmark in the history of Wilts & Dorset. A decision as to its future had been taken at Transport Holding Company headquarters at 10 Fleet Street, London – coincidentally just around the corner from Salisbury Court – one which, in effect, placed the seal on what Raymond Longman had begun. From 1 April 1964, the management of Wilts & Dorset Motor Services Ltd was to be merged with that of Hants & Dorset Motor Services Ltd. Upon the same date, Douglas W. Morison, general manager of Hants & Dorset, replaced Deacon as general manager also of Wilts & Dorset. The following month, Morison became a director of the latter also.

David Deacon replaced Thomas Gailey as chairman of Wilts & Dorset in February 1965, when Gailey stepped into the chairmanship instead of the Tilling Association Ltd, which had appointed him to the Wilts & Dorset board three years earlier. On 5 May 1965, the Wilts & Dorset board met at Newport, Isle of Wight, and approved the transfer of the firm's registered office from 8 Endless Street, Salisbury, to The Square, Bournemouth – the headquarters and registered office of Hants & Dorset. The registered office of Venture Ltd was also transferred to the same location.

left] The Bristol Lodekka, with its Eastern Coach Works body, was designed to achieve the lower clearance of a lowbridge double deck but without the discomfort of rows of four seats abreast on the top deck. Wilts & Dorset's first 17 Lodekkas were assigned to Salisbury city services, replacing the by now elderly Leyland TD5 Titans. The first six were Gardner-engined LD6Gs that arrived in 1954, but LMR740 (607), delivered early the next year, was a Bristol-engined LD6B. ANDREW WALLER COLLECTION

right] Wilts & Dorset cut out competition along the main road between Warminster and Salisbury by buying Harold Couchman's licence for this route in 1932, but for nearly 30 years he continued to serve the villages along the south bank of the river Wylye. In the 1950s, when the New Canal was still a two-way street, he used this wartime Bedford OWB, with an admirably complete destination display. THE OMNIBUS SOCIETY

left] White-outs can make driving across Salisbury Plain in the snow a hazardous affair, but the driver of OHR124 (623) is evidently coping as it passes Figheldean. This Bristol LD6G was new in 1956, the year in which Wilts & Dorset adopted the T-style destination box as standard for its double decks. Doing away with the 'via' blind saved weight at a time when fuel prices were rising. DAVID PENNELS

right] There was less need for coaches outside the summer season, so some were kept unlicensed for the winter at the back of Castle Street depot in Salisbury. EMW183 (274) was one of the first of the Beadle-bodied Bristol L6Bs to be refurbished by Wilts & Dorset's workshops in time for the 1957 season. Sliding vents took the place of half-drop windows, and the destination box was rebuilt, but at first these coaches retained their original red, maroon and cream livery. DAVID PENNELS

right] The 1950 Portsmouth Aviation bodies on GAM214-216 (295-7) were distinct in small ways from the Beadle products of the previous two years. The destination box was slightly more upright, and the anti-glare visor over the driver's windscreen was a typical Portsmouth Aviation feature. The streamline flashes, originally maroon on these coaches, were painted cream for the 1957 season. ANDREW WALLER COLLECTION

left] Bristol LS5G saloon OHR389 (589) leaves Endless Street at the start of a journey that will take it up the Bourne Valley to Tidworth, through Savernake Forest to Marlborough and over the hills to Swindon. It is passing the Woolpack Inn, which had moved lock, stock and barrels to make way for the bus station next door. In its old location it was the terminus of carriers' vans from Bourne Valley villages. Endless Street was so named because it led north beyond the walls of the mediaeval city of Salisbury. ANDREW WALLER COLLECTION

right] A Pewsey-based Bristol LS5G saloon, heading northwards up the Avon Valley, pulls away from a typical rural Wiltshire bus stop on the main road by Figheldean. LWV845 (569) was one of 25 of these single decks that Wilts & Dorset received in 1955-56. They had 41 seats and just one door at the front, unlike the dual-purpose vehicles that preceded them with what proved to be the impractical dual-door configuration. DAVID PENNELS

left] After Wilts & Dorset rebuilt Bristol L6B coaches GAM214-216 (295-7) in readiness for the 1958 season, it repainted them in an experimental 'cream-top' livery, which subsequently became the standard colours for the coach fleet. 295, now with sliding window vents and a simplified destination box, was photographed whilst parked up at Midhurst, Sussex, on an excursion. DAVID PENNELS

right] Eastern Coach Works carried out the first conversion to one-man-operation of a Wilts & Dorset Bristol LWL5G in July 1958. LAM744 (564), photographed at Endless Street two months later, retained its half-cab and bulkhead, but the company found this arrangement impractical. Starting in November 1958, the Castle Street workshops rebuilt all 15 of the type by removing the bulkhead and fitting the company's own design of full front. 564 was the last to be dealt with, in March 1960. DAVID PENNELS

left] Wilts & Dorset took the coach seats out of three of its dual-purpose Bristol LS5Gs and fitted them to new coaches in 1958. One of the vehicles that ended up with bus seats was KHR654 (552). It was photographed four years later in Cranborne, an early outpost in Dorset; the company put down a marker there (temporarily as it turned out) in 1915, with services to Salisbury three days a week, and once a week each to Poole and Ringwood. DAVID PENNELS

right] In June 1959 Wilts & Dorset and the Bristol Omnibus Co Ltd joined up two of their services to provide through buses between Salisbury and Swindon for the first time. Previously passengers had to change buses at Marlborough. KHR104 (391) ran the inaugural journey on the new service 709. Wilts & Dorset had two routes between Salisbury and Marlborough; it chose to link the more easterly service 9 with Bristol's 70 to avoid having to share the lucrative traffic between Salisbury and Amesbury with another company.
DAVID PENNELS

Amesbury-based LAM278 (561) passes through Figheldean on the 'back road' service 13 from Netheravon to Salisbury in July 1960. It was the second Bristol LWL5G converted to one-man-operation, in December 1958. The Wilts & Dorset bodyshop in Castle Street, Salisbury, turned out the 15 OMO conversions at the rate of about one a month. DAVID PENNELS

There was some discussion at this juncture about the perceived inadequacy of the Hants & Dorset workshop facilities in Southampton, and the possibility of their being replaced by an enlarged joint facility at the Central Workshops in Salisbury, which could be extended for the purpose. Warming to that theme, the directors envisaged that the proposed new workshops could also provide maintenance for the vehicles of the Thames Valley Traction Co Ltd.

With rationalisation very much in the air (despite the fact that Harold Wilson's first Labour government was now in power) it was thought that certain engineering functions could be performed on behalf of the Isle of Wight-based Southern Vectis Omnibus Co Ltd and the Brighton Hove & District Omnibus Co Ltd – all standardised in the Bristol-ECW vehicle mode.

It is not difficult to see how such projections came about. Thomas Gailey had represented BH&D upon the

The Flemington family, of Martin in Hampshire, ran one of the last of the true country carrier bus services to Salisbury – three days a week. They even had a joint season ticket with Wilts & Dorset, only valid on the big company's service on days when the independent did not run. Charles Flemington bought his first bus in the early 1920s and the family held on to the business until 1974. Between 1957 and 1962 they used this third-hand Bedford OB, GOR136, with body by Lee Motor Bodies of Bournemouth. DAVID PENNELS

Brighton Area Transport Committee when the co-ordination agreement with Southdown and Brighton Corporation came into effect in that Sussex resort. Thomas Pruett, appointed a director of Wilts & Dorset on 1 April 1966, had been chief engineer at BH&D since 1944, and that firm's general manager from 1948. In 1955 he had been appointed general manager of Thames Valley, by the Tilling Association Ltd.

The Tilling Association itself may well have been planning some years ahead, for the inclusion of Southern Vectis in the proposed maintenance plan presaged by some six years an arrangement whereby a future general manager (Peter Hunt) of the Hants & Dorset group of companies became 'Chief General Manager' of a 'Wessex & Wight Division' (after 1 April 1972), which was to include Southern Vectis and the newly merged Thames Valley and Aldershot & District companies (Alder Valley).

Meanwhile, on 12 April 1966, W.L.F. Henderson, chief engineer of Wilts & Dorset, was appointed additionally chief engineer of Hants & Dorset.

Somewhat belatedly, news that Brighton Hove & District had been part of the discussions leaked out into the excitable world of the bus enthusiast. One got hold of the wrong end of the information and, in an open postcard to Eric Surfleet – an ex-busman and proprietor of a well-known transport memorabilia shop at Lancing, Sussex – announced that all Brighton Hove & District's Bristol-ECW buses (recently merged with the Southdown fleet) were to be sent west to Portsmouth, which depot and its new occupants would be operated by Hants & Dorset. And all Southdown's Portsea Island-based Leylands were to be sent east to operate the ex-BH&D services in that part of Sussex – a neat and tidy maintenance proposition indeed.

The postman, himself an enthusiast, read the card and 'the news' was out. Way out, as it happened, for it overlooked the fact that BH&D never did become 'the property' of Southdown (in contrast to the manner in which Wilts & Dorset became subsumed under Hants & Dorset Motor Services Ltd), but merely the subject of a 'management agreement' with Southdown, similar to that which had been set up between Wilts & Dorset and Venture Ltd. The late Mackenzie and Cannon would have been amused none the less!

After a gap in new double deck deliveries of more than three years, the company received the first of a new flat-floor type of Lodekka, the FS, in the latter part of 1962. They replaced the last of the AEC Regents that had come from Venture and some early post-war Bristol Ks. 686AAM (648), an FS6B, was based at Andover. It has worked to Winchester on the joint service with Hants & Dorset, in whose bus station it is waiting for last-minute passengers. ANDREW WALLER COLLECTION

right] *Wilts & Dorset's first front-entrance double decks, and its first 70-seaters, were half a dozen Bristol FLF6Gs. The semi-coach seating of 467BMR (658) is clearly visible as it waits at Endless Street bus station. It was also the company's first bus to have the Cave-Browne-Cave heating and ventilation system, the most visible evidence of which was the pair of grilles on either side of the destination box.* ANDREW WALLER COLLECTION

below right] *Snow diverted GHR365 (301) from its normal morning peak route from Salisbury on 6 February 1963; instead of taking the exposed direct road to RAF Boscombe Down it drove down into Amesbury and pulled up outside the bus station. The bus was a standard 1950 Eastern Coach Works-bodied Bristol K5G; Wilts & Dorset modified the destination display to the T-form that it favoured from 1954.* DAVID PENNELS

below] *In June 1967 the organisers of the 'Salisbury Triumph' event asked Wilts & Dorset to provide a fleet of buses to ferry passengers to the cathedral from two temporary 'park-and-ride' sites on the city's outskirts. On a busy Saturday extra buses were drafted in from Andover, Amesbury and Pewsey to handle the predicted traffic. In the event loadings proved minimal, and many of the buses were sent home early. Andover-based Bristol FLF6B EMR295D (679) heads a line of Lodekkas waiting in vain in Stratford Road, alongside Hudson's Field.* DAVID PENNELS

Only a couple of years after the special order of 15 Bristol LWL5Gs was delivered their scheduled crew workings were rapidly being assigned to purpose-built 41-seat one-man-operated Bristol LS underfloor-engined vehicles. The company hastened to convert the LWLs to OMO. After an initial unsatisfactory conversion by Eastern Coach Works, it decided to deal with the remainder in its own workshops. First to be rebuilt with a full front and forward entrance was LAM110 (560), photographed with a Romsey driver at the wheel in the Hampshire town in May 1964. DAVID PENNELS

Wilts & Dorset assured its hold on the roads to Shaftesbury by taking over a handful of independents in the 1930s. It covered their old routes from outstations at Hindon, Bowerchalke and in the historic Dorset hill town itself. In the summer of 1965, LHR857 (566) one of the Bristol LWL5Gs that the company adapted for driver-only operation, stands before Shaftesbury Town Hall after arriving from Salisbury on the 27, which at that time followed the A30 via Wilton and Swallowcliffe. DAVID PENNELS

On 15 December 1967, the board was informed that it had been decided to abandon proposals for new central workshops in Salisbury. By way of a small compensation, a new washing and refuelling bay was approved and duly built.

In a year of mixed fortunes, 1968 saw further moves toward integration. Plans for a coordinated workshop for Hants & Dorset/Wilts & Dorset again came under review, this time by a panel of two; Morison and Deacon, and were under way when news came that the joint chief engineer W.L.F. Henderson had died in office. Between September and 30 November A. Reginald Smith acted as chief engineer, until Alan Gurley was appointed to the sadly vacated post. He was destined to become the last chief engineer of Wilts & Dorset.

There were plans for a new enquiry office at Pewsey on land specially purchased for it, but when the board perused the estimates, it was agreed that the expenditure was not warranted, and that project was abandoned also.

Also on the personnel front that year, Peter Fairweather was appointed operating superintendent at Salisbury in the place of J.W. Clay who had also died in office – as had A.E.C. Postlethwaite, the workshop superintendent at Salisbury. Altogether it was a depressing time at Wilts & Dorset. On a brighter note, however, the chief schedules clerk David J.N. Pennels was promoted on 1 December 1968 to the post of chief traffic assistant for the company.

It had now been decided fully to integrate the accounting and other administrative procedures of Wilts & Dorset with those of Hants & Dorset.

As from 1 January 1969, Wilts & Dorset became officially 'Hants & Dorset Motor Services Ltd trading as Wilts & Dorset' but, whilst Hants & Dorset services were mainly under the South Eastern traffic commissioners, the majority of Wilts & Dorset's remained under their Western counterparts.

From mid-1969 all new Wilts & Dorset buses were

left] Wilts & Dorset and Hants & Dorset started a limited stop version of their joint Salisbury-Bournemouth route in the mid-1960s, the 38A. A 1962 Bristol Lodekka FS6G was painted cream to promote the new service, which cut 22 minutes off the 100-minute journey time of the regular workings. 684AAM (646), waits to leave for Bournemouth at Endless Street bus station on 2 February 1966. DAVID PENNELS

below] The height restriction under the old Leighton House arch in Warminster Road, Westbury was no problem for a Bristol Lodekka FLF6G like AHR244B (662) on the Salisbury-Warminster-Trowbridge service, which became joint with Western National in 1948. The Bristol Omnibus Co Ltd took over the arrangement when Western National's Wiltshire operations were transferred to it in 1970. F.W. YORK

allocated Bournemouth registrations. For operational purposes, Wilts & Dorset had become the 'Northern Area' of Hants & Dorset Motor Services Ltd, and an enlarged map incorporating the services of both operators (those numbers for Wilts & Dorset prefixed W) now appeared at the back of timetables made available to the public.

The assets of Wilts & Dorset Motor Services Ltd were transferred to Hants & Dorset at the book values as on 1 January 1969. The latter also took responsibility for the liabilities. On the same date the securities of Wilts & Dorset were transferred from the Transport Holding Company to the newly created National Bus Company under the provisions of the Transport Act 1968.

As from 1 March 1969 all stores and supplies were ordered by Hants & Dorset. The transfer of vehicle log books to Hants & Dorset had been completed by the 31st of that month.

Wilts & Dorset's bank account with Lloyds Bank at Salisbury, that very building once the property of the Wilts & Dorset Banking Co Ltd, which latter had

suggested to William Graham and Maurice Coombes a suitable name for a bus service, way back in 1914, was closed on 30 April 1969 and all monies were thereafter credited to the Hants & Dorset account at the National Provincial Bank at Bournemouth. (There's another coincidence there for, on 1 January 1970, the NBC purchased the bus operations of the near 100-year-old Provincial Traction Co Ltd and placed its surviving services at Gosport & Fareham into the care of the Hants & Dorset group).

The title deeds and other documents of all Wilts & Dorset's freehold and leasehold properties were conveyed and assigned to Hants & Dorset Motor Services Ltd at book values as at 31 December 1968. In February 1970 799,999 £1 shares in Wilts & Dorset were formally transferred from the Transport Holding Company to the National Bus Company; and one ordinary £1 share from THC Bus Nominees Ltd passed to National Bus Nominees Ltd. There followed a conveyance to Hants & Dorset in accordance with the schedule submitted.

6
Crossing Boundaries: (a) Andover

A LITTLE Hampshire market town might not seem the obvious place for a company called Wilts & Dorset to set up its second most important centre of operations, but that is how things stood in the 1930s and 1940s. In its time Andover – one of the few places in Hampshire to retain a name of Celtic origin – had been on or near important crossroads. The Roman roads between Winchester and Cirencester, and between London and Sorviodunum (Old Sarum) met just northeast of the modern town.

Andover played host to a historic event in 994, a good two centuries before the city of New Sarum was founded on the banks of the river Avon, 18 miles to the south west. Olav Trygvason, having come to England at the head of an army of Viking raiders and, on receiving a payment of £16,000, made his peace, was brought to Andover by bishop of Winchester. There, sponsored by King Ethelred (the Unready), bishop Alphage confirmed him as a Christian, and he solemnly undertook to leave England and never return to it in war. Soon he became king of Norway, which, by whatever means of persuasion came to hand, he converted to Christianity. He is remembered there today as St Olav.

In the first half of the 19th century Andover's inns did a bustling trade from the 30 stage-coaches that called in on their way between London and the West Country every day, so they could change horses and let passengers slake their thirst and relax from the dust and tedium of the road. Stage-coaches between Southampton and Oxford also stopped in the town. This was all to change when the railways came and took the traffic away from the inns.

For a country town of its size the railways served Andover well. The line from London and Basingstoke opened in 1854, and was extended to Salisbury in 1857. Lines to Southampton (1865) and Swindon (1882) followed, providing direct links in four different directions. The existence of good railway links may have

In the mid-20th century the route from Salisbury to Andover, via Amesbury and Tidworth, was one of Wilts & Dorset's most heavily trafficked, but the company did not reach the Hampshire market town until 1927. Sixteen years before that the T.A.N. Syndicate had put four Commer WP4 buses on the Andover-Tidworth section. It was not the first to try the route, but increased fares on the competing railway line enabled it to achieve some success for around four years. DAVID PENNELS COLLECTION

made the town seem a less interesting prospect to early busmen than it might otherwise have been.

Andover's first motor bus service was a short-lived affair. William John Randall put a Dennis double deck on the road to Ludgershall and Tidworth in May 1906, but withdrew it only three months later. He could not compete with the cheaper fares that the railway offered. Five years later the T.A.N. Syndicate Ltd tried the route once again with four Commer saloons. Railway fares had gone up and the garrison at Tidworth had expanded. Army families found T.A.N.'s buses a handy way to ride the 10 miles to Andover for their shopping.

The T.A.N. garage was close to the site that the Wilts & Dorset bus station was to occupy in 1944. In a letter to David Pennels, L.G. Ford, who later ran a motor agency nearby, recalled: 'the T.A.N. bus was started by a Mrs Nicholls and her three sons. They came from Spain and lived at a house called Rothesay ... on the Andover-Weyhill road....This first service was used a lot by the villagers around Andover.' He said the Commer buses 'seemed to give a lot of trouble, hence Mrs. Nicholls giving them up.' It is not clear exactly when she did so, but local historian Derek Tempero believes the service lasted at least four years (see Bibliography).

Between 1914 and 1918 wartime restrictions on the supply of both motor vehicles and the petrol to run them made it hard to maintain bus services. By 1920 normality was returning, and, well before the arrival of Wilts & Dorset, new services were tried out between Andover and neighbouring towns. The Newbury & Andover Motor Company started to run every two hours between the two towns on 30 June 1920. It 'temporarily suspended' its service little more than a year later, by which time rivals had appeared on the route. Of these the most successful was Lewis Horne's *Pride of Andover*, which ran to Newbury every day until he sold out to Wilts & Dorset in April 1932.

Mobility Ltd, registered as a company on 28 February 1920, began a Tidworth-Andover-Winchester service. Post-war demobilisation reduced the traffic to be had in Tidworth and it cut the service back to Ludgershall-Andover-Winchester in 1921. The firm faced serious financial problems in 1923, and the liquidator offered it to Hants & Dorset Motor Services Ltd in December of that year. That company put a bus on the Winchester-Andover route as a stop-gap measure, but Anna Valley Motors Ltd eventually took over the ailing business in October 1924, still retaining the Mobility fleet name. In June 1927, Hants & Dorset bought the service from Anna Valley.

Wilts & Dorset paid £300 for Harold Roy Bartley and Charles Avery's Tidworth Motor Service in April 1929, which included services to Salisbury and Andover. The deal included a pair of charabancs and two saloons; all but HR74 (21) were sold on after only a few months, but Wilts & Dorset rebodied this 1919 Leyland with a second-hand saloon body in late 1929. When that wore out two years later, HR74 was turned into a lorry. It was known in this form as Betsy, and the company went on using it until 1948. DAVID PENNELS COLLECTION

It only held on to the Ludgershall-Andover section until November, passing it on to Wilts & Dorset, which had become the first of the 'territorial' bus companies to establish a long-term presence in Andover in May 1927, by starting a daily service from Salisbury via Amesbury, Tidworth and Ludgershall. At the time Andover still had fewer than 10,000 inhabitants, whose homes were just beginning to receive electricity.

The company was naturally keen to eliminate competition on what eventually proved to be a highly profitable route. In April 1929 it bought out Harold Roy Bartley's *Tidworth Motor Service*. Bartley started in the bus business at Sixpenny Handley in Dorset in about 1911. He moved to Tidworth in 1913, from where he ran to Salisbury and, infrequently, to Andover. In March 1932 Wilts & Dorset acquired the two stage licences of Sidney Shergold's *Allington Queen*, from Tidworth to Andover and to Salisbury. Sidney, whose brother Eddie was one of the founders of Silver Star, traded thereafter as Tidworth Coaches. Under that name he was to compete once more with Wilts & Dorset in the 1950s, with weekend express services from the army camps on Salisbury Plain.

Within days of Hants & Dorset reaching Andover from the south – by buying out Mobility – the Great Western Railway appeared from the north. It sustained a Newbury-Andover Junction bus service until February 1929. A GWR route from Hungerford did not last long; for just a few months in the summer of 1928 it wended its way through scattered villages on the North Wessex Downs that never generated enough traffic to support a profitable bus service.

The good railway links may go some way to explain why the bigger bus companies waited until 1927 to reach Andover. With the GWR, Wilts & Dorset and Hants & Dorset serving the town from three points of the

left] Herbert Henry Wolstenholme sold his Andover & District bus service to Wilts & Dorset in June 1930 for £1,650. It ran to Romsey every 90 minutes, Salisbury via Broughton in the morning, and Andover-Broughton in the afternoon. Three buses came with the business, including Dennis G UL9607, on the left, and Guy ONDF UK8818, which became nos. 48 and 49. The Guy became a familiar sight in the Fordingbridge area in the 1930s, where Wilts & Dorset used it on local services.
DAVID PENNELS COLLECTION

compass, the road from the east, which runs parallel to the railway line from Basingstoke, still lay open. In February 1928 Venture Ltd of Basingstoke began a regular service to Andover, only to be challenged three months later by the Aldershot & District Traction Co Ltd appearing on the same road. These two were jostling for territory east of Basingstoke as well. In return for concessions by Venture in that direction the Aldershot company withdrew from Andover in August. We tell the story of Venture, which Wilts & Dorset absorbed in 1951, in Chapter 7.

A handful of rural busmen, who had started services to Andover around 1920, kept going for some years yet. Among them were Harry Razey of Cholderton, Edwin Piper of Thruxton (*Amport & District*), Henry Tibble of St Mary Bourne, and Hedderly & Williams of Penton Mewsey. Wilts & Dorset bought out Sidney Williams, who survived A.J. Hedderly, in 1945. The Razeys took over Piper's service in 1946 and outlasted Wilts & Dorset M.S. Ltd. Tibble's son Oliver continued until 1969.

With its command of the substantial traffic from Tidworth and Ludgershall, Wilts & Dorset soon became the dominant operator in the town. It thus assumed a bigger presence in Hampshire than in Dorset. In late 1929 it started four cross-town services, each providing a bus every 30 or 60 minutes from the Guildhall. By mid-1930 the basic pattern of the company's Andover operations for the next 20 years was in place. It ran to Marlborough, Newbury — the route abandoned by the GWR, and Romsey. In June that year it paid £1,650 for Herbert Henry Wolstenholme's *Andover & District*, which ran to Stockbridge and Romsey up to eight times a day. Wilts & Dorset transferred one of his little buses, a 20-seat Guy, to Fordingbridge, where it became a familiar sight on local services in the 1930s.

The company also introduced a service across Salisbury Plain to Devizes, running four round trips a day, but this route evidently failed to generate enough traffic and it was withdrawn within a couple of years. Wilts & Dorset opened its first Andover garage in 1930. Arthur James Corp, who joined the company three years earlier from Bannister & Corp of Durrington, took charge

An Andover crew pose by one of the Leyland TD1 Titans allocated to the Hampshire town in the early 1930s. These top-covered double decks joined the Wilts & Dorset fleet just in time to take part in the launch and expansion of its Andover operations, including four one-way cross-town local services that served villages on the outskirts of the town; so that the bus on the Winton Road-Charlton service ran back through town to Clatford, thence back again and out to Amport, before returning to Winton Road. ARTHUR BLAKE, DAVID PENNELS COLLECTION

of operations. The Salisbury architects John Harding & Sons designed the premises to include local office, buffet and waiting room, but its location in Junction Road proved awkward; the centre of town was on the other side of a level crossing by Andover Town Station. To meet the need for an enquiry and parcels office in the town centre, the company bought a property at 29 High Street

The company displayed a wealth of information about other operators' services upon its enquiry office and waiting room on Andover High Street, which was conveniently located by the bus stop opposite the Guildhall. DAVID PENNELS COLLECTION

for £300. This also provided a waiting room and buffet by the main bus stop at the Guildhall.

Before the 1930 Road Traffic Act town authorities controlled bus operations by licensing individual vehicles to run on their streets. Salisbury police, for instance, issued little white enamel plates, bearing the licence number, which were fixed to the rear panel of the appropriate bus. Some Wilts & Dorset vehicles also bore Southampton and Bournemouth plates. Andover, with a population that reached 10,076 in 1931, seems to have found no need to do this until the new licensing regime was imminent. In 1930 the town clerk asked bus operators to apply for licences for the drivers and conductors of Andover buses. Wilts & Dorset listed 12 drivers, two of whom had worked for Andover & District, and one conductor.

Hants & Dorset and Venture, whose crew rosters covered varied duties based on Winchester and Basingstoke, sought licences for 41 drivers and 29 conductors between them. Lewis Horne had four driver/conductors. Smaller operators were feeling the pinch from Wilts & Dorset. In his response to the town clerk, George Henry Davidson wrote from Lower Clatford: 'In reference to time table required, I find that owing to Wilts & Dorset service on my run that it is no longer required except Friday and Saturday each week.'

Wilts & Dorset was busy consolidating its hold on the country around Andover, initiating or taking over further rural services in 1931, to Hungerford – which the GWR had tried and forsaken, to Broughton and to Redenham. It bought out Harry Gregory's service to Tangley, and then rented his garage in Hatherden, where it parked a bus overnight at no. 17 for a few years. In January 1931 Frank Holt of Hurstbourne Tarrant accepted the company's offer of £50, plus a job as a driver at £3 a week, for his Vernham Dean-Hurstbourne Tarrant-Andover service and a Hampshire County Council school contract.

Wilts & Dorset's Newbury service, begun in June 1930, proved more of a challenge to Lewis Horne than the GWR had done. He offered to sell the company five buses and his goodwill for £7,000, or one bus and the goodwill of his Newbury service for £2,250. He was invited to consider coordinating timetables on the Newbury road, but said he would continue to put a bus on the road ahead of Wilts & Dorset's whenever they ran. Indeed he added extra journeys, running up to seven round trips a day. Horne turned down the company's counter-offer of £1,000 for the goodwill of the Newbury

The company started four local services in Andover towards the end of 1929, radiating from the Guildhall to nearby villages like Lower Clatford. Among the buses that ran the Andover locals was MW3374 (62), a 1928 Leyland PLSC3 Lion. The Leyland bodies on this type normally had upright windscreens, but this was one of three with a revised design that soon became common across the bus industry. ARTHUR BLAKE, DAVID PENNELS COLLECTION

Among the saloons that came to Wilts & Dorset from Southdown in 1939 was one that had once been a familiar sight in the area, with Lewis Horne's Pride of Andover. OU7856 began life as a Thornycroft demonstrator; Horne ran it on his Newbury service, then sold it to Denmead Queen, which Southdown bought out in 1935. Wilts & Dorset sent the bus back to Andover, from where it is believed to have worked on contract to Hants & Dorset (as its No. AS201) on a rail-replacement service while work was in progress to strengthen the Newbury-Winchester line to carry heavy wartime freight from the Midlands to the south coast. DAVID PENNELS COLLECTION

service and one bus. Six months later the board agreed to offer him £500 for the goodwill of his Newbury service. The company carried the fight to the newly appointed traffic commissioners. It objected to his continuing services to Newbury, Vernham Dean and Stockbridge. He was refused a licence for Stockbridge, and in the end he sold the Newbury service to Wilts & Dorset in April 1932, for £450.

The Road Traffic Act required bus operators to license all the services they already ran and gave them an opportunity to contest their competitors' activities. This worked well against Lewis Horne, but proved less productive when Wilts & Dorset took on Robert Chisnell's *King Alfred Motor Services* in the Stockbridge and Broughton area. Together with the Southern Railway, it objected to part of his Winchester-Stockbridge service, on the ground that, on the shared road between King's Somborne and Stockbridge, it would draw custom away from the Andover-Romsey service.

The traffic commissioners thwarted Wilts & Dorset and Hants & Dorset when they tried to establish a link between Salisbury and Winchester via the Test Valley villages of Broughton and King's Somborne. Charles Emmence had for many years run three days a week from his base at King's Somborne to Winchester and once a week to Salisbury. After King Alfred's application for a Winchester-King's Somborne service was refused, Emmence proposed to run daily to Winchester. He also offered to sign a conditional contract with Wilts & Dorset for the sale of his goodwill if his application were granted. For Hants & Dorset, general manager William Wells Graham wrote to say his company was likely to favour sharing in the purchase.

In April 1932 Wilts & Dorset acquired the licences of Ernest W. Mare's *Speedwell Motor Coaches* for services from Broughton, to Salisbury three days a week and to Andover on Fridays. With the deal with Emmence already in its back pocket, the company then applied, jointly with Hants & Dorset, for a Salisbury-Winchester service. When the traffic commissioner turned them down they appealed against his decision, but without success, (see Freeman and Jowitt, 1984). Wilts & Dorset resolved to continue its support for Emmence's application to renew his existing

licences. (The company did establish a Salisbury-Romsey-Winchester service in the late 1940s, by combining its Salisbury-Romsey route with Hants & Dorset's Romsey-Winchester, in a joint service. In the event it was more than another 70 years – 2004 – before there was a through bus between Salisbury and Winchester via Broughton, run by the company's grandchild concern, the Wilts & Dorset Bus Company Ltd.).

Also in 1932, the idea was mooted that Wilts & Dorset and Hants & Dorset might take over Gordon E. Martin-Cooper's *Empress Coaches,* which ran from Stockbridge to Winchester and to Southampton. The two big companies agreed terms, but these did not suit Martin-Cooper; he stayed in business for another 19 years, eventually selling out to Basil Williams of Hants & Sussex in 1951.

There were two acquisitions that did take place in 1932, but with less ado: Sidney Shergold's Tidworth routes, mentioned above, and the three-days-a-week Nether Wallop-Andover service of Robert Elliott's *Iris Motor Services.* The Wilts & Dorset board minutes record two further acquisitions of independents' licences for services to Andover in July 1934 – Albert Millson from Kimpton, and Edwin Piper from Thruxton. However Piper continued to serve Thruxton until 1946.

By 1937 road traffic had increased to such an extent that Andover town council complained of buses causing congestion by the stop in the High Street, which was also used by Venture and by Royal Blue express coaches. The council suggested it was time to build a bus station and offered its support should Wilts & Dorset wish to build a new garage as well. The company bought a plot of land on West Street, on the same side of the level crossing as the town centre, but agreed not to develop it, apparently to give the council time to ponder other plans for the site. True to form it pondered long; it was not until 1950 that the council decided that the company could not develop the site.

So it was just as well that Wilts & Dorset had bought another site at 35-39 Bridge Street in March 1941. Within

right] At the end of 1940 Wilts & Dorset found itself with a fleet of nearly 40 aging ex-Southdown Leyland Titans with highbridge bodies too tall to cope with routes that went under low railway bridges. By February 1941 it had ordered 10 new lowbridge bodies. Andover-based UF7079 (25), once Southdown's 879, was one of three that went to Park Royal, west London, to be rebodied. THE OMNIBUS SOCIETY

below] Early in 1946 Venture asked for its Andover buses to be allowed to continue through the town centre to the Junction station, instead of turning around at the Guildhall. TV4957, a 1931 Brush-bodied AEC Regent that came from Nottingham Corporation in 1944 stands outside the station ready for a short working to Hurstbourne Priors. It later became Wilts & Dorset's no. 472. The Nissen hut behind the bus, the tall telegraph pole and the luggage trolley on the platform are all period items. JOHN SANTER

Wilts & Dorset held on to half a dozen of the eight piano-fronted Leyland Titans that came from Ribble Motor Services Ltd of Preston in 1939 and based them at Andover. They were in good enough condition to need only rebuilding, rather than rebodying. Eastern Coach Works did the job in 1944-45; it modernised the front of the top deck and fitted the company's standard destination equipment of the time. CK4225 (217) pulls out on to the A303 near Bulford Camp in August 1948, on the busy Andover-Tidworth-Salisbury service 8. JOHN SANTER

a month it had drawn up outline plans for a bus station there. Access from the street was very narrow, and traffic lights were installed to control the flow of vehicles in and out. There was also a parking lot for buses nearby.

In April 1943, Newbury & District raised once more the possibility of selling the business (see Chapter 3). Meeting on 28 July of that year, the Wilts & Dorset directors decided against the idea. Newbury & District's owners wanted a substantial payment for goodwill 'which it was considered inadvisable to entertain under prevailing conditions.' The Monmouthshire-based Red & White group bought Newbury & District instead, in January 1944.

World War II brought little change to the overall pattern of routes around the town, but there were additional buses to Tidworth and Salisbury, every 15 minutes at peak times, and more journeys to and from the Royal Air Force base at Middle Wallop, especially at weekends. Where traffic was lighter, wartime restrictions inevitably led to service cuts. Buses did not run to Hungerford so often, but in town the loss of even a minor service evidently stirred emotions. In March 1940 the town clerk asked the licensing authority to turn down the company's application to withdraw service between the Guildhall and Winton Road. He had to wait more than a twelvemonth for the regional commissioner's reply that 'in present circumstances the continuance of a service of little more than half a mile between terminals cannot be justified.' Undeterred by hardships elsewhere, Andover persisted, eliciting a response from the general manager in November 1944 to the effect that 'We are still extremely short of manpower, fuel and double deck vehicles, and until the position – particularly regarding manpower – is eased we are not likely to be allowed to recommence the local service.'

In February 1945, as the war in Europe approached its end, the company bought the goodwill of Sidney Williams' local operation at Penton Mewsey. Little more than a year later, after first checking with Newbury & District that it had no objection, it bought the licences of Percy Humphries, who ran from Fosbury to Hungerford, and once a week to Andover. Partly in consequence of this, Wilts & Dorset withdrew its Andover-Marlborough service via Ludgershall and ran twice a day between the two towns via Vernham Dean and Fosbury.

By 1949 the company, which came under state ownership the year before, was still recovering from wartime constraints. According to correspondence with the town council it had applied in December 1948 for a service between

Service 75 took minor roads between Andover and Tidworth, providing a daily service – mostly after midday - for the villages of Fyfield and Kimpton. The conductor helps passengers off the bus which has just arrived at Andover bus station. CHR475 (176) was the first of the 1939/40 Leyland TS8 Tigers to be rebuilt by Portsmouth Aviation after World War II; the only major visible alteration was the addition of new-style destination boxes.
DAVID PENNELS COLLECTION

Andover and Southampton. This would have run parallel to the railway and would certainly have raised eyebrows among Wilts & Dorset's railway shareholders, as well as those of Hants & Dorset. In the event no more was heard of the idea.

When Wilts & Dorset told Andover council in October 1949 that it had reorganised its five town services, objections arose to the use of the Guildhall as their terminus. Once more the issue was congestion in the town centre. For some months these services had to use the bus station, a little farther from the shopping centre. In the same month Wilts & Dorset bought more land at the rear of its

In the months before Andover's new bus station opened in October 1954, Andover Junction had to stand in as the terminus for out of town services. CHR478 (179), one of a dozen Leyland TS8 Tiger dual-purpose 32-seaters that were delivered early in World War II, stands on the approach to the station. Portsmouth Aviation rebuilt its Harrington body in 1949.
ANDREW WALLER COLLECTION

In 1949 congestion around the Guildhall prompted objections by Andover council to Wilts & Dorset using the area as the terminus for its local services. For a time they had to use the bus station instead. However, there was no sign of congestion when UF7411 (16) was photographed at the Guildhall stop. Wilts & Dorset built the body on this ex-Southdown Leyland Titan in its Salisbury workshops. JOHN SANTER

left] In June 1950 Venture received four new Guy Arab double decks with handsome Duple bodies. They did not stay long. When Wilts & Dorset took over management of Venture in 1951 they were transferred to Newbury & District. HOT354, the last of the four, is parked in Andover on a private hire contract while still with Venture. G.F. ASHWELL, COLIN MORRIS COLLECTION

below left] Delivered less than three months before World War II began, BWV671 (174), a Harrington-bodied Leyland TS8 Tiger, started life as a 32-seat dual purpose saloon. In 1942 the seats were re-positioned along the sides of the bus, to make room for 20 standing passengers in the middle. The Wilts & Dorset bodyshop put the seats back in their original position after the war, remodelled the destination display and fitted sliding vents to the windows. It was photographed on a private hire contract at Finkley Down Farm, near Andover. DAVID PENNELS COLLECTION

below] Tree branches somewhere along the Salisbury-Andover road may have dented the roof of GAM10 (293). Around the end of 1949, when this Bristol K5G was new, Eastern Coach Works stopped fitting destination boxes over the rear platform; fuel consumption was a serious issue and this saved weight. In 1955 service 76 was extended to Basingstoke. ANDREW WALLER COLLECTION

Bridge Street site. Coincidentally nationalisation soon resolved the issue of the Guildhall bus stop. When Wilts & Dorset took over management of Venture Ltd in 1950, the Basingstoke buses were soon allowed to use the bus station, and the town services were permitted once more to terminate at the Guildhall. Beside the trunk services from Basingstoke, Venture brought with it an Andover local route, to Picket Piece, which had started in 1946 at the town council's request.

Amid local fanfare Wilts & Dorset finally opened a modern bus station and garage on 6 October 1954 at the Bridge Street site, near the place where the T.A.N. Syndicate had once kept its vehicles. *The Southern Daily Echo* said 'Andover has a bus station now which is second to none in

right] Wilts & Dorset rebuilt AMW482 (154) in 1950 with a full front and proudly operated it on a Salisbury-Yeovil service, but when the bus was transferred to Andover depot the drivers there were far from happy. The full front made it harder to see the side of the road as they pulled in at bus stops, so the Leyland LT7 Lion tended to be left behind in the depot. The resulting low mileage did not please the chief engineer. It is parked at Andover Junction in September 1954, when the town's bus station and depot were being rebuilt. DAVID PENNELS

above] Andover's new bus station opened with fanfare on 6 October 1954. The 12.35 departure on service 8 to Salisbury was the first to use the new premises, but other routes were kept away until the next day. The clock shows it is midday; the bus is already on its stand, partly hidden by the rather aged motor car, perhaps belonging to a dignitary arriving for the ceremony. THE OMNIBUS SOCIETY

above] Company officers, in town for the ceremonial opening of Andover bus station on 6 October 1954, pose for the camera. On the left is W.H. Tryhorn, chief engineer, next to Jack G. Welling, former general manager of Venture Ltd who became area traffic superintendent for Basingstoke and Andover. Wearing the hat is Harold William Mills, traffic manager, and on the right George H. West, who was in charge of Andover depot. DONALD BEALING COLLECTION

left] One of Andover depot's Bristol KSW5Gs pulls up Old Sarum Hill, the last incline before the gentle slope down to Salisbury, on the well-patronised service 8. The advertisement on its side proclaimed the self-confidence that pervaded the bus industry in the 1950s, when the motor car was still a luxury for many people. HMR689 (350) was new in 1952 and stayed with Wilts & Dorset until 1967. DAVID PENNELS

below] JWV383 (384), one of the fifteen 1953 Bristol KSW6Bs that had platform doors, arrives in Salisbury at the end of its journey from Andover via the RAF station at Middle Wallop. This was the more direct route between the two places, but it never ran as frequently – or carried as many passengers – as the route via Tidworth. DAVID PENNELS

the country for a town of its size, and for the size of the station itself it is the most modern in the south of England.' Offices and waiting area were all concentrated in a central island building, so waiting passengers could stay under cover until boarding their bus.

Andover's population passed the 15,000 mark early in the 1950s, which were a heyday for the bus. Plenty of people who wanted to travel had no car of their own. To tap into this demand Wilts & Dorset ran tours from its new bus station. At a busy summer weekend they were advertised for as many as seven, eight or even 10 different destinations, as far afield as the Wye Valley, Stratford-upon-Avon and Eastbourne. In 1962 there was even a conducted tour of London Airport.

Wilts & Dorset believed another way to attract more passengers was to enable them to travel between towns without a change of bus. With this in mind, in 1955 it joined its Salisbury-Middle Wallop-Andover route to

those for Basingstoke and Newbury. However, the Basingstoke service had to be divided at Andover once more when driver-only buses were introduced. A one-man saloon met the demand between Salisbury and Andover, but passenger loadings on the Basingstoke side demanded a double deck, so a conductor had to be carried. Driver-only double decks still lay in the future. Salisbury-Newbury started out as a double deck service, but a saloon later proved sufficient for the whole journey.

The more rural services remained a problem. Never able to attract enough passengers to generate a profit,

some of them only ran on certain days of the week, and could only be staffed by drivers working on their rest days. This applied particularly to the downland country northwest of Andover, on the roads to Marlborough and Hungerford. At the end of 1959 Wilts & Dorset completely revised its services in this area. Under the new arrangement Andover drivers no longer had to work what were now Saturday-only services to Marlborough and Hungerford. Andover buses ran no farther than Vernham Dean or Oxenwood. Instead Pewsey depot was assigned a little network of routes so that Wiltshire villages would not be deprived of even a once-a-week bus. Villagers from beyond Oxenwood who wanted to travel to Andover had improved facilities but had to change buses. The link was a lifeline for some of them. Roly Clarke, who grew up in Oxenwood, said his mother had the Andover Co-op send her weekly groceries on the Wilts & Dorset bus; she wanted to keep earning her Co-op

above] Wilts & Dorset believed that wear and tear on country roads would incur higher maintenance costs for underfloor-engined buses than for those with engines in the traditional place at the front. With this in mind, and much to the surprise of many in the bus industry, it placed a special order for 15 front-engined 39-seat Bristol LWL5G saloons in 1954. Three years later KWV935 (555) was about to leave Andover to negotiate the narrow lanes around Vernham Dean and Linkenholt. DAVID PENNELS

above right] Three LD6B Lodekkas with enclosed platforms joined the Wilts & Dorset fleet in January 1956, but they were not fitted with doors until September that year. They were found to be unsuitable for Salisbury city services, so they were assigned to country routes, and then transferred to Andover depot. MMW411 (614) was the last Lodekka to be delivered with a deep radiator grille. All subsequent vehicles of this type came with a shallower grille. DAVID PENNELS

below right] Romsey Square was a meeting point for red Wilts & Dorset buses going to Salisbury and Andover and green Hants & Dorsets bound for Southampton and Winchester. For a time in the mid-20th century they ran jointly between Winchester and Salisbury as service 66. Hants & Dorset made a brief foray up the Test Valley to Stockbridge in the early 1920s, but this road became a Wilts & Dorset preserve long before Bristol L6B GMR31 (310) was working the 83 to Andover in August 1960. DAVID PENNELS

left] The remote Wiltshire village of Oxenwood was never likely to generate much traffic, but Pewsey depot laid on a double deck for the Saturdays-only journey on the 17 to Marlborough, crewed on this occasion by driver Farr and conductor Vears. This was part of a revised pattern of services introduced at the end of 1959 to avoid Andover-based crews having to work on rest days to provide through journeys to Marlborough. GHR366 (302), a Bristol K5G, was new in 1950. DAVID PENNELS

below] In April 1963 JWV381 (382) passes No. 46 High Street, Amesbury – where E.M. Coombes set up in business in 1914 – on its way from Andover to Salisbury, one of Wilts & Dorset's most frequent inter-urban services. The bus had suffered an accident a few months earlier; during repairs it was fitted with the T-shaped destination display, the only Bristol KSW6B that the company modified in this way. PETER RELF

dividend. At the end of the 1950s the company charged between 9d and 2/- (about 4p and 10p) for a parcel, depending on how heavy it was. The maximum weight was 28 pounds (12.7 kilograms).

Like its neighbour Basingstoke, Andover was declared a London-overspill town in 1961. By the mid-sixties extensive new housing estates were going up to the north of the town's ring road. For many of the Londoners, moving out of low-grade and overcrowded accommodation in the capital, there were no jobs on the doorstep. Nor were shops close at hand, so transport had to be provided. In 1966 Wilts & Dorset revised its town services to meet the needs of residents on River Way, the first of several big overspill estates to be built on Andover's northern periphery. A few years later, after Henry Tibble's son Oliver gave up his Pioneer Motor Services, the company extended some journeys on the Picket Piece route to St Mary Bourne.

By happenstance the bus service was not all that Wilts & Dorset provided for the new estates. Casting around for a way to meet the new residents' spiritual needs, the Rev. Bryan Apps, the curate at St Mary's Church, hit on the idea of buying an old double deck bus and fitting it out as a mobile church. So a 1950 Wilts & Dorset Bristol was selected, bought for the going rate of £150, and adapted for its new role thanks to the generosity of a local businessman.

The space below the stairs where the conductor used to lodge his ticket box formed a handy niche for a statue of the Virgin Mary. The church was downstairs and the top deck was used for Sunday school and other meetings. During the week the bus rested up at a local flour mill.

Over time it took on a patina of white flour, which had to be washed off before its Sunday outings. This did the paintwork no good, so the staff at the Wilts & Dorset depot volunteered to repaint it.

If you saw what looked like a Wilts & Dorset bus in Andover between 1966 and 1968, apparently heading for 'Sunday School' or 'Young Wives', you were not hallucinating. It must have been GMW195, a Bristol KS6B in retirement from the more arduous role of conveying fare-paying passengers around Basingstoke.

7
Crossing Boundaries: (b) Venture and Basingstoke

ONCE WILTS & DORSET reached Andover in 1927, that town remained the eastern limit of its penetration into Hampshire for the best part of a quarter of a century. The only exceptions were joint services with Hants & Dorset, to Winchester and Southampton. Venture Ltd, of Basingstoke, came to Andover early the next year, extending its Basingstoke-Whitchurch service six miles to the west, and briefly taking in Stockbridge as well.

Venture had begun as just that, a venture, in May 1926, to carry the workers at John I. Thornycroft & Co Ltd's vehicle-building works. It was hastened by the General Strike, but apparently what set it in motion was the need to find a way for the factory's workers to travel home and back in their allotted lunch break. The works director was Thomas I. (Tom) Thornycroft, younger son of John Isaac Thornycroft, and local legend has it that his wife, Gladys Evelyn Thornycroft, asked: 'In that case why don't we run a bus?'

She became Venture's first chairman. Her fellow directors were Arthur W.H Dalgety, Master of Foxhounds at the Vyne Hunt, the first managing director, and Fred E. Jordan, accountant at the Thornycroft works, whose son Ken became company secretary later in the year. Tom Thornycroft was technical adviser to Venture, but became chairman after his wife died tragically in October 1927 at the age of only 33. He chaired the board until the Red & White group bought up the company just before the end of World War II.

Running the Basingstoke factory and chairing the bus company were just two of Tom Thornycroft's many achievements. Born on 2 November 1881, he showed an early interest in applying petrol engines to cars and boats. In 1908 he won the motor boating event in the London Olympics. His craft, *Gyrinus II*, was the only one to complete the course in the rough conditions, helped by his foresight in recruiting two crew members to bail the water out. All three were awarded gold medals. Perhaps not surprisingly, the event has never been included in the Olympic programme since.

In the same year he drove a Thornycroft car in the Tourist Trophy Race, completing the course at an average speed of 44.1 miles per hour. In 1928 he won a bronze medal in the 'London to Brighton Run by Cars of the Old Brigade', driving Thornycroft's 1895 Steam Wagon No.1. His stoker was Norman Endacott, a boyhood friend, by now works manager at the firm's Basingstoke factory. The pair of them had teamed up to drive the steam wagon in the 1890s, when the law still required a red flag to be carried before a powered vehicle. Tom Thornycroft overcame the difficulty by carrying the flag whilst riding a bicycle. To quote Alan Townsin (2001): 'Tom

The sculpturesque figure of John I. Thornycroft lends a proprietorial hand to the rear of his 'Steam Wagon No. 1'. His son Tom is at the helm. Since Tom was just 14 years old when the vehicle was constructed, this was probably a 'tenth anniversary' commemorative photograph. With a wheel-base of just 5 ft, wooden-spoked wheels, chain-drive on the front axle and swivelling rear-axle steering, this forerunner of the many fine Thornycroft vehicles which followed must have been quite a handful to drive.

COLIN MORRIS COLLECTION

A Venture Thornycroft rests by the Crown Inn at Old Basing, where Royalists endured a three-year siege during the English Civil War. OT4785 (no. 5) was a typical example of Venture's 20-seat buses of the 1920s. It was new in 1927, the very year that Venture began running to Old Basing. The company had to face down competition from Aldershot & District before ensuring its hold on this route. ALAN LAMBERT COLLECTION

Thornycroft was a charismatic figure, well regarded within the works and beyond, and perhaps the most adventurous of the family members.'

Venture began with a share capital of £3,000. This was doubled in 1928, then increased by another £3,000 in 1929, and up to £14,000 in mid-1930. Town services in Basingstoke were always an important part of the operation, carrying people to and from work at the Thornycroft factory, Wallis & Steevens road roller works and the town's clothing factories.

The company's first two out-of-town bus routes went to Overton and Reading. The Overton service was extended first to Whitchurch and then to Andover; by 1930 there was a Basingstoke-Andover bus every 30 minutes. The Great Western Railway had a branch line from Reading to Basingstoke, but Venture took the opportunity of the General Strike, which started on 4 May 1926, to launch what it called 'an emergency service' to Reading. However, faced with competition from other

bus operators, as well as the railway (the strike was over in mid-May), Venture reduced it to Sundays only in 1927 and dropped it altogether two years later.

Like independent operators across the country, Venture flourished by filling in gaps between big companies, but at first it sparred with the Aldershot & District Traction Co Ltd for the territory east of Basingstoke. When it was barely six weeks old Venture threw down the gauntlet by pushing out as far as Hartley Wintney. Aldershot & District saw its opportunity to retaliate in May 1928 by extending its Aldershot-Basingstoke service westwards to Andover. Each drew back the following August: Aldershot & District agreed

In 1930 Venture received its first Thornycroft 32-seaters. Though new that year, OU5659 (no. 19) already looks dated as it stands at Newbury Wharf bus station waiting to drive the few miles south to Whitway, across the Berkshire-Hampshire county boundary. This was a short working of the Whitchurch-Newbury service, for which Venture garaged a bus in Newbury. THE OMNIBUS SOCIETY

OU826, Venture's only six-wheeler, began life as a Thornycroft demonstrator with first Bournemouth then Liverpool Corporations. Its size and its clerestory roof gave rise to its name with Venture busmen, the 'Showboat'. More prosaically this 40-seat Thornycroft FC was numbered 20 when it joined the Venture fleet in 1931. It lasted until 1937. The destination screen reads 'Bramley', a route kept busy by workers at the army ordnance dump there. ANDREW WALLER COLLECTION

to withdraw the Andover extension, and Venture dropped its Hartley Wintney service.

A year earlier Venture had started another service into Aldershot & District territory, through sparsely peopled country to Alton, but this did not bring the two into conflict. At first Venture was competing with the Basingstoke and Alton Light Railway, but this was never a big earner; indeed the track was lifted in 1916 and shipped to France for use by the army, and was only relaid in 1924. The Southern Railway closed the line to passenger traffic in September 1932, leaving Venture alone between Basingstoke and Alton. Longer term, this made Alton Wilts & Dorset's most easterly destination.

Venture had a busy year in 1929. It pushed southwards to Alresford, where it linked up once more with the Aldershot company's service to Winchester via Farnham and Alton. The Venture directors also made the first of two approaches to their eastern neighbour about a possible sale of the business. Aldershot & District baulked at the suggestion that Tom Thornycroft should have a seat on its board.

Venture started once-a-week services to Newbury, via Whitchurch, and to Winchester. Soon it went to Newbury three days a week; in 1931 it began a daily service to the Berkshire town via Kingsclere. Winchester, well served by rail from Basingstoke, proved a harder nut to crack; the city council refused Venture a licence to run there every day and its Winchester service came to an end in 1931. R.A. Chisnell's *King Alfred* had extended its Winchester-Whitchurch-Overton service to Basingstoke in October 1928

Venture approached Aldershot & District again in 1933. The asking price of £40,000 made it easy for Aldershot to resist any temptation there might have been to expand westwards. The following January Ken Jordan, now Venture's general manager and secretary, met Raymond Longman to enquire whether Wilts & Dorset might be interested.

Longman asked Aldershot & District and Thames Valley, Venture's northern neighbour, whether they would object to the company making a bid, provided it coordinated services where Venture had been in competition with them. Thames Valley raised no objection, but Aldershot & District said Venture was in its territory and Wilts & Dorset should not negotiate. However, it was agreed that Wilts & Dorset should make a tactical bid of £10,000. Venture rejected it. As far as

Wilts & Dorset was concerned, there the matter rested until 1950.

Dalgety retired from Venture's board in 1933 and F.E. Jordan in 1935, three months after his son had resigned as general manager and secretary. Jack Welling, the traffic superintendent, was promoted to traffic manager and secretary. With a new team in charge Venture sought to strengthen its position to the north of Basingstoke. In 1936 the board discussed bidding for a controlling share in Newbury & District. This company had united the operations of three local independents in 1932. The matter does not appear to have been pursued any further.

Then the traffic commissioners turned down Venture's bid to take over Edith Kent's *Kingsclere Coaches*, which was based at Baughurst and served both Basingstoke and Newbury. Instead she sold out to Newbury & District in 1937. The Kent family, Edith and her sons William and Fred, dominated the bus business in the Kingsclere and Baughurst area for around ten years up to 1937, each running their own operation. The Great Western Railway briefly challenged Edith Kent's hold on the Kingsclere-Newbury road with its own bus service in the late 1920s, and even ran briefly to Basingstoke, but then decided to cut back its road activities.

Venture's opportunity to gain a firm foothold on the villages between Basingstoke and the Berkshire border came a few months after Mrs Kent had sold up. It took over William Kent's stage services in October 1937. (He had absorbed his brother Fred's service in 1935). This gave the company a new route to Newbury and a service to the Berkshire village of Aldermaston, later famous as the site of the Atomic Weapons Research Establishment, as well as substantial traffic between Basingstoke and the Hampshire villages around Tadley and Baughurst.

At first Venture's buses were all Thornycroft 20-seaters. By 1936 it had 27 Thornycrofts, including nine 32-seaters and a six-wheeler, known as the 'Showboat', which had 40 seats. Two coaches, a little Ford that only lasted about four years with Venture and a Leyland Lion that arrived in 1936, were the only vehicles of another make that the company had ever had. Everything was to change in 1937.

left] A publicity shot of one of the half-dozen AEC Regents that Venture bought in 1937. When it decided to buy double decks Venture found it hard to choose between AEC and Leyland, so the matter was decided at a lunch. Representatives of each manufacturer were invited, and slips of paper bearing the letters A or L were drawn from a silver bowl. When the score reached a level 5-5, the fate of the £12,000 order hung on the 11th slip. It bore an A. BOU697 became Wilts & Dorset's no 427 in 1951. COLIN MORRIS COLLECTION

below] Venture's first pair of diesel-engined saloons arrived in 1938. They bore some resemblance to London single decks of the early 1930s, with chassis by AEC of Southall and bodies by Park Royal. COT548 (no. 35), parked at Newbury, shows the fuller destination display that Venture began to specify at the time. THE OMNIBUS SOCIETY

With only single decks, Venture had to run duplicate buses on its busiest routes, particularly westwards to Andover and northwards to Bramley. Occasionally traffic was so heavy that four vehicles were required for one journey. This meant expensive 'dead mileage' running empty in the other direction, so for the first time the company decided to buy double decks. The choice came down to two chassis builders, the Associated Equipment Company (AEC) and Leyland. It was hard to choose between them so Venture organised a lunch with representatives of the two companies and the editor of *The Commercial Motor*, at which lots were drawn.

AEC, which built buses for London Transport, won the draw and the order for six Regent double decks. These promptly went to work on the Andover road and other busy routes. Thenceforth AEC became Venture's principal bus supplier. A number of second-hand AECs also joined the fleet in 1940 and 1944, so that when it passed to Wilts & Dorset in 1951 all but two vehicles were of that make. The last of the Thornycrofts was withdrawn in 1948.

Two weeks after Britain declared war on Germany in September 1939 Venture cut back its weekly mileage by 30 percent. It suspended less profitable routes and reduced the number of journeys on others. With more double decks on the road there was less call for duplicate buses. This also helped to handle the extra traffic generated by the number of evacuees in the area. However, desire to save costs to help the war effort may not have been the principal motive for the service cuts; at the annual general meeting in December 1939 shareholders learned that Venture had made a trading loss of £755.

above] Sidney Huntley & Son's Oakley-Basingstoke service dated from 1921, four years before Venture appeared on the road. They competed for traffic for many years until the Huntleys gave up the route in 1948. However, they held on to Basingstoke-Kingsclere and Basingstoke-Hannington services until they were sold to Wilts & Dorset in 1952. Like many small independents in the 1930s the Huntleys used Chevrolet 20-seaters. JH1025 lasted into the 1940s, to appear with wartime white mudguards and masked headlamps. THE OMNIBUS SOCIETY

The war meant that there were more patients and visitors travelling back and forth to Park Prewett Hospital, on the north western outskirts of Basingstoke. In April 1940 the police took Venture and the conductor

above] After 1940 Britain geared all its productive capacity to the war effort. Civilian vehicle building had to stop, but a small number of chassis remained incomplete on the production line. In 1942 the government let them be completed and allocated to bus companies deemed to be in need of them. Venture received two of these 'unfrozen' AEC Regents, with bodies built to the austere standards laid down by the Ministry of Supply. ECG646 became Wilts & Dorset's no. 445, but retained its old destination blinds with Venture service numbers. DAVID PENNELS

above] Like bus companies across the country Venture hired women to take the place of men called up to the armed services. Health and safety rules were not what they have since become: so there was nothing out of order for a wartime timetable cover to show a conductress – Setright ticket machine at her waist - balancing on fog light bracket and starter handle to wind the destination blind. DAVID PENNELS COLLECTION

"FREEFOLK" OF ENGLAND

left] A Venture bus starred in this scene that was used to stir patriotic English hearts in World War II. For wartime propagandists the name of the village was sheer serendipity. Two smartly dressed schoolchildren hail BOU701, one of Venture's 1937 AEC Regents, outside Manor Cottages, Freefolk. Besides being used for propaganda, this photograph, taken from a wartime calendar, also featured on the cover of Venture timetables. The bus became Wilts & Dorset's no. 431. COLIN MORRIS COLLECTION

of the last bus to Park Prewett to court for carrying 48 passengers on a 31-seater. He was fined 10 shillings (50p) and the company £2. Later in the year Venture put another vehicle on the main cross-town service, between the hospital and Kempshott, so there was a bus every 20 minutes in the afternoon and early evening. Like Wilts & Dorset, Venture had to cope with new traffic generated by the war effort while facing vehicle shortages and diversion of some services. In 1942 the Basingstoke-Tadley-Baughurst-Newbury service was diverted northwards from Brimpton to reach Newbury along the Bath Road, avoiding the RAF base at Greenham Common. Extra journeys were added from Basingstoke to Tadley, which was close to the airbase being built for the US Army Air Force at Aldermaston.

Venture conveyed civilian workers to the army's explosives depot at Bramley Camp, as well as providing transport for people along the route with jobs in Basingstoke factories, and meeting the spare time needs of military personnel at the camp. The Alton route called for extra journeys to serve the RAF station at Lasham, and a new Whitchurch-Andover service was added to meet the needs of a big army camp at Barton Stacey; this followed a more southerly road than the main Andover service.

To cope with the volume of traffic Venture borrowed no less than 30 buses from other parts of the country at different times between 1940 and 1945. Fourteen of them came from London, six from Morecambe in Lancashire, and five apiece from Manchester and East Kent. At the end of 1944 it acquired a dozen more AEC Regents from Nottingham Corporation.

On 1 March 1945 Red & White United Transport Ltd bought out Venture Ltd. From then until 1950 the directors came from the Chepstow-based company. Buying Venture was part of an eastward thrust by the group; it had taken over Newbury & District Motor Services Ltd in January 1944, and was to buy South Midland Motor Services Ltd, of Oxford, seven months after Venture. The heart of the group's activities lay in southeast Wales. John Watts started his business 1921, and registered Red & White Services Ltd eight years later. It stretched across the English border into Herefordshire and Gloucestershire, with a group of routes based on

Stroud, and in 1939 it acquired Cheltenham District Traction Ltd.

The five years of Red & White control of Venture coincided with the country's emergence from wartime austerity. Few people had cars and for most of the population the bus was the only means of local transport, so there were plenty of passengers. However, new vehicles were still hard to come by. Until the first new buses arrived in 1947 Venture made do with its prewar fleet, the second-hand double decks it had acquired in 1940 and 1944, and a pair of 'unfrozen' AEC Regents it had received in 1942. (Early in the war vehicle

manufacturers had been told to halt civilian production, which left a handful of unfinished chassis on the production line. These were 'unfrozen' in 1942 and allocated to the bus operators judged to be most in need of them).

A postwar landmark for Venture was the restoration of the service to Winchester in April 1946, after a gap of 15 years. The first bus out of Basingstoke was well loaded and so many passengers queued for the second journey that a relief bus had to be hastily found. Publicity for the new service related it to the visit to Winchester in May by King George

above] Early in World War II London Transport needed to borrow buses from the provinces, but the tables soon turned and London buses appeared around the country helping out provincial operators. Venture borrowed no less than 14 ST-class buses from London Transport between 1941 and 1946. GK6239 (ST963) stayed with the company from January 1942 to January 1946. THE OMNIBUS SOCIETY

right] GH3815 was one of two London Transport AEC Regals that Venture bought in 1940 to cope with extra wartime traffic. It wears Venture's pre-1945 two-tone red livery, but with wartime headlamp masks and white-rimmed mudguards. As it pulls into the bus stand in Basingstoke it still looks for all the world like the Green Line coach (T188) that it had once been. THE OMNIBUS SOCIETY

left] Odiham Motor Services Ltd gave up its bus services in February 1966, including the Basingstoke-Long Sutton route. It became Wilts & Dorset's service 110, pointing a finger southeast of Basingstoke at Aldershot & District territory. There were three journeys each way on Wednesdays and two on Saturdays. About twenty years earlier Odiham MS's Duple-bodied Bedford OB EOT404 waited to leave for Long Sutton from its stand in Wote Street. Tony Hancock was appearing in 'The Rebel' at the cinema. ANDREW WALLER COLLECTION

VI and Queen Elizabeth, who had won the hearts of many Britons by the way they related to peoples' wartime sufferings, still fresh in the nation's memory. As John Pearce comments in *Venture Limited*: 'For the rest of Venture's existence the Winchester route always seemed to be regarded as a prestige service.' Indeed, even after Wilts & Dorset took over, the usual bus on this route was the last of the AEC Regents to join the fleet, no. 500. Could there be a connection? Near the Winchester terminus still stands that Winchester landmark, the statue of King Alfred. The sculptor was Hamo Thornycroft, Tom's grandfather.

Early in 1946 Andover's town clerk wrote to Venture to ask if it could route its buses into the town along a different road, and also run a service to Picket Piece, an outlying settlement to the east of Andover. Local services there had hitherto been a Wilts & Dorset preserve; no doubt seeing a good opportunity, Jack Welling, now Venture's general manager, responded immediately. He welcomed the town's ideas and used the occasion to point out that the travelling public wanted Venture buses to continue to Andover Junction. The Guildhall terminus, he wrote, was some distance from the station and inconvenient for passengers wanting to take the train. Within a couple of weeks the company sent in its proposed new timetables, which were in use just three months later. Given Wilts & Dorset's slower response to wartime submissions about a local bus service, the town council must have been impressed.

Now that Newbury & District and Venture were both part of the Red & White group it was only natural that the two should rationalise local services based on the Berkshire town. They combined two Venture routes with one of Newbury & District's to create a joint cross-town service between Shaw, effectively a Newbury suburb, and the Hampshire downland villages of Burghclere and Whitway.

The Venture management had more trouble with the Alresford route. It was hard to reconcile the requirements of scattered villages along the road both with one another and with cost-effective operation. Jack Welling told Basingstoke Rural District Council that this route had set the company more problems than the rest of the

system combined, and he proposed to hand over some workings to an independent, Oswald Porter, of Dummer.

In November 1948 Venture bought the freehold of a timber yard in Wote Street, Basingstoke, as the site for a future bus station. For a few years after Wilts & Dorset took over, buses were parked in the old timber sheds, under cover but open to the elements all around.

When the Tilling group was nationalised in 1948 under the British Transport Commission, the Red & White directors were faced with a decision: should they hold out for their independence, or if the company were to be nationalised anyway might they get a better price by selling of their own free will? The outcome might have been different had they waited, but in February 1950 the 10 companies in the group passed to the BTC, which promptly arranged for Wilts & Dorset to enter into a management agreement with Venture Ltd. Wilts & Dorset was to hire the assets, retain the receipts and pay the expenses of Venture Ltd from 1 January 1951. The Wilts & Dorset board formally approved this arrangement on 28 November 1950. It was altered, retrospectively, in February 1952, so that the aggregate receipts and expenses were apportioned between the two companies on a mileage basis, making it a 'joint operation'. The need first to establish Venture's tax

King George VI was due to visit Winchester soon after Venture launched its service to that city in 1946 – a fact the company made use of in its advance publicity. It continued to use its newest buses on this route, like 1947 AEC Regent FOT201, later to become Wilts & Dorset's no. 480. In this publicity photograph, Venture general manager Jack Welling boards the bus. Lydney Coachworks, also part of the Red & White group at the time, built the body to Weymann design. DAVID PENNELS COLLECTION

Venture bought five diesel-engined AEC Regals in 1938, three coaches and two saloons. It added another dozen, all but two of them coaches, in 1947-48. One of the prewar batch, COT550 stands alongside a 1947 saloon. A postwar coach is parked behind. All three had apparently been on 'relief car' duties, perhaps on hire to Associated Motorways or Royal Blue for busy summer weekend work. PM PHOTOGRAPHY

Map of the final route network of Venture Ltd, Basingstoke, before it was taken over by Wilts & Dorset. COLIN MORRIS

position may have lain behind the delay in finalising the arrangement.

At its meeting on 24 November 1953 the Wilts & Dorset board agreed to take on Venture's debit balance, but the share capital was not to be increased to cover this. The board returned to the relationship with Venture on 13 May 1958, discussing whether to make a subvention to Wilts & Dorset's subsidiary. The directors instructed the secretary to raise the issue with the Tilling Association: should they make Venture Ltd a dormant company? It survived, in name alone, long enough to have its registered office transferred in December 1965, along with Wilts & Dorset's, to The Square, Bournemouth, as part of the Hants & Dorset group.

Wilts & Dorset took over a company with a fleet of 46 buses, more than half of them double decks, a small network of seven town services in Basingstoke, and country routes stretching out to the north, west and south. North and west these served Aldermaston, Newbury and Andover, and to the south they went to Alton, Cheriton and Winchester. There were also relatively local routes out of Alton and Newbury, where Newbury & District had come under the control of the

Thames Valley Traction Co. Ltd. Apart from the main Basingstoke depot in Victoria Street, and the newly acquired Wote Street premises, Venture had garages at Whitchurch, which dated from 1930, and Baughurst. It also kept a vehicle each in Newbury & District's main depot and Aldershot & District's Alton garage.

When Venture took over Bill Kent's services in 1937 it needed a new garage at Baughurst. Tom Thornycroft specified a single-span 'Belfast' roof, reflecting his experience of such a structure at the Thornycroft works. A Belfast truss is a technique for building a strong but lightweight 'girder' out of small sections of wood, with lattice-work support and nailed joints. (The company that moved into the premises in the 1990s preserved the roof, and called the building Lattice House.) The garage was built on the site where Edith Kent had kept her buses. Wilts & Dorset kept on the outlying premises at Baughurst until the end, unlike the Whitchurch garage, which it closed in 1955 when the Salisbury and Basingstoke services to Andover were joined up to form route number 76.

In its first year Wilts & Dorset made only minor alterations to Venture's old services. They were

left] Venture found it hard to meet the disparate needs of villages along the Alresford road. Jack Welling, the general manager, told district councillors he proposed to hand over some workings to Oswald Porter, of Dummer. This independent was already running as far as Preston Candover, a route he acquired with Henry Nobbs' Nobby Bus Service in 1945. Porter's Bedford OWB (FRU149) – built to wartime utility specification for Charlie's Cars, of Bournemouth – was working the route in 1951. It had spent more than three years with King Alfred in Winchester before joining Porter's fleet. J.F. HIGHAM COLLECTION

right] Two buses parked in Basingstoke, both with bodies by Willowbrook of Loughborough. The rear view of the pair shows distinctly the external difference between the highbridge layout, with central gangway on the top deck, and lowbridge, with sunken gangway along the offside. ECG646 (445) was new to Venture in 1942. UF7421 (256), came from Southdown in 1939 and was rebodied six years later. DAVID PENNELS

below] Most of the dozen elderly AEC Regents that Venture acquired from Nottingham Corporation passed to Wilts & Dorset management in 1951. Venture had their bodies reconditioned by Portsmouth Aviation or Reading & Co Ltd, also of Portsmouth. Park Royal-bodied TV4493 (465) is on a Basingstoke local service via 'Elly Lilly Wks'. What the U.S. pharmaceuticals company Eli Lilly made of this is not recorded. DAVID PENNELS

the Conservative government, which had defeated the postwar Labour administration in the previous year's general election, passed the Town Development Act, which was to transform Basingstoke, and many other towns, for ever. London County Council, Hampshire County Council and Basingstoke Borough Council reached an agreement under the terms of this act to turn the town into an important business area. By 1961 its population had swollen to nearly 26,000. Ten years later this had doubled. Inevitably this demanded a complete revision of town bus services.

But first there was some reorganisation along the road to Kingsclere and Newbury. On the last day of 1952 Wilts & Dorset paid £1,500 to buy the three remaining stage licences of S. Huntley & Son of East Oakley, for services to Kingsclere and Hannington; Huntley had sold his Basingstoke-East Oakley licence to Venture in 1948. Wilts & Dorset only took over operations the following May, launching a through service via Kingsclere to Newbury, jointly with Thames Valley. This brought an end to the service to Newbury via Tadley, Baughurst and Brimpton, which dated in one form or another from 1937. It now terminated at Baughurst, and Brimpton was left to Thames Valley's

renumbered by the addition of 100, so the 1 became the 101, and so on, but the Picket Piece service was numbered 72, alongside other Andover locals.

Basingstoke's population in 1951 was just under 17,000. This was around 4,000 more than when Venture started up in 1926, but it was still a small market town which offered employment in the Thornycroft works and other local factories. All this was soon to change. In 1952

left] UU6650, which began life in 1929 as London General's T35, received a fresh coat of paint from Wilts & Dorset in 1950, but still bears the Venture name and fleet number. It kept its original Chiswick-built body to the end, rebuilt by Reading of Portsmouth in 1946. The open platform at the rear avoided the need for an emergency door. Parked behind it is one of Venture's smart new Guy Arab double decks, which soon all passed to Newbury & District. ANDREW WALLER COLLECTION

below left and right] Before and after: Venture's ex-Nottingham AEC Regent TV4957 (72), in Red & White-style livery, negotiates the snow in Basingstoke. Within a year or so its Brush body had been refurbished, with sliding vents replacing the half-drop windows. In July 1952 Wilts & Dorset had just painted what was now its no. 472 in its new colours when the camera caught it turning into Wote Street. DAVID PENNELS COLLECTION

below] Venture gave a new lease of life in 1945 to three aged buses it had acquired during the war by sending them to Blackburn for new bodies by East Lancashire Coachbuilders. When the chassis of an ex-Chester Corporation bus wore out three years later, Venture transferred its body to JO5401, ex-City of Oxford Motor Services, which was caught by the camera when working a schoolchildren's special as Wilts & Dorset's no. 441. DAVID PENNELS

A curious change in the first year of Wilts & Dorset's stewardship was the extension four times a day of the Basingstoke-Aldermaston service to the hilltop Berkshire village of Beenham. It was not served by Thames Valley, but clearly lay within its territory as it is north of the A4 Bath Road. Services that only ran two or three days a week, largely intended for shoppers, were gradually reduced. In 1959 Basingstoke-Steventon was abandoned altogether. However, when Odiham Motor Services Ltd gave up its bus services in February 1966, Wilts & Dorset took over its Basingstoke-Long Sutton route. It also continued to the end the twice-weekly run to Hannington and Wolverton, which had replaced Huntley's service.

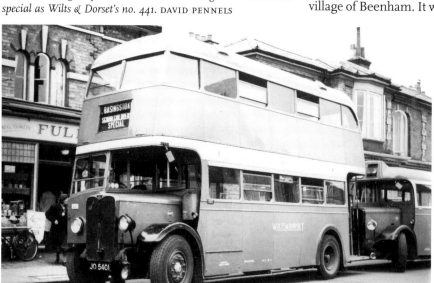

Newbury operation. As part of a general reorganisation of local services in mid-1953 Baughurst-Basingstoke was extended through the town to Worting, enabling Wilts & Dorset to replace J. & T. Wood's *Empress Motor Service*, for which it paid £1,000.

By 1958 Venture Ltd was making losses sufficient to cause the Wilts & Dorset board to consider subvention payments (cash to help keep the company afloat) to Venture. The board explored with the Tilling Association the possibility of making Venture Ltd a dormant company. Instead, Wilts & Dorset

right] *Company employees do not always transfer their loyalties as fast as their managers do when a firm changes hands. Wilts & Dorset repainted Venture AEC Regal coach GCG816 in its red and maroon coach livery after it became its new owners' no. 495 in January 1951. However, working to Brighton on an August Bank Holiday excursion in 1952, its driver opted to keep up tradition by turning his destination blind to 'VENTURE'.* DAVID PENNELS

below] *BAD30 pulls out of a full bus park on Victoria Street, Basingstoke, on a June Saturday in 1953. Besides two other AEC Regents, there are Leyland and Bristol buses behind it, and a saloon – half a dozen vehicles originating with operators in six different counties. No. 485 was the first of three Regents with all-metal Weymann bodies and Gardner engines that joined the Venture fleet from Cheltenham*

District Traction in 1947. Wilts & Dorset modified its destination display to its own standard in 1950. DAVID PENNELS

purchased from Venture property at Crane Wharf and Basing Road, both in Basingstoke.

Town services were reorganised once more in December 1959, and again four years later, although the 1963 changes were postponed for five months because road-building fell behind schedule. By this time the expansion of the town was seriously under way. A map of the proposed development showed that Basingstoke was to be planned with the motor age in mind. An east-west dual carriageway was to pass between the town centre and the railway station, with a ring road connected to it. Vehicles were to reach the centre only by these roads, while other routes into the town would be blocked off.

The detailed plan emanated from the Basingstoke Development Group, which comprised a director of town development, an architect, an engineer and a surveyor. They provided for a large number of routes, each linking one housing estate or factory to the centre. Writing five years later in *Bus and Coach*, Alan Townsin commented: 'An experienced traffic man from a bus operator would have spotted their uneconomic nature almost at once.' Fortunately for Wilts & Dorset there was just such a man to hand, area traffic superintendent Jack Welling, who had been Venture's traffic superintendent back in the early 1930s, and became its traffic manager and secretary in 1935. In the Red & White years he was general manager. He was active in local politics too, a member of the borough council and an alderman, and Mayor of Basingstoke in 1955-56.

After Wilts & Dorset objected to the proposals in October 1962 it was given assurances on the routes and stops that its buses could use. They were to be allowed along some streets scheduled for pedestrian areas, and link roads for buses were to be provided where the provisional plan had shown they would have to stop short of the centre.

Writing before bus lanes became commonplace, Alan Townsin continued: 'Thus, the idea that buses were to

be operated over roads forbidden to other vehicles was expressed. This document is regarded as particularly significant by the Wilts & Dorset management – indeed it could almost be described as the bus operator's charter.'

David Pennels, who was responsible for planning timetables and work schedules, recalls that Jack Welling wanted to put buses into new estates as soon as there were roads. The first major development was South Ham. To Popley, which came later, 'initially a one-man single decker was enough, but very soon you couldn't see through the bus.' The company opted, where possible, for cross-town circular routes, clockwise and anti-clockwise, to serve housing and industrial estates on either side of the loops. Also, with one-man operation in mind, it wanted to avoid dangerous and time-consuming reversing. There was minimum standing time at the outer termini, with longer layovers at the bus station to provide, if necessary, for crew changes.

While the government and the town were working on Basingstoke's expansion Wilts & Dorset also set about the lengthy business of sorting out its property portfolio there. It was already in correspondence with Hampshire County Council in 1954 about the proposed bus station site, but it did not legally acquire the Victoria Street garage from its Venture subsidiary until the 1960s. Then it sold it to the Borough of Basingstoke

above] *UF7384 (130), the last of Wilts & Dorset's Leyland TD1 Titans in passenger service, lurks under an old timber shed at Wote Street, Basingstoke. It began life in 1931 as Southdown's no. 884, passed to Wilts & Dorset in 1939 and saw out the last of its days in Venture country before retiring in March 1955. 130 was rebodied in 1945 by Willowbrook, whose utility design included a peculiar sideways overhang above the cab.* LONDON TROLLEYBUS PRESERVATION SOCIETY

The one-man Bristol LWL5Gs, or 'conker boxes' as they became known, were distributed about Wilts & Dorset's depots and outstations, from Blandford to Basingstoke, for drivers did not generally favour them. However, in ice and snow they were far happier at the wheel of a front-engined LWL than piloting an underfloor-engined LS, with its front wheels set back. LAM745 (565) waits at Wote Street, Basingstoke, to drive southwards to New Cheriton in July 1959. DAVID PENNELS

One of Wilts & Dorset's first batch of underfloor-engined Bristol LS6Gs, delivered in 1952, waits outside the Wallis & Steevens works. Specialising in steam traction vehicles, road rollers and road making equipment, in its time this was one of Basingstoke's biggest employers. JAM226 (522) retains its original coach livery and seating even though it is only on a local service. DAVID PENNELS

right] One of Venture's ex-Nottingham AEC Regents, TV4952 (74), ended its days as a breakdown truck-cum-tree lopper. Hants & Dorset's engineers carried out the conversion in 1950, and Wilts & Dorset later modernised its front end. It even swapped the old radiator with a more modern one taken from a postwar bus. P. YEOMANS, PSV CIRCLE

The ex-Venture service 107 to Alton required one bus to be kept at Aldershot & District's depot in the Hampshire town. GMR27 (312), last but one of Wilts & Dorset's Bristol K5Gs, stands alongside an Aldershot Dennis Loline. The later Bristol Ks had flexibly mounted engines, which gave passengers a more comfortable ride. PETER TREVASKIS

in 1965 for £38,000. It formally acquired the Venture properties at Crane Wharf and Basing Road in 1959. The following year the British Transport Commission approved plans for a new depot, which was to be alongside the bus station. According to Wilts & Dorset board minutes the estimated cost of the project was £93,150. The contractors had to drive reinforced concrete piles 30 feet into the ground to support the structure because it was on the site of the former basin of the Basingstoke Canal.

The new bus station, depot and workshop were opened in a blaze of local publicity on 28 June 1962. Appropriately enough, the first departure was worked by a Basingstoke crew on service 101 to Bramley Village. But they needed a freshly painted bus, so a Salisbury-based Bristol Lodekka – RWV526 (633), fitted for the occasion with Basingstoke destination blinds, but still with its Salisbury area advertisements – was provided for the occasion. The bus station was designed to handle 180,000 departures a year. Wilts & Dorset's 13 country and eight town services accounted for 150,000 of these, and other operators for the remainder. In 1965 part of the adjoining Wote Street site was sold to the borough. The transfer of another piece of land from the town to the company permitted further expansion of the bus station in 1968.

As the town continued to expand, local services had to be repeatedly revised. When Hants & Dorset finally absorbed Wilts & Dorset in 1972 there were no less than 22 local services criss-crossing Basingstoke.

8
Camp Services: Silver Star and Wilts & Dorset

BY THE TIME Edwin Maurice Coombes created his Wilts & Dorset Motor Service in 1914 the army was already well-established on Salisbury Plain. Much of its transport was still horsedrawn. What motors there were had to plough through dust or mud on unmetalled roads and tracks.

After the military disasters of the Crimean War the army realised it needed better training, and more extensive land upon which to conduct it. The Military Lands Act of 1892 gave the Secretary of State for War powers to buy and lease land. Salisbury Plain was chosen because it was sparsely populated, its chalky soil dried quickly so horses would not be bogged down in it, and it was within striking distance of London, Aldershot and the port of Southampton. Between August 1897 and December 1899 the army bought 45 properties. The first was at West Lavington. A big area at Tidworth soon followed, and by the outbreak of war in 1914 this was the largest base on Salisbury Plain. Like many of the camps, Tidworth had its own railway branch both for military freight and for troops going home on leave. At one time the Midland & South Western Joint Railway earned more revenue from Tidworth than from all its other stations combined.

The war brought a huge concentration of British and Empire troops to the Plain. New Zealanders and Canadians encamped at Bulford, and Australians at Larkhill. In the Wylye valley, west of the Plain, there were 15 camps at Codford and others at Sutton Veny, near Warminster. War meant that fuel supplies for civilian use were limited and new vehicles were hard to come by. However, soldiers could make weekend trips to Salisbury and elsewhere by hired charabanc.

Eddie Shergold and Ben White had been friends at school and, after war service, worked together for the Great Western Railway before returning home to set up in business in 1923. They bought their first bus that year, a Ford T registered HR9447, and ran it from Allington to Salisbury three days a week. Pitt & Sons of Fordingbridge built the polished aluminium body with a canvas hood that folded down in good weather. DAVID PENNELS COLLECTION

In the 1920s restrictions eased and tar macadam surfaces improved the roads out of all recognition. For the first time bus companies could offer reliable regular services between the camps and nearby towns. At first Wilts & Dorset was just one of a handful of operators serving the Plain. It returned to Larkhill in September 1922 and Tidworth, Bulford and Netheravon within the next year. Competition for traffic was intense and in 1926 the company sent two rebodied ex-War Department Crossley tenders as 'chasers' to Larkhill, where Wilts & Dorset maintained a small garage until 1937.

Relations with the army were not always sweet. In November 1931 the board heard that a Captain Learmont of the Royal Artillery had made derogatory remarks about Wilts & Dorset's service to Larkhill. Lt Col Gilbert Szlumper, one of the Southern Railway's representatives on the board, agreed to take the matter up. He was well placed to pull rank, should it be needed. Within a month or so Raymond Longman, the company secretary, met the garrison adjutant. The board's minute book recorded: 'It was hoped a more favourable view of the company's operations would now ensue.'

Wilts & Dorset consolidated its hold on the Plain by buying out Bannister & Corp in 1927, giving it a base at Bulford. Bartley & Avery's *Tidworth Motor Service* followed two years later, securing for the company a virtual monopoly on the busy Salisbury-Tidworth-Andover route. Faced with this powerful presence, several smaller operators gave up local bus services on

Shergold & White's second bus was based on an ex-War Department Crossley tender. The chassis bore Lancashire registration B9396, and it had a 14-seat saloon body. In an early example of Eddie Shergold's flair for publicity, the front wheels were painted with an eight-pointed silver star. Not many bus companies legal address was on military premises: 'Silver Star Garage, Porton Exp[erimental] Camp'. DAVID PENNELS COLLECTION

the Plain. Then the 1930 Road Traffic Act accelerated the process, replacing local-authority bus service licensing with a national system of regional licensing bodies. But not all the independents gave up; the best known of these was Shergold & White's *Silver Star*.

The jolting carrier's cart was already creaking into history when William Shergold bought up Joseph Rowden's village carrier business in 1922. The horsedrawn van took people to market on Tuesdays and Saturdays from the three Winterbournes, a cluster of villages about three miles northeast of Salisbury. Shergold's purchase launched what turned out to be not just a market day affair but a highly successful concern that lasted for another 40 years. His son Eddie and an old schoolfriend, Ben White, came home from South Wales, where they had been working on the Great Western Railway, to help run the business. In September 1923 they put together what money they had or could borrow to buy their first bus, a 14-seat Ford T.

The little bus, with fold-back canvas roof, went to work three times a day between Allington, Porton Camp

and Salisbury, taking in Joseph Rowden's old patch at Winterbourne Dauntsey. Ben White suggested they call it Silver Star, the title of a waltz that was popular at the time. The name must have appealed to Eddie Shergold, who had been a sailor on the destroyer *HMS Morning Star*. They timed their bus so it could take children to school in Salisbury, and carry scientists who lived in the city to work at Porton Camp. Wilts & Dorset had started a daily service up the Bourne valley from Salisbury to Tidworth earlier the same year, via the Winterbournes and Allington. Rival independents on that road mostly ran to Salisbury only on market days: Harry Razey from Cholderton, John Armstead from Newton Tony, and Thomas Lee from Winterbourne Gunner – whose widow carried on the business after he died in 1935, until Silver Star eventually took it over in 1949.

In 1926 Shergold & White started another service, from Salisbury via Amesbury – the prime Wilts & Dorset route – to Sling. By 1927 they had a garage on War Department land at Porton Down. There they kept what had now become a fleet of five vehicles, including two Crossleys and two Albions, one of them with 26 seats. The fifth was a Rolls Royce Silver Ghost chassis which they converted themselves to a six-wheeler, then sent to Fulham for Wray's Motor & Body Co to build the coachwork. Two years later they bought their first Leylands, a Tiger and a Lion, both 32-seaters. From then

Silver Star lined up its latest coaches in a 1930s publicity shot. WV5823, at the head of the line, was a 1934 Leyland Lion showing Weymouth as its destination. Behind it is MW8981, showing Bournemouth. This was Silver Star's only AEC. Leyland Tigers MW4774 and MW8982 bring up the rear, with their blinds wound to show London and Southampton. So there was nothing new about the idea of conveying troops to different destinations when Silver Star fought its battles in the traffic courts in the 1950s. DAVID PENNELS COLLECTION

Eddie Shergold, in the bow tie, and Ben White pose in front of a shiny silver-coloured coach in about 1935. Starting out as school friends, their business partnership lasted 40 years. Ben White was responsible for the high quality of the fleet's turnout and maintenance, while Eddie Shergold drummed up business. DAVID PENNELS COLLECTION

until they sold out to Wilts & Dorset in June 1963, Shergold & White were loyal Leyland customers. All but three of the vehicles they bought new thereafter were Leylands, and all but two of those they acquired second hand.

The 1930 Road Traffic Act changed the nature of the bus business. Every stage or express service, and every excursion pick-up point and destination, had to be licensed by the new traffic commissioners. They heard licence applications from Salisbury operators in mid-1931. Over the next two or three years this spelled the end of a number of small independents' market-day services. Silver Star, in the person of Eddie Shergold, ultimately emerged as a vigorous player of the new system, even if he faced a couple of setbacks to start with.

He sought licences for three stage services, and for excursions from Salisbury and Porton Camp. Two daily services were approved, Allington-Porton Camp-Salisbury, and Salisbury-Amesbury-Bulford-Sling, but the third was refused. This was unfortunate for Silver Star, which had just had 'Salisbury-Amesbury-Bulford Camp-Tidworth-Andover' emblazoned on the glass louvres above the windows of a brand new bus. Wilts & Dorset was well established on this route, and the Traffic Commissioner held that Silver Star had appeared on it too recently to justify the licence. He approved the excursions from Porton Camp, and in 1933 from Bulford Camp, except for one important clause. Silver Star added excursions from Durrington in 1934 by acquiring the licences of Albert Hawkins, who had sold his twice-weekly Salisbury market service to Wilts & Dorset two years earlier.

Not for lack of trying, Silver Star never gained a licence to pick up excursion passengers in Salisbury. Wilts & Dorset inspectors kept a beady eye on its coaches when they stopped at Blue Boar Row with a load of football fans heading for a Saints match in Southampton; were they picking up any passengers in the city? The clause that the traffic commissioner deleted when he granted the Bulford licence read: 'Application is made for permission to convey men of HM Forces only stationed at Porton Camp, Bulford Camp, Larkhill Camp, to Victoria, Oxford and Aldershot when general leave is granted. These tours to be for the period of leave up to twenty-one days.' What would the commissioner have made of the battles that Salisbury Plain coach operators waged in the traffic courts 20 years later?

If tour licences to coincide with military leave were hard to come by in the 1930s there was plenty of scope for operators to vie with one another for private hire contracts to carry army bands around the country. Military musicians had exacting requirements, but the distances they travelled ensured that the money to be earned made it worthwhile. Silver Star had a healthy slice of this market right up to the end. Some of its coaches had specially large roof racks to carry the bands' instruments. Other independents intent on staying in business, like Edmund Stanfield of Figheldean and Joseph Whitmarsh of Netheravon, competed to offer servicemen weekend excursions to London, but for all of them this business came to an untimely end in 1939.

Like Wilts & Dorset, but on a much smaller scale, Silver Star had to find extra vehicles in a hurry in 1939, to convey workers to military construction sites on Salisbury Plain. It lighted on half a dozen Leyland TD1 Titans, surplus to the needs of Yorkshire Woollen District Traction, of Dewsbury. HD4154, with masked headlamps but no white patches on its mudguards, picks up passengers at Blue Boar Row in Salisbury. THE OMNIBUS SOCIETY

Three of Silver Star's best single decks were requisitioned by the War Department in 1940, leaving Shergold & White with a handful of aged saloons, including a pair of ex-Southdown 1929 Tilling-Stevens passed on by Wilts & Dorset. One of them was UF5076 which soldiered on until it was nearly twenty years old, with its Harrington body virtually unaltered. W.J.HAYNES

Storm clouds of war might billow over the European horizon in the mid-1930s, but the efforts of a maverick politician called Winston Churchill had yet to persuade many of his colleagues to take them seriously. Despite Ramsay MacDonald's 1935 White Paper recognising 'the security of armed force' some army camps were as yet empty and offering bus companies very little traffic. Silver Star was in any case finding it hard to staff its Sling service. Understandably, given the importance of the Andover route that passed that way, Wilts & Dorset was quite ready to take it over in 1937. It paid £1,500 for the goodwill of Salisbury-Sling, together with excursion licences from Bulford.

As the decade drew towards its bitter end the nation's leaders at Westminster faced up to what now seemed inevitable war. This confronted Shergold & White with new demands. Like Wilts & Dorset, they were called upon to provide transport for construction workers erecting new army camps around Salisbury Plain. In order to ferry workers to a militia camp at Winterbourne Dauntsey, later known as Figsbury Barracks, they bought their first double decks – six 51-seat Leyland Titans came from the Yorkshire Woollen District Traction Co Ltd, of Dewsbury.

Just three weeks after war broke out Silver Star became a limited company, Shergold & White Ltd, with Edward W. Shergold and Bernard F. White as its directors. The War Department requisitioned three of their single decks in 1940, so the double decks, now ten years old, had to bear the brunt of the greatly increased traffic. Once more the Plain became the temporary base for troops from abroad. The United States Army took over Tidworth Barracks in 1942, and used many other camps around the Plain.

The country drew breath when war ended in 1945, but the early post-war years were still a time of hardship and austerity. Hot war yielded to the Cold War, as the West squared up to Soviet communism. For a time it seemed possible that Europe would become a battlefield once more. War-weary Britain still had big military commitments: restoring a semblance of normal life to the shattered continent, striving to keep the peace in the Middle East, and policing what was still called the British Empire. The US Army pulled out of Tidworth Barracks in April 1946, almost a year after Germany's defeat. Now the British army could once more base large numbers of troops in Tidworth, conveniently located as it is on the edge of the Salisbury Plain Training Area.

Silver Star's Leyland Titans were worn out, as were three even older saloons, two of which came third-hand from Wilts & Dorset in 1940, but, given how hard it was to obtain new buses in the early post-war years, these aged vehicles soldiered on for a year or two more. A new double deck arrived at the end of 1946 and a coach in September 1947, but otherwise Shergold & White had to make do with second-hand buses until it could set about steady modernisation of its fleet in the 1950s. In 1949 they took over the Winterbourne & East Gomeldon Motor Service from Martha Lee, whose smart Dennis Falcon bus had served the Gas School at Figsbury. The route was close enough to Silver Star's for it to be an easy matter to combine them.

With all the tasks that still faced British forces, a volunteer army – like that between the wars – no longer sufficed. Parliament passed the National Service Act in July 1947, so every fit young man had to join one of the services. When the Act came into force in 1949 the term was 18 months, but with the outbreak of the Korean War in 1950 National Service was extended to two years. Between 1949 and May 1963, when the last enlisted soldier was demobbed, the army alone took in 1,132,872 conscripts.

Thousands of them spent time at Tidworth, Bulford, Larkhill or one of the 20 or more other camps around Salisbury Plain. What were they to do at weekends? The army was mindful of troop morale. No doubt it also wanted to avoid crowds of young men in uniform roaming the streets of nearby towns with little to keep them out of mischief. So it issued them with 36- or 48-hour passes to travel home to their families and loved ones. The lucky ones had 72-hour passes.

From 1947, when fuel was still rationed, Wilts & Dorset laid on special buses to the mainline stations at Salisbury and Andover Junction, so troops on weekend leave could go to London and beyond by train. Company inspectors called at the camps on Thursdays to sell through bus-and-train tickets to Waterloo. When the railways were nationalised on 1 January 1948 the state-owned system retained the Southern Railway's 50 per cent share in Wilts & Dorset. As part of the Tilling group the bus company itself became publicly owned eight months later.

Under the post-war Labour government, the authorities favoured the road-rail facility over direct coach services between the camps and London or other centres. From the soldiers' and airmen's point of view, this was less than ideal. National Servicemen earned little, and wanted to travel home as fast, as often and as cheaply as possible. The portion of the fare for the train journey was set by British Railways and the road-rail connections were often just too slow. The market was ripe for more nimble independents to move in on the act.

Local operators, like Edmund Stanfield and his son Dudley, and Joseph Whitmarsh's *Avon Coaches*, sought to run express services directly from the camps. Silver Star soon joined the fray. If they could persuade the

Silver Star replaced some of its aged double decks in 1949 by buying younger second-hand models like COX966, a Leyland TD4C Titan that came from Birmingham Corporation. Basically a standard all-Leyland product, its straight staircase and offside destination display betrayed its Birmingham origins. Resplendent in new silver paint, with red waistbands, it waits at Blue Boar Row to leave for Porton Camp.
ANDREW WALLER COLLECTION

Licensing Authority to authorise such services they would obviously challenge Wilts & Dorset's hold on the lucrative weekend leave market. As a starter, Wilts & Dorset gained licences in 1949-50 to run feeder services to more distant railheads, Portsmouth for the South-East, Bristol for trains to South Wales, and Cheltenham and Oxford for the Midlands and North.

The Stanfields applied unsuccessfully in 1949 for an express licence between RAF Netheravon and London. Two years later Avon Coaches were granted licences for express services from Netheravon to London and Birmingham, only to have them revoked when Wilts & Dorset and the Railway Executive appealed against them. 'Seemingly the existing rail feeder arrangements were considered adequate,' wrote David Pennels. After the Conservatives returned to power in 1951, the licensing regime began to ease, not least because of realities on the ground; for example, one November Sunday night that year Wilts & Dorset laid on 35 double-deck departures from Andover Junction between 11 pm and 2 am – room for 1,900 seated passengers. All but nine of the buses, manned by crews from Andover, Amesbury and Pewsey, were full. Salisbury depot supplied an average of eight buses to meet trains there, mostly to convey soldiers back to Blandford Camp.

Wilts & Dorset and the independents all cashed in on the weekend express bonanza in the 1950s. At first the Licensing Authority favoured the big company; early in 1951 it allowed Wilts & Dorset to run a Boscombe Down-London express, but turned down Silver Star's application for excursions that would in effect offer a Boscombe Down-London service at weekends.

Once it became involved, Silver Star made much of the running. Eddie Shergold and Bernard White set about creating a network of weekend express services that covered the country. They went to London, Swansea, Glasgow, Newcastle-upon-Tyne, Birmingham, Liverpool, Manchester and many other cities. Whitmarsh, for all his pioneering effort, fared less well than his rivals, and

left] HWV793, Shergold & White's first Leyland Royal Tiger, is bound for Birmingham on a forces weekend leave express from Tidworth. This coach was rebodied by Harrington in 1956 after its original Leyland body was badly damaged in a fatal accident near Rugby. After June 1963 it continued to work weekend express services for Wilts & Dorset as its no. 904. DAVID PENNELS

below] Silver Star's OHR281 waits to leave Tidworth for Manchester on a weekend express duty. Shergold & White bought a pair of these Leyland Tiger Cubs in 1956, and the owners' sons each drove one of them. The central entrance made it difficult for the driver to supervise loading and collect fares, so they were sent to Locomotors of Andover in 1962 to have their doorways moved to the front. DAVID PENNELS

in 1958 he sold out to Dudley Stanfield's *Tourist Coaches.*

After 1951 express operations gathered pace. By early 1952 Wilts & Dorset, Tourist, Avon Coaches, Silver Star and Sidney Shergold's *Tidworth Coaches* were all licensed to run weekend expresses to London, but from different camps. Wilts & Dorset shared the traffic from Larkhill with Tourist, from Tidworth and Perham Down with Tidworth Coaches, and from Bulford with Silver Star. The company could also pick up passengers at Tilshead, on the western side of Salisbury Plain. Silver Star had pick-up points at Porton Camp and the Winterbournes.

The 1950s were Silver Star's heyday. In the ten years from 1951 it took delivery of 11 underfloor-engined coaches and three dual-purpose vehicles, which were designed for local bus work during the week and express duties at the weekend for soldiers going on leave. With their distinctive bodies, mostly built by Thomas Harrington, of Hove, painted in silver livery with red lettering, they became a familiar weekend sight in many parts of England. On several occasions they came in pairs, which meant that Michael Shergold and Gordon White, Eddie and Ben's sons, could drive one each.

In August 1952 the government appointed a committee to look into the licensing of road

above] Only two months old, Silver Star's RAM620 approaches St Thomas Bridge on its way into Salisbury in April 1958. This was the last of the three dual-purpose Leyland PSUC1/2 Tiger Cubs that the Porton Down independent bought; the driver could now take the fares on weekday operations into the city, and the vehicles were available at weekends to carry troops on leave to different parts of the country. DAVID PENNELS

left] Wilts & Dorset's 39-seat underfloor engined Bristol LS6G dual-purpose saloons like JAM418 (528) began to arrive at the end of 1952, in time to handle the bulk of the weekend express traffic from Salisbury Plain. They were painted red below the waistline and maroon above, with ivory flashes. On weekdays they ran local stage services from their home depots. The two-door arrangement was not a success, so the company soon panelled in the rear doorway and added two more seats. DAVID PENNELS

Sidney Shergold's Tidworth Coaches was the first of the operators competing for traffic on Salisbury Plain to put an underfloor-engined coach on the road. This Duple-bodied AEC Regal IV, photographed at Hampshire Cross on 12 September 1958, was in service just ahead of Silver Star's first Leyland Royal Tiger and a few months before Wilts & Dorset's first Bristol LS6G was delivered. DAVID PENNELS

passenger services. It reported the following year. Under the heading 'Camp Services' (a term still innocent of *double entendre* in those days), it found that there had indeed been instances of the railways and nationalised bus companies opposing independents' applications for weekend leave services. 'It is claimed that, the independent operator having established the need for the service, the controlled company has then applied for the licence for itself and has not been opposed by the railways.' The nationalised companies, it said, 'had some reason for thinking that policy favoured the road-rail schemes in which they were already cooperating rather than the direct road services for which the 'independents' were applying; and it is no unusual feature of proceedings before the Licensing Authority for an established operator to claim that the new service applied for by a rival is unnecessary but that if the Licensing Authority

considers need to be proved, the established operator has the stronger claim to provide it.'

Up until November 1952 Wilts & Dorset's coach fleet consisted entirely of front-engined half-cab vehicles. There were a dozen postwar Bristols and about the same number of prewar Leylands, together with more than 20 dual-purpose Leylands delivered in 1939-40. Almost all of these seated only 32 passengers. It was hard to accommodate more with any degree of comfort within the vehicle dimensions that the law permitted at the time. These restrictions were eased in 1950. At the same time manufacturers were designing the underfloor-engined vehicles that were to sweep half-cab saloons and coaches off the roads by the mid-1960s.

Wilts & Dorset's first underfloor-engined Bristol LS (Light Saloon) dual-purpose 39-seaters – with coach seats in a bus shell – arrived in November 1952. This was some months after Tidworth Coaches and Silver Star took delivery of their first underfloor-engined vehicles. The new Bristols immediately displaced most of the petrol-engined Leyland Tiger coaches. Within 16 months the company had 37 of these new vehicles. They were all painted in the smart red, maroon and ivory coach livery, which reflected Southdown design even though the link

above] The company used the old airfield at High Post - where once Salisbury-built Spitfires took flight – to pose its vehicles for official photographs. Bristol LS6G JWV262 (549) shows off its new single-door configuration after Wilts & Dorset rebuilt it in 1955. DAVID PENNELS

right] Wilts & Dorset introduced a simplified coach livery, with no maroon paint, in 1958. RMR524 (703) was one of six of the new Bristol MW6G coaches delivered that year. The drivers called them 'cream tops'. The MW (for 'Medium Weight') had a more conventional chassis than the LS that it succeeded. 703 is parked in Brighton after running a weekend express from Salisbury Plain army camps to the Sussex coast. ANDREW WALLER COLLECTION

Joseph Whitmarsh's Avon Coaches, from Netheravon, took the initiative early to establish weekend express services from Salisbury Plain, but he sold the business to Tourist Coaches in 1958. However, his Daimler coach with locally built body by Heaver of Durrington, was still going strong in June that year, waiting to pick up soldiers going on weekend leave to Plymouth at Hampshire Cross, in Tidworth.
DAVID PENNELS

between the two companies had long since been severed. The Bristols were delivered with a door at the front and another at the rear, but the company rebuilt them all in 1955 to remove the rear door, which left too little leg room for the corner seat behind it, raising the seating capacity to 41. The 39th soldier might have put up with cramped legroom, but for use on private hire, tours and excursions the rebuilds effectively added three extra seats.

Through the 1950s and much of the 1960s the LS remained the workhorse for Wilts & Dorset's weekend expresses. All of the type survived to be transferred to Hants & Dorset legal ownership in March 1969, still 'trading as Wilts & Dorset' for another three years. Newer Bristol MW (Medium Weight) coaches started to arrive in 1958. These were known to the drivers as 'cream tops' because of their simpler red and cream livery. A fleet of Bedfords, the standard coach for many independent concerns, arrived in 1965-70. Until 1968 these were all 41-seaters. Then came the six-wheel VALs, with seats for 49 passengers.

Flushed with success on the London road, Wilts & Dorset applied for services to Birmingham and the north. In mid-1953 new services were approved from

Boscombe Down, Netheravon camps and RAF Upavon to Birmingham, and Boscombe Down, Tidworth and Perham Down to Liverpool, Preston, Manchester and Leeds. The three independent rivals also gained new licences: Tourist for Larkhill to Birmingham, Manchester and Liverpool, Tidworth Coaches for Tidworth-Birmingham and Tidworth and Perham Down to Manchester and Liverpool, and Silver Star for Bulford, Tidworth and Perham Down to Birmingham, Manchester and Liverpool.

So Wilts & Dorset and the three independents were now well-established express operators from Salisbury Plain. Avon Coaches maintained its licences but became less forceful in pushing for new ones. A struggle for supremacy ensued, with keen competition in booking passengers, and intense rivalry on the road. But the fiercest battles were fought out in the traffic courts, as each applied time and again for new services and variations to existing ones, and raised objections to their

Edmund Stanfield of Figheldean had a share in a Milnes-Daimler bus as early as 1914. In the 1950s, he and his son Dudley vied with Wilts & Dorset for weekend express traffic from army camps. At that time the Stanfields used mainly Leylands, including this PS2 Tiger, photographed at Figheldean in May 1960, with Upavon, Netheravon and Larkhill on its destination blind. The licensing authority may have been less than pleased when they flirted with the title 'Pirate Coaches'. They opted instead for 'Tourist Coaches'. DAVID PENNELS

Heavy traffic on Silver Star's forces weekend leave service to London often called for a double deck. To cut down draughts on the long late night journeys, two Leyland Titans were sent to Heavers of Durrington to have platform doors fitted. Ex-Maidstone & District GKL763 was already 16 years old when its Weymann body was modified in 1956. During the week it continued with regular stage bus work between Salisbury and Bourne Valley villages.
DAVID PENNELS

rivals' applications. They fought for additional picking up and setting down points, new, extended and alternative routes, revised timetables, linking conditions, and the removal of restrictions. Though the fares were modest the value of regular weekend express traffic made it worth the operators' time and the lawyers' fees.

Early on both the traffic commissioners and the operators accepted that each camp should be the preserve of one concern, except where there were equal claims on the traffic. So Boscombe Down was regarded as a Wilts & Dorset camp, Larkhill as Tourist's and Bulford as Silver Star's. That was until Silver Star thought otherwise. Not the pioneer of weekend express services, it was however apparently the first to see that the future of the business lay in linking feeder services from a dozen or more camps to a network of express routes covering much of the country – initially from an interchange on public land at Hampshire Cross, Tidworth.

By doing this, Eddie Shergold made an important contribution to the way the express services developed;

the one camp/one operator arrangement was much more likely to lead to the 'wasteful and uneconomic competition' that he regularly cited when Silver Star lodged objections to other operators' applications. In 1959, when the Licensing Authority had 74 cases concerning Salisbury Plain express services to consider at a public hearing, Silver Star appeared as applicant or objector in 65 of them. So eager was he to promote the express services that even in his later years Eddie Shergold would turn up at army camps week after week, driving his Bentley or a Leyland Tiger Cub. Armed with a ticket machine, he did his best to ensure the passengers chose Silver Star, and he supervised departures.

Silver Star's coaches were more consistently well presented than those of rival independents, and more eye-catching than Wilts & Dorset's standard Bristols. When they were at remote locations between the Friday night journey out and the Sunday night return, they gained high visibility in other parts of the country by being hired out to local concerns. Most of Silver Star's coaches were needed for express services every weekend. When a double deck was used as well it was a legal requirement that a conductor be carried. If more vehicles were needed they were

One of Silver Star's 1955 Leyland Tiger Cubs, MMR553, rests in Yorkshire after a Friday night drive from Salisbury Plain. Not all the passengers rode in such a modern vehicle; parked behind the Fray Bentos hoarding is AAM756, Silver Star's 1936 Leyland Tiger. Wilts & Dorset did not retain MMR553; instead it became Western National's no. 3805 painted in Royal Blue livery. Years later it passed to a preservationist, and emerged resplendent in its original colours. ANDREW WALLER COLLECTION

right] *London Transport's RTL305 was the last of Silver Star's second-hand Leyland Titans. It was only ten years old when it arrived in Porton Down in 1959 from a dealer in Stratford-on-Avon. Wilts & Dorset had no need of non-standard double decks when it took over Silver Star in 1963, but KGU263 found its way in 1965 to Ledgards for another two years on the road with the Leeds independent.* DAVID PENNELS

hired in from other operators like Pride-of-Sale (Manchester), Excelsior (Bournemouth) or Hollands Tours (Birmingham). On the longest run, to Glasgow, a relief driver had to take the wheel for part of the journey. Gordon White recalled that a Pride-of-Sale driver would take over from him between Knutsford and Carlisle. Silver Star coaches laying over at their remote destinations were hired out to local independents like Morris Bros in South Wales, Sunniways Coachways Ltd, Crown Coachways or Kenilworth Coaches in Liverpool. 'The Manchester boys would do a Yelloways Saturday [journey] to Cheltenham' and sometimes a Silver Star would do a run to Pwllheli for Crosville Motor Services Ltd.

On 13 November 1957 Shergold & White changed the official name of their company to Silver Star Motor Services Ltd. In the same year they stole a march on Wilts & Dorset by applying for an express licence for a service to convey Ministry of Supply employees between their homes on a new housing estate at Bemerton Heath, on Salisbury's northern outskirts, and their jobs at Porton

Down. Wilts & Dorset, which had preserved its monopoly on Salisbury local services since taking over Sparrow & Vincent in 1933, objected to the application. So did British Railways; the workers had previously had either to change buses in Salisbury or transfer from bus to train to reach Porton Down. The camp authorities supported Silver Star, and the licence was granted. Wilts & Dorset and the railways appealed to the Minister of Transport, but their objections were dismissed.

Two years later it was Silver Star's turn to object to a local change proposed by Wilts & Dorset, a joint service with the Bristol Omnibus Co Ltd between Salisbury and Swindon, to run via the Winterbournes and Allington. In reality the change did no more than link the two publicly owned operators' existing services, which had previously met at Marlborough. The new through service was approved, and just five months after it was introduced all three operators agreed to coordinate their timetables to provide more evenly spaced timings up and down the Bourne Valley.

VAM944, Silver Star's second Leyland Atlantean, heads into Salisbury with its doors open. These rear-engined buses were ahead of their time as far as Wilts & Dorset was concerned; it never owned such a vehicle. Instead, when Shergold & White sold out to the company in June 1963, the three bus-seated Atlanteans went to the Bristol Omnibus Co. Ltd. Running them for a year was no doubt helpful experience as Bristol worked on the design for its own rear-engined double deck which made its first appearance in 1966. DAVID PENNELS

the 61-seater, with its coach seats, its radio and its public address system, ultimately proved to be a white elephant.

Then, in October 1962 Eddie Shergold died

Also in 1959, less than a year after Leyland announced the production model of its Atlantean rear-engined double deck, Silver Star became the first independent operator in the country to buy one. In each of the next three years it bought another. The 1961 Atlantean had coach seats, and Silver Star hoped to use it on weekend leave express duties. Sadly for the company, the Licensing Authority turned this down, so

and, as David Pennels wrote: 'it became obvious that he, virtually, *was* Silver Star, for his passing marked the beginning of the end of the company.' Pennels summed up his achievement like this: 'Quite apart from anything else, to have taken on all comers in the Salisbury Plain express war, and won, was no mean feat. He was a man who "went big".' The end was not long in coming. Ben White, who had looked after maintenance of the buses,

Ladies take their tea in the Cadena Café while Silver Star buses line up outside on Blue Boar Row for afternoon workings to Porton Camp and Allington. The dual-purpose Leyland Tiger Cub PHR829 later became Wilts & Dorset's no. 901, but the Leyland Atlantean behind it, VAM944, went to Weston-super-Mare to work for the Bristol Omnibus Co Ltd. DAVID PENNELS

had decided to retire.

In mid-May 1963 reports surfaced in the local press that Silver Star had agreed to sell its goodwill and assets to Wilts & Dorset.

In January 1963, Silver Star Motor Services Ltd told Wilts & Dorset that its owners wished to dispose of the

undertaking. The Transport Holding Company gave its permission for negotiations to take place. The 'merger', as it was termed, took place at midnight at the end of Tuesday 4 June 1963. Wilts & Dorset took over the assets of Silver Star, including two leases for its premises at Porton Down – one of which was set to be developed into an important maintenance facility for Wilts & Dorset/Hants & Dorset.

Wilts & Dorset integrated the stage and express timetables with its own services, and acquired a fleet of 23 buses and coaches. It kept six coaches and the three dual-purpose vehicles, one of which was already being painted red in the company's workshop as the takeover took effect. The three Atlantean buses were transferred to the Bristol Omnibus Co Ltd, which used them for a year: the associated chassis builder, Bristol Commercial Vehicles, was to start creating is own rear-engined double deck in 1965, so having the Atlanteans on hand was an opportunity to learn how they fared and how the design might be improved upon. Most of the other coaches went to the Western National Omnibus Co Ltd to serve as reliefs on Royal Blue express services.

The acquisition added hugely to the volume of Wilts & Dorset's weekend express traffic. Just as Silver Star had done latterly, it concentrated its main Friday departures at Aliwal Barracks in Tidworth. Troops came in by feeder services from other camps to join the coaches that fanned out to different destinations. Salisbury depot provided the bulk of Wilts & Dorset's coaches, but Amesbury contributed too, and an Andover driver brought in passengers from Barton

A peaceful farewell: Salisbury Market Place seems deserted as RAM620, a 1958 dual-purpose Leyland Tiger Cub, waits at Silver Star's bus stop on Blue Boar Row in the last days of Shergold & White's operation, 3 June 1963. After midnight the next day this Harrington-bodied bus was to become Wilts & Dorset's no. 903 for the last six years of its working life. DAVID PENNELS

In the heart of Silver Star country, PMW386 passes Idmiston church only a month after it became Wilts & Dorset's no. 902. Fitted with coach seats and painted in dual-purpose livery, it was still available at weekends for armed forces leave express services. The turning to the left of the church, not visible in this picture, used to lead up to Idmiston Halt, on the Salisbury-London line, used by workers at the Porton Down Chemical Defence Experimental Establishment. A.J.DOUGLAS

Bere Regis & District, one of the UK's biggest independents with more than 100 vehicles, was Wilts & Dorset's main competitor on weekend express services from the big army camp just outside Blandford. This Plaxton-bodied AEC Reliance, bought second hand the previous year, was caught on camera in September 1960 as it headed through Salisbury on its way to Liverpool.
DAVID PENNELS

personnel. Besides the Salisbury Plain camps there were troops and airmen wanting to go home for the weekend from Middle Wallop, Barton Stacey, Stockbridge and Worthy Down in Hampshire, from Knook Camp and Warminster to the west of the Plain, and from Blandford Camp in Dorset. At peak times Wilts & Dorset sometimes needed 15 or 16 coaches to meet demand at Blandford, and on Sunday night it might have to lay on a double deck to convey soldiers back there from Bristol.

Stacey and Middle Wallop before heading off to Manchester. John Lewis, who drove an Amesbury-based coach to Preston, recalls that on a busy Friday there would be ten or a dozen coaches lined up on the barrack square. At Bristol Temple Meads, on a Sunday night, there could be four or five Wilts & Dorsets heading back to the Plain.

Coaches also exchanged passengers at other stops en route, avoiding unnecessary duplication when only a few people from different camps were going to a particular destination. In practice the independents had a freer hand, even if the licensing authorities might not always have approved. John Lewis started his journey to Preston at Wilton, picking up more passengers at Boscombe Down and Larkhill, before heading for Tidworth, where he would meet up with another feeder from Bulford. His coach was then timed to meet the Liverpool vehicle at Cirencester, to exchange passengers. They met up again at Whitchurch, in Shropshire, at a truck-drivers' café, which stayed open for them of a Friday evening even if bad weather caused delays. In those days there was no M5 or M6 motorway to speed them northwards. Gordon White used to drive the Manchester and Liverpool service for Silver Star. He recalls how he would meet up at Knutsford with Peter Budden, of A.E. Budden & Sons. They told one another how many passengers they had for the two cities, and then one would say: 'You take my Manchester and I'll take your Liverpool.'

Serving the needs of forces personnel demanded that days and times of operation be flexible. Coaches normally left the plain on Friday/Saturday and returned on Sunday/Monday. Most of the express services ran consistently for a decade or more, but a few were laid on to meet the requirements of particular regiments stationed temporarily on the Plain. One such was Tidworth to Dagenham, Bedford and Northampton, which Wilts & Dorset, Silver Star and Tidworth Coaches shared between them in 1955.

Between them the coach companies catered to a potential market of perhaps some 30,000 armed service

The independents kept a wary eye on each other and on Wilts & Dorset. At one time or another these included Bere Regis & District, Berridge & Sons of Warminster, P.J. Card of Devizes, Empress Coaches (Stockbridge) Ltd, A.E. Budden & Sons of West Tytherley, Taylors of Sutton Scotney and A.H. Razey's *Amport & District*. Bere Regis & District served Blandford Camp, running to London, Birmingham, Manchester and Liverpool. P.J. Card ran from Warminster to London and Bristol. Berridge & Sons were licensed for a service to Dundee, and objected when Wilts & Dorset applied for a similar route. Later they withdrew the objection after the company agreed only to go to Dundee at Berridges' request. A.E. Budden & Sons were a strong presence in the Hampshire camps, to the east of the Plain. Besides Liverpool and Manchester, they had licences for Leeds, Newcastle, Glasgow, Edinburgh, London, Swansea and Bristol, the last to be operated on a rota basis with Taylors of Sutton Scotney.

John Lewis said the regular passengers did not give much trouble. Servicemen were more interested in reaching home on the outward journey, and happy to fall asleep on the way back to camp. In those days coaches did not have toilets. John Lewis recalled one problem on a run to London: 'I had a couple of WRAC girls one day and one of them wanted to use the toilet. I had to stop at the young men's YMCA for two young ladies to use the toilet.' Evidently the company's experience of troops' behaviour reflected what happened elsewhere. In 1962, five years after Wilts & Dorset extended its Brighton service to Dover, there was an exchange of letters with the East Kent Road Car Co Ltd about what passengers could be picked up in Kent. Evidently their behaviour also concerned P.W. Dodge, of East Kent. He wrote: 'Though you do, as we do, experience misconduct and damage from troops stationed locally, you do not find this to be the case on your Express Services.'

Gordon White agreed that troops on weekend leave were generally well behaved. If there was a disturbance one of their own number would step in to keep them under control. But the Saturday hires to other operators were not always so well disciplined. On one Liverpool to Manchester run, he recalled, 'a bloke called his mother-in-law an old cow'. Fisticuffs ensued. He stopped the coach and left the belligerents at the roadside. The coach was on hire to Sunniways.

Both Wilts & Dorset and the independents sought extra business for their coaches rather than have them stand idle between Friday night and Sunday evening. Helping other 'group companies', the large territorial operators, was a regular feature of Wilts & Dorset drivers' long-distance runs. After parking up for the night in Preston in the wee small hours of Saturday, John Lewis had to be up bright and early to drive his coach from Blackpool to Newcastle, via Bowes Moor, Durham and Chester-le-Street, on hire to Ribble Motor Services Ltd. He returned light to Preston in the afternoon. If not required for Newcastle, the coach would often be used to help out on the Liverpool-Pwllheli express service. Tidworth Coaches and Silver Star also helped out on services to Pwllheli.

On occasions, this mutual assistance might become a tad more questionable. 'We were well known at Chester, because we would help out,' John Lewis recalled. 'The inspector would know that we were coming in at elevenish' on a Friday night. 'If you were on time you could pick 10 to 15 passengers' for Birkenhead or Liverpool. After an evening out in Chester these civilians must have missed the last Crosville bus home. For the inspector who asked the Wilts & Dorset driver to take them it was 'anything to get them out of Chester town square.... We were breaking the law in that we were carrying passengers uninsured. Their ticket is their insurance... We didn't actually charge them at all. We left it to their discretion when they got off... It went into the hat, but we lost out if we didn't get a tip because we had to pay a penny each through the [Mersey] tunnel.'

Wilts & Dorset's London coaches regularly ran back to the West Country on hire to Royal Blue. An Amesbury-based coach ran to Brixham, in south Devon, after unloading its passengers. Coach and driver would wait in London until 11 pm, then load up at Victoria Coach Station. On the westward journey drivers changed over at Salisbury and the coach

continued to Brixham. Then it would go back to Exeter 'to see if we could get a load to go to London or Salisbury'. Another driver used to do the Royal Blue working to Salcombe, and an Andover driver took a coach to Newquay. At peak times an Amesbury driver sometimes drove as far west as Penzance for Royal Blue.

Competition on the road with the independents was a constant feature of the weekend expresses, but the Licensing Authority tempered this with conditions attached to some of the licences. Stanfield's Larkhill-London licence contained the proviso: 'Wilts & Dorset Motor Services Ltd. to operate the first and subsequent alternate vehicles; D.F. Stanfield to operate the second and subsequent alternate vehicles. Traffic from Rollestone [two miles west of Larkhill] to be shared with Wilts & Dorset Motor Services Ltd.' The alternate departures arrangement with Tourist Coaches was unusual, but many of the express licences restricted the destinations to which an operator could carry passengers from particular camps.

Wilts & Dorset served Sheffield and Leeds, but it was not allowed to drop off passengers there from Tidworth, Perham Down or Ludgershall. This was the preserve of Tidworth Coaches and Tourist Coaches. Silver Star was not allowed to pick up any passengers from Boscombe Down until two hours after the last Wilts & Dorset coach had left the RAF station. The Licensing Authority's rules did not prevent a bit of freelance competition by the drivers. John Lewis said Dudley Stanfield used to check up on his Preston coach when he pulled up on the Packway at Larkhill. 'He used to come and stand in front of my bus, to see who was getting on ... If I could poach a couple of Londoners and change them at Aliwal I would.' On the London service 'the race was between Tidworth Coaches and ourselves. If we could get to London before Tidworth Coaches, we had the same lads next week. So we were a little bit dirty in our route. If we didn't have anybody for Camberley... we'd turn off at the Cricketers and go across by Ascot and pick up the M4 into London, which was unofficial but it was quicker. It was the same when we left Tidworth, we'd go [via] Grateley and go across to miss the level crossing in

Keeping a vehicle idle in London from Friday night to Sunday evening would be a poor return on investment, so Wilts & Dorset's weekend leave coaches were often hired out to work express services to the West Country on a Saturday. SWV689 (708), a 1959 Bristol MW6G, waiting for duty at Victoria Coach Station, even displays 'ROYAL BLUE' on its destination blind. ANDREW WALLER COLLECTION

Ex-Silver Star Leyland Leopard WWV564 (909) leads a private hire convoy of 20 coaches out of Bulford Camp on 1 July 1965; half were going to Southsea and half to Bognor Regis. New in December 1960, this was the newest of the nine Silver Star vehicles that Wilts & Dorset absorbed into its own fleet. Seven other coaches were handed on to the Western National Omnibus Co. Ltd to help out with Royal Blue express services. DAVID PENNELS

Andover, and straight through to Stockbridge, which would give you another 20 minutes on Tidworth [Coaches].'

They may have fought one another for passengers, but this left no ill feeling between the drivers from different operators. If his own coach was parked up in London for the weekend, John Lewis might catch a lift home on Friday night on an empty Tidworth Coaches vehicle. On a Sunday the Tidworth driver might head back to London on a Wilts & Dorset coach travelling up light. The express drivers saw themselves as a bit special. 'We were a different breed,' John Lewis said. Drivers accustomed to the more easygoing excursion and private hire business did not thrive on the competitive edge of express work. All the coach drivers took pride in their appearance. 'On our trips from Blackpool Coliseum Coach Station to Newcastle, we'd stand in front of our vehicle on hire to Ribble and we'd get the customers because we had a reliable vehicle... They saw a Wilts & Dorset. We had our white tops on. We had clean shirts on Saturdays.'

Drivers staying away from home were given an allowance of about £3.50 for bed and breakfast. The four drivers who took turns on the Preston run stayed at the home of a Ribble driver called Bert and his wife Mabel, who was 'one in a million.' John Lewis recounted: 'We had a key to the house. We had a room with a chest of drawers and the four drivers had a drawer each. Our clothes were washed and placed in the drawer for our next visit. So we got out of our pyjamas and she would wash them and iron them and put them back in the drawer for us... We would always have a clean shirt for Saturday... Supper was always laid and we just put a note on the table if we were doing a Saturday job. She would call us for breakfast... We were treated as family members.'

It was not so comfortable everywhere. 'When I did the Penzance job I used to sleep in the back of the garage in the coach... But that was always a nice warm garage that Royal Blue had in Penzance, and they used to look after us very well.... You couldn't do it in London because if you parked at Vauxhall Bridge the police checked the coach. You had to have digs.' Another driver saved his allowance when he went to Colchester by staying with his aunt in the town. On the very long routes, like those to Glasgow or Edinburgh, operators had to provide a relief driver, who would take over between Knutsford and Carlisle. Wilts & Dorset's services to Scotland did not run every weekend, only as demand justified them, depending on which units were stationed on Salisbury Plain at the time.

However the army transport office at Bulford was one of the company's best private hire clients. It called for coaches to carry large bodies of troops about the country. Sometimes this involved journeys from airfields beyond the company's home territory, like Lyneham or Brize Norton, to carry units as far north as Glasgow.

Licences for the express services listed timing points along the route as well as all the scheduled stops. That way the police could tell if a coach had exceeded the speed limit. At first the licences set the speed between timing points at an average of 24 miles an hour, but around the late 1950s this was increased to 30 mph. The longer routes had to be licensed by three or even four different regional authorities. Drivers and passengers alike had an interest in reaching their destinations as fast as possible.

In those days there was no system of points to be lost on a licence if a driver was caught going too fast. Speeding was what John Lewis called an occupational hazard. 'We didn't tend to exceed the speed limit until the hat had gone round. We sort of stuck to 30 or 40

miles an hour until one of the people would say 'Come on, John,' and I would say 'Who's going to pay the fine?' and the hat would go round to pay the fine. Some of the lads kept the drivers in cigarettes.' He was stopped one weekend between Ormskirk and Preston, but was let off with a caution. He forgot to tell the driver making the same trip a week later. He was caught and fined. 'I never lived that down with Mick, but we still see each other.'

Gordon White was stopped for speeding between Swindon and Marlborough one Sunday night when he was 30 minutes ahead of his scheduled time. He turned around and went back to warn the other Silver Star drivers heading south. They all waited awhile in Swindon, but he said the police caught the Wilts & Dorset and Tidworth Coaches drivers.

Just as they had when road-rail facilities began in 1947, Wilts & Dorset inspectors, like 'Bing' Tiller from Salisbury and Len Penney from Pewsey, still visited the camps on Thursdays, together with their 'express conductors', to sell tickets for the weekend services. Even so, it was hard to predict how many coaches might be needed for the return journey. Many passengers only bought singles, or hitched a lift one way. John Lewis explained: 'They were National Servicemen and they

didn't have the money. A lot of times they were buying singles up and mum and dad paid for their fare back.'

The inspectors kept their ears to the ground; sometimes they suggested possible new express routes if a regiment was being transferred from a part of the country that the company did not already reach. 'Bing' Tiller relished the contact with the army; he would visit the traffic office in Endless Street once a week and greet his colleagues with the old sergeant major's cry of 'stand by your beds'.

Drivers had insert Setright ticket machines specially adapted by Wilts & Dorset to cope with higher fares than those required on local services. John Lewis took sixty to seventy pounds on Sunday nights coming down from Preston, 'and we used to get jumped as well to make sure we'd done our job properly, by a duty inspector from Salisbury. They'd come out as far as Cirencester sometimes.'

Traffic was so heavy on Sunday nights from London and Bristol that conductors went along to issue tickets. 'We used to take a conductor up with us to London, and he would travel from Victoria through to Staines with us.' He would issue tickets for one coach at Victoria, travel to Staines to take fares on a second vehicle, then transfer to a third for the rest of the way back to Salisbury Plain.

'It was the same at Bristol Temple Meads. We used to take a conductor to Temple Meads on a Sunday evening and he would do tickets at Temple Meads and do as many as possible. If he could fill the first coach we

OHR280, now in Wilts & Dorset colours, passes a line-up of the mixed types of vehicle used for weekend express services from Salisbury Plain. They include another Tiger Cub coach, and two dual-purpose vehicles – a Bristol MW6G and a third ex-Silver Star Tiger Cub. DAVID GILLARD

would leave with all our fares taken.... We left Temple Meads sometimes with two or three sat on the floor. The conductor was stood at the front with you all the time because he couldn't get a seat.'

In spite of the rivalry between operators, fares were co-ordinated between them. The most expensive fares were to Edinburgh and Glasgow, at £3 return in 1958. A single to Preston cost 27 shillings and sixpence (£1.37½) and a return £2. A Birmingham return was just £1, and a single 14 shillings (70 pence), lower than the flat fare for a journey within that city today.

If a coach broke down far from home, the local company would provide a substitute. 'The best one I had was a Scottish vehicle,' John Lewis said. 'I broke down on the way to Newcastle, and Ribble hadn't got a vehicle so they lent me the Scottish vehicle which I brought to Salisbury for a week, and then it worked its way back the following weekend across to Newcastle... And I had a Midland Red vehicle. They were all their own vehicles, and the gearboxes were so different.'

Demand for weekend leave services fell off after the end of National Service. Regular soldiers now often lived in married quarters near their barracks, and, like the rest of the population in an increasingly affluent country, more and more of them drove their own cars. Either way they had less need of a coach service to take them home on leave. Even so, the express services continued through the 1960s and passed to Hants & Dorset Motor Services Ltd along with the rest of Wilts & Dorset's activities. After the merger, as Gordon White put it, 'the tin hat' was put on express services. Hants & Dorset had virtually no experience of this type of operation, having agreed with Royal Blue back in the 1920s not to run express services from Bournemouth. Some of the Plain expresses survived into the mid-1970s, but the heart had gone out of the business.

above left] GCG815 (494), one of a pair of AEC Regents delivered to Venture in 1948, rests at Basingstoke after working into town on service 136. For a few years in the early 1950s this was the only route that took Wilts & Dorset north of the notional boundary line with Thames Valley Traction. It crossed the A4 London-Bath road at Aldermaston to serve the hilltop village of Beenham, in Berkshire. ANDREW WALLER COLLECTION

above right] Former Wilts & Dorset buses from Basingstoke garage were spared from retirement for a few months in 1973, to help out when Hants & Dorset took over King Alfred bus services in Winchester. Bristol KSW5G HMW448 (ex-W&D 362) was fitted with a King Alfred destination blind to run on a Winchester local service. DAVID PENNELS

above] A pair of Bristol LS saloons, still in Wilts & Dorset red, took the place of King Alfred's green buses on Winchester Broadway in 1973. LAM964 (W&D 573) bears the Hants & Dorset fleetname but betrays its Basingstoke connection by half-showing Ramsdell as its 'destination'. Bringing up the rear is JMR13 (ex-535), displaying 'Broadway' in good King Alfred style, but still bearing its original owner's Tilling-style fleetname below the windscreen. SOLENTSLIDE

right] In 1967-1968 Wilts & Dorset converted its first eight Bristol MW6G coaches, by then nearly ten years old, to stage bus use. They appeared in red livery with cream window surrounds, with bus-type destination boxes and 'PAY AS YOU ENTER' signs alongside the door. RHR853 (802, renumbered from 702 in 1971) stands by for a local working out of Andover. DAVID PENNELS

above left] Within sight of St Thomas's Church, in whose shadow Wilts & Dorset had its registered office from 1917 to 1940, Bristol Lodekka LD6B NHR909 waits at the Castle Street terminus of city service 64 in the 1970s. On weekdays a bus made the 11-minute journey every half hour. Renumbered 420 by Hants & Dorset in 1971, the 60-seat bus still wears its original Tilling-style fleetname. It was new in 1956 as Wilts & Dorset's no. 619. BRISTOL VINTAGE BUS GROUP

above right] The British Transport Commission's lion-and-wheel logo was proudly emblazoned on the manufacturers' plate displayed on the platform of Bristol Lodekkas. This one belonged to Wilts & Dorset's LMW914 (611), built in 1955. DAVID PENNELS COLLECTION

left] Salisbury market is in full swing across the road as a Bristol LS5G saloon loads up for Laverstock, not that the destination blind would offer the unfamiliar passenger such useful information. It was left to the specially painted stop sign to identify service 254 as the one for Laverstock via Wain-a-long Road. NAM117 started life as Wilts & Dorset's no. 577, but became no. 784 when Hants & Dorset renumbered the fleet. DAVID PENNELS

below] Wilts & Dorset placed this board outside its ticket office on Blue Boar Row, Salisbury, to publicise its excursions in the late 1940s. DAVID PENNELS COLLECTION

Bristol L6B coaches like EMW284 (279), with 32-seat Beadle body, were a common sight on Wilts & Dorset's tours and excursions in the 1950s. Withdrawn by the company in 1962, this one has survived in preservation, and was photographed in Warminster in 2005. JOHN SANTER

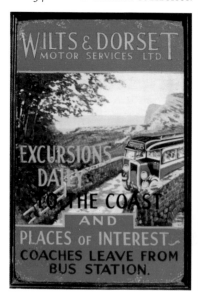

right] *Eastern Coach Works completely redesigned the coach bodies on Bristol MW6G chassis for the 1962 season. With wrap-round windscreen and rear windows, it was more flamboyant than its predecessor, but some thought the style less elegant. 673AAM, one of three MWs delivered in May 1962, stands empty at Aliwal Barracks, Tidworth. Originally no. 715, it was renumbered 5 in 1971; the blue disc by the fleet number shows it was based at Salisbury.* DAVID PENNELS

right below] *From mid-1969 all new vehicles for what had become 'Hants & Dorset trading as Wilts & Dorset' were registered in Bournemouth instead of Wiltshire. WEL803J, a 1971 Bedford VAL70, bears blue and orange discs above its fleet number to show it is from Andover depot. It is leaving Aliwal Barracks, Tidworth, on its way to Manchester. Note the old-style fleetname on the front, and the contemporary version on the side.* DAVID PENNELS

left] *Up until the 1930 Road Traffic Act towns and cities licensed the drivers of buses plying their streets.*

left] *Just two months before the Wilts & Dorset name disappeared from the buses in October 1972, Hants & Dorset painted one of its own saloons in Wilts & Dorset livery and transferred it to Salisbury. SRU973 (1783), a 1956 Bristol LS5G, stands at Endless Street bus station before going up the Bourne Valley into former Silver Star country.* DAVID PENNELS

left below] *In the 1960s there were but three journeys a week from Shaftesbury to Newtown – two on Tuesdays and one on Saturdays. XMR955 (808), a 1962 Bristol MW6G with standard 43-seat Eastern Coach Works body, waits before Shaftesbury Town Hall to leave for Tisbury, in the Nadder Valley, and the small community of Newtown that lies to the west of it.* BRISTOL VINTAGE BUS GROUP

Cap badges worn by Wilts & Dorset bus crews and inspectors.

below] Under the 1930 Road Traffic Act every PSV driver or conductor had to wear a numbered badge. The HH prefix was for the South Western Traffic Area, covering Wiltshire, Dorset and points west, whilst KK was for the South Eastern TA, including Hampshire.

above left] For a short period in the mid-1960s Bristol offered no medium-size chassis for single decks, so Wilts & Dorset – like many Tilling companies - plugged the gap with Bedford saloons. Then came the Bristol LH type ('Lightweight, horizontal-engine'). XEL835K (renumbered 531 in 1971) was one of ten LH6Ls with six-cylinder Leyland engines supplied to the company in 1969-1970. It is passing through Andover bus station on its way from Newbury to Salisbury. DAVID PENNELS

left] Wilts & Dorset bought Bedford coaches for the first time in readiness for the 1965 season. Three of the five Leyland-engined SB13s acquired that year stand newly delivered and ready for service at Bellevue, Salisbury. Fitted with the Duple Bella Vega body, this type was widely used by small independent operators across the UK, but was not so popular with the bigger territorial bus companies. DAVID PENNELS

25 Years Service badge worn by driver Cecil Wicks of Salisbury, who was PSV driver no. HH31199. WICKS FAMILY COLLECTION

Lapel badge worn by bus crews.

above right] A busy scene at Aliwal Barracks in Tidworth as a mixed bag of Bedford coaches, and one Bristol MW6G, load up for the regular weekend express departures for army personnel and their families to different parts of Britain. Compare the livery on LMR733F (53), a 1968 VAL70 with Viceroy body by Duple Northern, on the left, with that of the 1971 coach beside it. The brakes tended to wear out fast on the VALs, so they had to be relined frequently. DAVID PENNELS

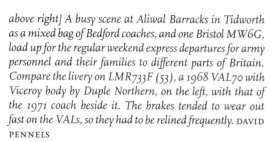

right] LMR740F (820) waits at Whiteparish on service 66 to Winchester. It was the last of the half-dozen Willowbrook-bodied Bedford VAM70 saloons that Wilts & Dorset bought in 1968, which had Bedford diesel engines. They were designed to carry 40 seated passengers and another 19 standing. The front-end design had by now become almost an industry standard across the UK. DAVID PENNELS

left] The three Leyland Tiger Cub dual-purpose vehicles that came to Wilts & Dorset from Silver Star appeared at first in the company's cream-top livery, but when they were repainted for bus-only duties only the waistband remained cream. Former Silver Star driver Doug Tillyer, still based at Porton Down, stands by PMW386 waiting for the next departure from Endless Street bus station. This was one of two vehicles retained at its old garage on Ministry of Defence land. DAVID PENNELS

below] Two former Silver Star coaches, just converted by Wilts & Dorset for one-man-bus operation in 1969, wait at Salisbury to take over new duties at Blandford, which was responsible for the 50-mile Salisbury-Weymouth service. Harrington-bodied Leylands SAM47 and WAM441 (907 and 908) were new in 1958 and 1960, the first a Tiger Cub and the other an L1 Leopard. DAVID PENNELS

right] Ex-Silver Star Leyland Leopard WWV564, with veteran driver George Hackett in charge, called in at Hants & Dorset's Winchester bus station to provide a photo opportunity for the bus enthusiasts who had hired it for the day. Wilts & Dorset equipped it for one-man-operation by fitting the 'PAY AS YOU ENTER' sign and providing for a ticket machine beside the driver, but it kept its coach seats. The 1971 renumbering scheme assigned it the memorable no. 999. DAVID PENNELS

below] After Thomas Tilling Ltd's bus interests were nationalised, most of the firms concerned adopted a standardised fleetname style, with deeper first and last letters framing the rest, which were underlined. The original version was of a plain sanserif pattern. The next one featured serifs, but this, the final slimmed-down logo, introduced in the early 'fifties, survived until NBC imposed its image upon the industry. DAVID PENNELS

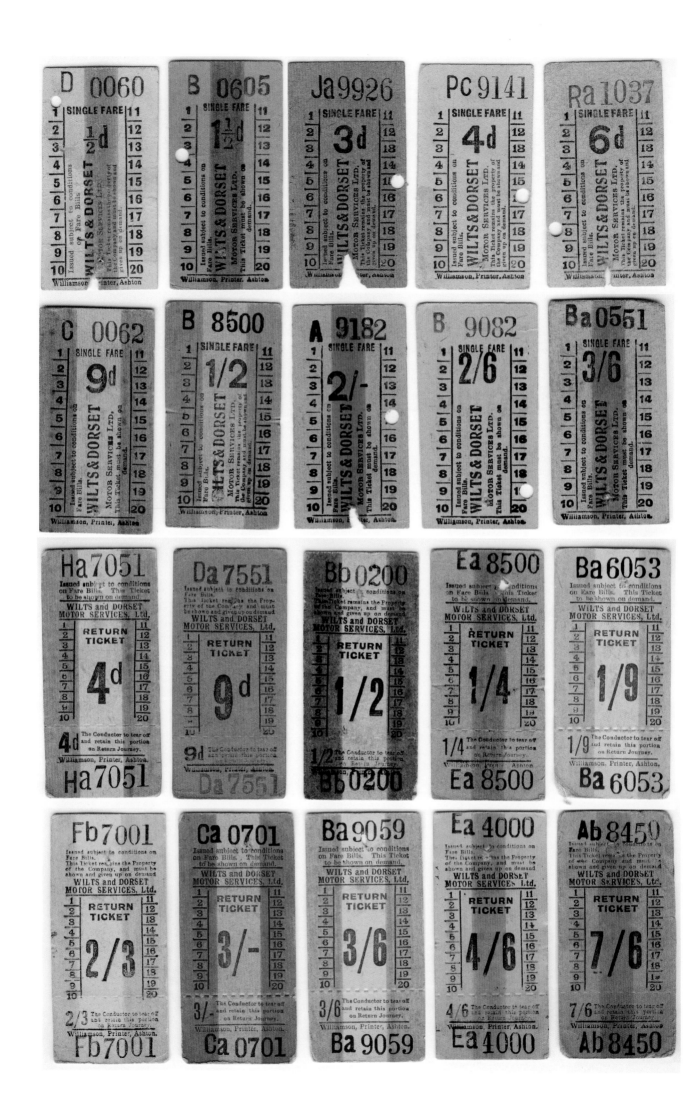

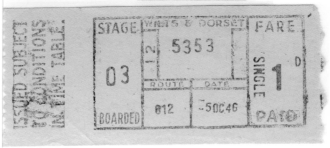

[above] Setright and TIM tickets (see Appendix E);
[...] tour brochure from the early 1950s,

Hobnob Press

PO Box 1838, East Knoyle, Salisbury SP3 6FA

phone 01747 830015   mobile 07946 068892
john@hobnobpress.co.uk   www.hobnobpress.co.uk

DISTRIBUTING BOOKS ON BEHALF OF HOBNOB PRESS, EX LIBRIS PRESS,
WILTSHIRE RECORD SOCIETY AND WILTSHIRE BUILDINGS RECORD

with compliments

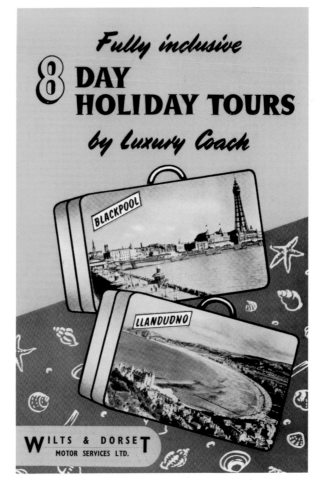

Fully inclusive
8 DAY HOLIDAY TOURS
by Luxury Coach

BLACKPOOL

LLANDUDNO

WILTS & DORSET
MOTOR SERVICES LTD.

Silver Star lapel badge. DAVID PENNELS
COLLECTION

More than 40 years after its demise, Silver Star still commands the loyalty of enthusiasts. A pair of Shergold & White's Leylands, kept smartly turned out by preservationists, returned to their old haunts. Atlantean 1013MW stops by the church in Winterbourne Earls, and MMR553, a Tiger Cub dating from 1955, pulls up at Blue Boar Row in Salisbury.
DAVID PENNELS

above] Metal plates like this were fixed at the head of timetable cases at rural bus stops.

above] Bus stop posts displayed fare stage numbers, to help drivers and conductors. It also enabled savvy passengers to check that their tickets were correctly issued. This one was at Amesbury.

below] In the 1920s and 1930s Wilts & Dorset topped up its revenues with advertising on the back of its tickets.

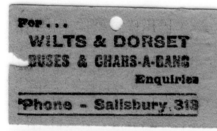

9
A Far from Fine Finalé (1970-1972)

THE AFFAIRS of the, as yet, extant Wilts & Dorset Motor Services Ltd, now incorporated within and accommodated by Hants & Dorset, can only be reviewed as part and parcel of that now enlarged company. In 1970, Edward Heath's Conservative government came to power. It didn't much like the National Bus Company but, hard pressed with other legislation and a damaging fight with the nation's miners, could not find an opportunity to dismantle it. Instead it imposed upon NBC's officers the need to ensure that its subsidiary companies halted a nationwide drift into the red. Part of that problem came from new legislation enshrined in the Act which brought the NBC into being; a revision of bus drivers' hours. From March 1970, more than 5½ hours' driving without a 30-minute break was prohibited. In addition, within a 14-hour day, no driver was to be permitted to be at the wheel for more than 10 hours. Today that seems both safer and reasonable, but the practice of maintaining the timetables by offering drivers considerable overtime and opportunities to work rest days promptly ceased. Neither company nor crews found this financially advantageous. Many drivers quit; a recruitment drive followed but, inevitably, the suspension of some services led to outright cancellation.

The public response was a noticeable increase in the use of alternative means of transport throughout the enlarged Hants & Dorset area. The company's expenses were swollen by the wages of extra staff, employed to sustain less extensive schedules, subscribed to by fewer passengers. During 1970, costs had reached £4.9 million, whilst the receipts totalled £4.7 million. It was Hants & Dorset's first ever loss.

The following year, the National Bus Company itself economised by reducing its ten operational areas to six. At Hants & Dorset, as traffic continued to fall, there was no option but to introduce fare increases. In 1971 the combined Hants & Dorset/Wilts & Dorset companies carried four million fewer passengers than in 1969. What had been a combined fleet of 770 vehicles at the end of 1969 was down to 670 by June 1971. Because there were now fewer buses to maintain, a decision was taken to reduce the size of the engineering facilities. Wilts & Dorset's central workshops in Salisbury were to handle

above] Since it had such a big fleet of LS-type Bristols, Wilts & Dorset waited until 1961 to buy saloons of the next model, the MW (medium weight). XMR952 (805), one of a batch of 10 MW6Gs that took more than a year to be completed, stands at Endless Street bus station. The 6G in the type designation signified that it had a Gardner 6HLW (six-cylinder) engine. ALAN LAMBERT

left] After 1962 the only coaches that Wilts & Dorset bought were Bedfords. BMW137C (912) was one of five SB13s new in 1965. They had Leyland engines and Duple Bella Vega bodies, a type favoured by independent operators across the UK. The company used them on express services as well as excursions. 912 is at Bournemouth bus station, standing by to work a Hants & Dorset tour to Southampton Docks. DAVID PENNELS

right] By 1967 Wilts & Dorset's vehicle policy already reflected Hants & Dorset practice. At the time there was no suitable lightweight saloon available from Bristol; to plug the gap operators turned to Bedford for saloons. Wilts & Dorset bought two in 1967; when still new, the first of the pair of Leyland-engined VAM14s, HHR943E (813), picks up passengers at Blue Boar Row on the Salisbury local service to Laverstock. Strachans built the Pacemax body at their factory in Hamble, Hampshire. DAVID PENNELS

below] Bedfords were lighter and less expensive to buy than the Bristols that had been Wilts & Dorset's standard coaches between 1948 and 1962. The 1967 vehicle programme allocated £22,500 for five Leyland-engined VAM14 coaches with Viscount bodies by Duple Northern, Blackpool. HAM501E (915) was the first of the five. The type was widely used by independent operators but less popular with the big territorial companies. DAVID PENNELS

above] In the mid-1960s the Labour government had set about 'rationalising' the nation's bus services, but on the ground anomalies crept in aplenty. Where 'Silver Star' was once emblazoned upon the brow of this Leyland Tiger Cub the lettering was for Wilts & Dorset, yet on the side it bears the title 'Charlie's Cars'. The company had loaned it to the Bournemouth coach operator in 1966, only to hire it back again. Inspector Fred Ayles briefs the driver of OHR280 (Wilts & Dorset's 905), before he sets out from Endless Street bus station on a Wilts & Dorset excursion. DAVID PENNELS

right] In the autumn of 1971 Hants & Dorset renumbered its own buses, and those it inherited from Wilts & Dorset, into a common series. On 4 September it was the turn of WWV564 (909), which started life as Silver Star no. 39, to become H&D's no. 999. The company rebuilt the rear of its Harrington Cavalier coach body in bus style after a lorry ran into the back of it in 1969, whilst it was parked in Wilton Road, Salisbury, on a private hire contract. DAVID PENNELS

only docking procedures, and Southampton would deal with all major overhauls. In the Wilts & Dorset area, the garage and a dwelling house were sold, together with workshops and a disused café at Salisbury, and some property at Blandford.

The economies were, however, working. The company's trading results for the four weeks ending 30 October 1971 showed a distinct improvement – the balance had gone into the black at £1,653. NBC measured the ongoing performance of its subsidiaries at that time by the total working expenses per hundred 'car' (bus) miles. The use of the word 'car' reflected the fact that in March 1968 the British Electric Traction Company's United Kingdom bus interests had also been nationalised (somewhat reluctantly) and transferred to the THC. The word 'car' was very much the common parlance among the now ex-BET officers accommodated by the National Bus Company – as it always was at Wilts & Dorset too, with its historic Southdown connection. Stanley 'Jim' Skyrme, for instance, who became a Wilts & Dorset director in 1968 (until 1970) was an ex-general manager with BET's Southdown Motor Services Ltd.

Nevertheless, the Hants & Dorset/Wilts & Dorset total working expenses per car mile for the 44 weeks ending 30 October 1971 were £20.17p, which put the company on a par with the United Counties Omnibus Co Ltd (the range nationally went from £17.04 to £26). Twenty other NBC

left] WAM441 (908), one of a pair of Leyland L1 Leopards that came from Silver Star, continued to work on weekend express services for a while. By 1969 younger models had taken their place and the company adapted them for use as stage buses in red and cream dual-purpose livery. Passengers board at Endless Street for the thrice-daily limited stop Bournemouth service 38A, which at the time was normally the preserve of sister vehicle WWV564 (909). DAVID PENNELS

below] Bristol MW6G coach no. 705, RMR992, took a hit amidships in 1968. Wilts & Dorset took the opportunity to convert it into an experimental bus with two doors and standing room for 25. It kept its hinged door at the front, but folding doors were fitted just forward of the rear axle. Like many a bus that did not quite measure up to requirements, it found itself on school duties. DAVID PENNELS

subsidiaries had proven more expensive to run, 20 less so.

It now becomes necessary to insert a pen picture of the Hants & Dorset/Wilts & Dorset general manager and director, Douglas W. Morison:

Douglas Morison was the son of W.J. Morison, draughtsman and engineer with Thomas Clarkson Ltd of Chelmsford, and chief engineer with the National Steam Car Co Ltd, the National Omnibus & Transport Co Ltd and Eastern National; designer also of the World War II Bristol-built T2-type gas trailer (see Chapter 4) and the Essex bus-washing machine which became standard among Tilling Group subsidiaries. Whilst a young man, Douglas Morison joined the National group of companies as a 'management cadet' – a group of four which included Robert Bushrod who became traffic manager for Wilts & Dorset from 1945 to 1953 and in 1950 its assistant general manager also. Morison was appointed assistant traffic manager with Hants & Dorset in 1936 and was (apart from military service in World War II) set to spend the rest of his career with that company – something of a record in the industry.

As a member of the Army Supplementary Reserve, he was called up three days before the outbreak of war in September 1939. He was told that his job would await him on his return and, unlike the unfortunate Maurice Coombes in 1919, was to discover that it was just as he was promised. Morison served in the Royal Engineers, rising to the rank of major. He fought in the field in North Africa with the 1st Army and was grievously wounded – he lost the lower part of one leg; and such was his poise and bearing thereafter that no-one would have guessed it – and became a staff officer in the UK until, in May 1944, he returned to Hants & Dorset, where he was promoted to traffic manager the following year and assistant general manager soon thereafter.

above] Two Bristol-Eastern Coach Works Lodekkas display Tilling group standardisation as they cross Bournemouth Square and approach the bus station in April 1970. Wilts & Dorset's 479BMR (670), a red 60-seat FS6B arrives from Salisbury. Unlike the green Hants & Dorset 70-seat front-entrance FLF6G behind it - on a local service from Poole – the Wilts & Dorset retains a cream band below the top deck windows. A.J. DOUGLAS

The company's last Wiltshire-registered buses were seven rear-engined Bristol RELL6Gs delivered in 1969. They took advantage of new rules allowing longer buses. MMW354G (824) is at Upavon on a through journey to Salisbury. On most journeys the 10 from Devizes was timed to meet the bus from Marlborough for passengers to change for Salisbury. The two-door RELL seated 45 passengers, but three of them — front-entrance dual-purpose buses, seated 50, two more than Wilts & Dorset's double decks of 40 years earlier. DAVID PENNELS

In 1958, he was invited to attend an interview at the Fleet Street headquarters of the Tilling Association Ltd, where he discovered that he had the strong backing of – Raymond Longman. Accordingly, he became the general manager and a director of Hants & Dorset with effect from 1 July of that year.

Douglas Morison's fondest memories of his time as general manager included the intellectually stimulating exchanges in the various sittings of the traffic courts, but also the rapport he established with the staff and, in particular the union representatives. The latter was at its most challenging during the period in 1950 – whilst he was traffic manager – when many Hants & Dorset employees, and some from the Bristol Tramways & Carriage Co Ltd, formed the National Busworkers' Association. The NBA promptly went head to head with the National Union of Railwaymen members, leaving him to enact the role of an avuncular referee.

Morison never did forget the debt of gratitude he owed to Raymond Longman and therefore to the Wilts & Dorset organisation. In an interview in 1994, he spoke of Longman's 'forceful personality' and of his own time as general manager and director also of Wilts & Dorset Motor Services Ltd.

One of the Wilts & Dorset staff impressed at the time with the veracity of this stance was David Pennels, who recalled being among a group addressed by Douglas Morison as he unwittingly stood with his back to a window. Shafts of sparkling sunlight danced about his broad shoulders as he spoke – not the sort of mesmeric performance one is likely to forget. Others, however, had different plans for Wilts & Dorset and Morison in particular.

What happened next, as the existence of Wilts & Dorset Motor Services Ltd was drawing to a close, provides a curious and loud echo of what befell Maurice Coombes just a few years after its foundation.

I make no apology for quoting verbatim from *Hants & Dorset: a history*, (Morris; 1996):

There now took place the most controversial incident in the history of Hants & Dorset Motor Services Ltd. On Tuesday 14 December 1971, Douglas Morison arrived at NBC's Wilbury Road, Hove office to deliver to the board his managing director's report on the economic situation 1971-75; together with its numerous detailed appendices, a weighty and detailed set of documents [which I have perused] – to be told five minutes before the meeting that he had been 'removed from the board by the National Bus Company with effect from the previous day – December 13.

This bombshell was compounded on 17 December when NBC circulated a memo to the general managers of its other subsidiaries: 'Hants & Dorset ... announces

I was very concerned to keep the identity of the separate companies alive, particularly Wilts & Dorset, because it meant so much from the staff relationship point of view. Hants & Dorset was *not* swallowing up Wilts & Dorset, which was, of course, their fear. So I did run Wilts & Dorset as a separate concern.

This shot of a Swindon-bound Bristol RELL6G reflects changes wrought in the 1960s. The Bristol Omnibus Company renumbered its bus routes in 1967, so the joint Salisbury-Swindon service became the 470, instead of 709. From mid-1969 new Wilts & Dorset buses like TRU946J (845) were registered in Bournemouth instead of Wiltshire, reflecting Hants & Dorset practice. ANDREW WALLER COLLECTION

right] In June 1971, Hants & Dorset bought 33 second-hand Leyland Panthers from Maidstone & District. Sixteen of them went to what was still separately identified as Wilts & Dorset, although the two companies were steadily being integrated. The 33 entered service in four different liveries. JKK204E, numbered 693 in the new Hants & Dorset series, was assigned to Basingstoke, where it appeared smartly painted in Wilts & Dorset red. ANDREW WALLER COLLECTION

below] All but two of Wilts & Dorset's last seven Bristol MW6Gs, delivered in 1966, were dual-purpose vehicles. The emergency door was open as EMR301D waited on the bus stand on Hungerford High Street in the 1970s, perhaps to give the driver a through draught on a baking

hot day. Little clue was offered as to its destination, unless you knew that the 216, formerly 16, went to Burbage and Pewsey. Wearing the Hants & Dorset fleetname above the window and renumbered 836, it had been Wilts & Dorset's no. 726. ANDREW WALLER COLLECTION

the early retirement of its managing director, Mr D.W. Morison, on December 31 as part of the forward planning arranged within the company'. This was not just inaccurate, it was totally untrue, because there was no other reorganisational plan from *within* the company, beyond the one set out in the forecast he had taken to Hove – the one which was at no stage consulted.

The method of his dismissal and, more importantly, the reason for it simply mystified him. He had *not* decided to take 'early retirement' because his retirement proper was just 18 months away. Bus crew members of the No. 2 Branch of the National Union of Railwaymen ceased working for two hours to hold an emergency meeting and 'registered our disgust at the treatment of Mr Morison by the NBC'.

Neither did anyone at the NBC have the courtesy to offer an explanation. Was the forthcoming plan for the 'Chief General Manager' set-up in an advanced stage and Morison was seen to be in the way? Had room to be made for ex-BET men in such a plan? Or was Douglas Morison seen to be 'dragging his feet' in response to repetitive demands for reams of photocopied notes to keep the enlarged staff at NBC busy?

Whatever the reason, the handling was without grace. A highly respected busman and dignified war hero could

have been 'kicked upstairs' to see out his remaining 18 months with honour. Instead, like his assailants in World War II, those responsible kept their heads below the parapet. In one sense Douglas Morison became the winner: he simply outlived them.

The bland statement in the Hants & Dorset minutes for that fateful meeting of 14 December 1971 put on record also that, with effect from 31 December, the Salisbury workshops of Wilts & Dorset would be closed – 'as a result of which the majority of the engineering workers at that establishment had been declared redundant and would be leaving the company's service'. They also 'noted' the names of all those Hants & Dorset/Wilts & Dorset employees aged 65 or over!

With effect from 1 February 1972, Peter C. Hunt became general manager of Hants & Dorset/Wilts & Dorset, and a director on 28th of that month. An ex-BET officer, he had served as area manager at Chichester and then Brighton for Southdown, and came south again, to Bournemouth, from the Yorkshire Traction Co Ltd – a BET Omnibus Services Ltd subsidiary. Yorkshire Traction's working expenses per car mile for the 44 weeks ending 30 October 1971 had been £21.03p, in other words, more than Hants & Dorset's.

On 27 March 1972 the directors were informed that negotiations were in progress for the sale of 139-143 Castle Street, Salisbury to Sadia Water Heaters Ltd – as indeed happened two months later.

Wilts & Dorset Motor Services and its subsidiary Venture Ltd both ceased to trade with effect from 1 April 1972, and all their services were then provided officially by Hants & Dorset Motor Services Ltd. It was at this point that Michael Wadsworth, Hants & Dorset's, and effectively Wilts & Dorset's last, traffic manager made his now familiar decision. Told of the Wilts & Dorset staff's dismay – even those about to be made redundant

AEL5B began life as a Hants & Dorset coach (no. 897, later 1011). It still bore the legend across the front 'HANTS & DORSET HOLIDAY TOURS' after it was transferred, albeit briefly, to the Wilts & Dorset fleet in 1972. Photographed at Endless Street bus station in May of that year, the 39-seat Bristol MW6G had its new fleetname on the side and now bore the number 11. DAVID PENNELS

– at the loss of the firm's traditional identity, Wadsworth simply announced 'Fine, in that case we'll go red!'

The last vehicles actually delivered in Tilling red, and bearing Wilts & Dorset fleetnumbers – but not fleetnames, were six Bristol RELL saloons which arrived as late as November 1972. Eastern Coach Works was presumably using up its stocks of traditional Tilling paint. The red which Hants & Dorset then adopted, instead of its traditional green, was NBC's bland poppy red – it looked like an undercoat. It is difficult to believe that this truly compensated the Wilts & Dorset aficionados any more than it dismayed those of Hants & Dorset.

As was to become increasingly common when the NBC subsidiaries entered the next decade, Wilts & Dorset could not be declared officially 'dead and buried' until tax clearance had been granted. A series of extremely short meetings, usually with just three officers present, thereafter took place at Hove, 3 Thorn Walk or 12/14 Queen Victoria Street, both in Reading. Obliged to attend this pale shadow of a Wilts & Dorset board were David Deacon, Frank K. Pointon, who took the chair by agreement on most occasions, Peter Hunt and George Carruthers, the last person to be appointed a Wilts & Dorset director – on 1 April 1973. Also in attendance

was either Desmond Finley or Roger Wigmore, making a return to some Wilts & Dorset business for the first time in 14 years.

At 4.30 pm on Friday 12 March 1976, Frank Pointon (in the chair), George Carruthers, Peter Hunt, secretary Desmond Finley and I.M. Read, regional finance officer, met at 3 Thorn Walk, Reading. The profit and loss account for the year ending 31 December 1975 was read to the members of the board and approved. The meeting lasted less than three minutes.

This is the last minute on file and would therefore appear to represent the last act of the directors of Wilts & Dorset Motor Services Ltd, a company set up just over 61 years previously at Amesbury.

The fleetname 'Wilts & Dorset' was set to reappear, for both market-potential and sentimental reasons, some ten years later when, following the Thatcher government's Transport Act 1980, the unloved National Bus Company was undone and its subsidiaries divided into saleable bits. Hants & Dorset was split up into five parts plus a secretarial unit. The operational company covering much of Wiltshire, eastern Dorset and south-west Hants became the Wilts & Dorset Bus Co Ltd. The history of that undertaking belongs elsewhere.

Appendix A
Company Officers

CHAIRMEN

Percy E. Lephard	1915-1919	Raymond Longman	1949-1962
Frederick Sutton *	1919-1926	George McKay	1962-1964
Percy E. Lephard	1926-1937	Thomas W.H. Gailey	1964-1965
Alfred E. Cannon *	1937-1939	David S. Deacon	1965-1972
George Cardwell	1939-1948	Frank K. Pointon *	1972-end
Stanley Kennedy	1948-1949		

* Acting chairman. Frank Pointon chaired each meeting at the request of those present.

DIRECTORS

Percy E. Lephard		1915-1938
A. Douglas Mackenzie	Worthing MS/Southdown	1915-1927
Alfred E. Cannon	Worthing MS/Southdown	1915-1952
George H. Davis		1915-1924
Frederick Sutton		1915-1926
William Fielden		1926-1952
Raymond I.H. Longman		1927-1962
George Cardwell	Thomas Tilling Ltd/T&BAT	1931-1948
Charles D. Stanley	BAT Ltd/T&BAT	1931-1942
Ralph G. Davidson	Southern Railway	1931-1946
Gilbert S. Szlumper	Southern Railway	1931-1932
Herbert A. Short	Southern Railway	1932-1936
John C. Chambers	Southern Railway	1936-1939
Charles W.G. Elliff	Southern Railway	1939-1944
Stanley Kennedy	Thomas Tilling Ltd	1942-1949
John C. Chambers	Southern Railway	1944-1949
Herbert A. Short	Southern Railway	1946-1949
Frederick P. Arnold	Tilling Association Ltd	1949-1958
William H.F. Mepstead	British Railways (SR)	1949-1960
Charles P. Hopkins	British Railways (SR)	1954-1956
James W.J. Webb	British Railways (SR)	1954-1956
Maurice A. Holmes	Tilling Association Ltd	1955-1962
H.E. Barber	British Railways (SR)	1956-1963
Stephen A. Fitch	British Railways (SR)	1960 (1-19 April)
Percy A. White	British Railways (SR)	1960-1963
George McKay	Tilling Association Ltd	1962-1964
David S. Deacon	Tilling Association Ltd	1962-1964
Thomas W.H. Gailey	Tilling Association Ltd	1962-1965
Frederick P.B. Taylor	British Railways (SR)	1963-1968
Douglas W. Morison	Hants & Dorset MS Ltd	1964-1971
Ian R. Patey	Tilling Association Ltd	1964-1965

David S. Deacon	Tilling Association Ltd	1965-1973
Bernard Griffiths	Tilling Association Ltd	1965-1966
Thomas G. Pruett	Tilling Association Ltd	1966-1968
George A. Weedon	British Rail (SR)	1968-1970
Stanley J.B. Skyrme	National Bus Company	1968-1970
Ray St C. Sandall	National Bus Company	1970 (Jan-Dec)
Clifford A. Rose	British Rail (SR)	1970-1971
Ian R. Patey	National Bus Company	1971-1972
Llewelyn S. Edwards	British Rail (SR)	1971-1972
Peter C. Hunt	Hants & Dorset MS Ltd	1972-end
Frank K. Pointon	National Bus Company	1972-end
George Carruthers	National Bus Company	1973-end

MANAGING DIRECTORS/GENERAL MANAGERS

A. Douglas Mackenzie	1915-1927	Joint Managing Director
Alfred E. Cannon	1915-1924	Joint Managing Director
George H. Davis	1924	Joint Managing Director
Raymond I.H. Longman	1942-1946	General Manager - ran the company as Secretary 1924-1942
Raymond I.H. Longman	1946-1962	Managing Director
David S. Deacon	1962-1964	General Manager
Douglas W. Morison	1964-1971	General Manager (also of Hants & Dorset)
Peter C. Hunt	1972-end	General Manager (also of Hants & Dorset)

SECRETARIES

A. Douglas Mackenzie	1915-1919	V.H.Brooks (acting)	1949 (1-31 Oct)
George H. Davis	1919-1924	Roger Wigmore	1949-1960
Raymond I.H. Longman	1924-1942	Desmond G. Finley *	1960-end
R.E. Herridge	1943-1949		

* Appointed additionally Secretary of Hants & Dorset in 1965, Shamrock & Rambler Coaches Ltd 1966-1973 and Gosport & Fareham Omnibus Company from 1970.

TRAFFIC MANAGERS

A. Bertram Wells	1921-1927	George Carruthers *	1960-1964
S.J. Hall	1927-1944	Stanley Bartlett	1964-1967
Robert F. Bushrod *	1944-1953	J. Michael Wadsworth	1967-end
Harold W. Mills *	1953-1960		

* Bushrod, Mills and Carruthers were appointed additionally Assistant General Manager in 1950, 1955 and 1964 respectively, Carruthers also of Hants & Dorset.

CHIEF ENGINEERS

George Wallis *	1921-1935	W.L.F. Henderson *	1961-1968
George R.E. Wallis *	1936-1949	A. Reg Smith (acting)	1968 (Sept-Nov)
W. Ingham *	1949-1950	Alan Gurley *	1968-end
W.H. Tryhorn	1951-1961		

* George Wallis was initially known as Garage Manager when transferred from Amesbury in 1921. His son George R.E. Wallis was Maintenance Engineer when first appointed in his father's stead. Ingham was Works Superintendent. Henderson was appointed additionally Chief Engineer of Hants & Dorset 1966-1968, a position also held thereafter by Alan Gurley.

Appendix B
Bus services

June 1925, low ebb of mid-1920s

--	Salisbury-Amesbury-Larkhill-Netheravon
2	Salisbury, St Mark's Church-Wilton
2C	Salisbury, Market Place-Skew Bridge
3	Salisbury-Ringwood-Bournemouth [HD]
4	Salisbury-Whiteparish-Southampton [HD]
--	Fordingbridge-Southampton
8	Salisbury-Allington-Tidworth
9	Salisbury-Winterbourne Gunner

1925 and 1932 lists
During the 1920s service numbers were
changed several times. Salisbury City and
Andover local services are omitted from the
March 1932 list; the number 23 was duplicated.

Joint services shown as follows
[AV] Thames Valley & Aldershot Omnibus
    Co Ltd (Alder Valley)
[BO] Bristol Omnibus Co Ltd
[HD] Hants & Dorset Motor Services Ltd
[ND] Newbury & District Motor Services Ltd
[SN] Southern National Omnibus Co Ltd
[WN] Western National Omnibus Co Ltd

March 1932. T&BAT and SR investment

1	Salisbury-Amesbury
2	Salisbury-Amesbury-Larkhill-Shrewton
3	Salisbury-Amesbury-Bulford-Larkhill
4	Salisbury-Amesbury-Devizes
5	Salisbury-Amesbury-Marlborough
6	Marlborough-Pewsey-Devizes
7	Salisbury-Winterbourne-Tidworth
8	Salisbury-Amesbury-Tidworth-Andover
9	Andover-Marlborough
10	Andover-Redenham
11	Andover-Broughton
12	Andover-Newbury
13	Andover-Hungerford
14	Salisbury-Whiteparish-Romsey
15	Salisbury-Lockerley-Romsey
16	Salisbury-Whiteparish-Southampton [HD]
17	Salisbury-Ringwood-Bournemouth [HD]
17A	Fordingbridge-Rockbourne
17B	Fordingbridge-Woodgreen-Breamore
17C	Fordingbridge-Hyde
18	Salisbury-Woodfalls
20	Salisbury- -Dorchester-Weymouth
21	Salisbury-Bowerchalke-Shaftesbury
22	Salisbury-Odstock-Coombe Bissett
23	Salisbury-Netherhampton
23	Andover-Stockbridge-Romsey
24	Salisbury-Warminster-Trowbridge [WN]
	+ Added by May 1932: Salisbury-Fovant

July 1939, the eve of World War II

1	Salisbury-Amesbury
2	Salisbury-Amesbury-Larkhill-Shrewton
3	Salisbury-Amesbury-Bulford-Durrington
4	Salisbury-Amesbury-Devizes
5	Salisbury-Amesbury-Marlborough
6	Salisbury-Amesbury-Netheravon
7	Salisbury-Winterbourne-Tidworth
8	Salisbury-Amesbury-Tidworth-Andover
9	Andover-Marlborough
10	Andover-Redenham
11	Andover-Broughton-Houghton
12	Andover-Newbury
13	Andover-Hungerford
14	Salisbury-Whiteparish-Romsey
15	Salisbury-Lockerley-Romsey
16	Salisbury-Whiteparish-Southampton [HD]
17	Salisbury-Ringwood-Bournemouth [HD]
17A	Fordingbridge-Rockbourne
17B	Fordingbridge-Woodgreen-Breamore
17C	Fordingbridge-Hyde
17D	Fordingbridge-Cranborne
18	Salisbury-Woodfalls
18A	Redlynch-Woodfalls
19	Andover-Stockbridge-Romsey
20	Salisbury-Blandford-Dorchester-Weymouth
21	Salisbury-Bowerchalke-Shaftesbury
23	Salisbury-Netherhampton

24	Salisbury-Warminster-Trowbridge [WN]
25	Salisbury-Fovant-Shaftesbury
26	Salisbury-Middle Wallop-Andover
27	Salisbury-Woodford Valley-Amesbury
27A	Salisbury-Great Durnford
28	Salisbury-Old Sarum
29	Woodfalls-Nomansland
30	Andover-Kimpton-Tidworth
31	Upavon Village-Upavon RAF
32	Devizes-Easterton
33	Devizes-Beechingstoke
34	Salisbury-Hindon
35	Salisbury-Tisbury-Shaftesbury
36	Tisbury-Newtown
37	Salisbury-Hindon-Mere
38	Salisbury-Winterslow direct
39	Salisbury-Grimstead-Winterslow

Salisbury city services to:
Wilton, Ditchampton, St Marks Church,
Devizes Road, Laverstock and Harnham
Andover local services to:
Aerodrome, Amport, Tangley,
Winton Road, Lower Clatford

	+ Added about September 1939:
40	Blandford-Blandford Camp

January 1952, the height of post-war activity for the UK bus industry

	Interurban and country services
1	Salisbury-Woodfords-Durnford-Amesbury
2	Salisbury-Amesbury-Larkhill
2A	Salisbury-Amesbury-Larkhill-Tilshead
2B	Amesbury-Larkhill-Greenlands Camp
3	Salisbury-Amesbury-Bulford-Larkhill
4	Salisbury-Old Sarum
5	Salisbury-Amesbury-Upavon-Marlborough
6	Salisbury-Amesbury-Netheravon
7	Salisbury-Amesbury-Boscombe Down
8	Salisbury-Amesbury-Tidworth-Andover
9	Salisbury-Tidworth-Marlborough
10	Salisbury-Amesbury-Upavon-Devizes
11	Devizes-Easterton
12	Devizes-Beechingstoke-Pewsey-Burbage
13	Amesbury-Ablington-Netheravon
16	Pewsey-Hungerford
17	Pewsey-Marlborough
18	Upavon Village-Upavon RAF
21	Blandford-Blandford Camp
24	Salisbury-Warminster-Trowbridge [WN]
24A	Warminster-Sutton Veny
26	Salisbury-Tisbury-Hindon
27	Salisbury-Fovant-Shaftesbury-Yeovil [SN]
27A	Salisbury-Fovant-Shaftesbury
28	Salisbury-Tisbury-Shaftesbury
29	Salisbury-Bowerchalke-Shaftesbury
30	Salisbury-Odstock-Coombe Bissett
31	Tisbury-Newtown
32	Salisbury-Winterslow direct
33	Salisbury-Farley-Winterslow
34	Salisbury -Dorchester-Weymouth [SN]
36	Salisbury-Lockerley-Romsey
37	Salisbury-Whiteparish-Southampton [HD]
38	Salisbury-Ringwood-Bournemouth [HD]
39	Salisbury-Rockbourne-Fordingbridge
40	Salisbury-Woodgreen-Fordingbridge
41	Fordingbridge-Hyde
44	Salisbury-Woodfalls-Redlynch
45	Salisbury-Woodfalls-Nomansland
54	Salisbury-Mere-Wincanton-Yeovil [SN]
54A	Salisbury-Hindon-Mere
54B	Chicklade-Lower Pertwood
66	Salisbury-Romsey-Winchester [HD]
68	Andover-Bullington-Winchester [HD]
68A	Andover-Barton Stacey-Winchester [HD]
68B	Andover-Crawley-Winchester [HD]
71	Andover-Amport
73	Andover-Redenham
75	Andover-Kimpton-Tidworth
76	Andover-Middle Wallop-Salisbury
77	Andover-Middle Wallop-Broughton
80	Andover-Newbury
80A	Andover-Faccombe
81	Andover-Hungerford
82	Andover-Conholt
83	Andover-Stockbridge-Romsey
83A	Andover-Leckford-Stockbridge
84	Andover-Great Bedwyn-Marlborough
97	Salisbury-Cranborne-Poole [HD]

	Ex-Venture country services
101	Basingstoke-Bramley
102	Basingstoke-Longparish-Andover
102A	Basingstoke-Overton limited stop
103	Basingstoke-Oakley
103A	Basingstoke-East Oakley
104	Basingstoke-Andover Down-Andover
104B	Whitchurch-Overton Mills
105	Baughurst-Tadley-Bramley Camp
105A	Baughurst-Silchester-Bramley Camp
107	Basingstoke-Lasham-Medstead-Alton
107A	Alton-Medstead-Wield
107B	Basingstoke-Lasham-Alton
109	Basingstoke-Preston Candover-Cheriton
109A	Basingstoke-Ellisfield-Cheriton
110	Basingstoke-Oakley-Steventon
111	Basingstoke-Winchester
111A	Basingstoke-Winchester
117	Basingstoke-Hartley Wespall
131	Shaw-Newbury-Whitway [ND]
131A	Shaw-Newbury-Whitway [ND]
132	Whitchurch-Drayton Camp-Andover
134	Basingstoke-Silchester-Baughurst
135	Whitchurch-Newbury
136	Basingstoke-Baughurst-Beenham
136A	Basingstoke-Baughurst-Beenham
137	Basingstoke-Baughurst-Newbury

	Salisbury city services to:
46	Netherhampton
55	West Harnham
56	Milton Road
57	Meyrick Avenue
58	Coronation Road
59	Heath Road
59A	Woodside Road
60	Wilton-Ditchampton
61	Waters Road
62	St Mark's Church
63	Railway Station
64	St Francis Road
65	Laverstock
67	Quidhampton-Wilton-Ditchampton

	Andover local services to:
69	Hedge End Road
70	Rooksbury Road
72	Picket Piece (ex-Venture 4A)
74	King George Road
78	Tollgate Road
79	Lower Clatford

	Basingstoke town services, ex-Venture
103B	Queen Mary Avenue-Sandys Rd
106	Grove Road-Little Basing
106A	Grove Road-Hatch Lane
108	Queen Mary Avenue-Grove Rd
108A	Queen Mary Avenue-Grove Rd
112	Thornycroft works-Kempshott
113	Thornycroft works-Queen Mary Avenue
114	Thornycroft works-Grove Road
127	Kempshott-Park Prewett
127A	Kempshott-Park Prewett

July 1972, the end of Wilts & Dorset Motor Services Ltd's separate existence

	Interurban and country services		*Salisbury city services to:*
1	Salisbury-Woodfords-Durnford-Amesbury	51	Bemerton Heath
2	Salisbury-Amesbury-Larkhill- Tilshead	52	Bemerton Heath
3	Salisbury-Amesbury-Bulford-Larkhill	53	Bemerton Heath
4	Salisbury-Old Sarum	54	Laverstock
5	Salisbury-Amesbury-Upavon-Marlborough	55	West Harnham
6	Salisbury-Amesbury-Netheravon	56	Netherhampton
7	Salisbury-Amesbury-Boscombe Down	57	Meyrick Avenue
8	Salisbury-Amesbury-Tidworth-Andover	58	Gainsborough Close
9	Salisbury-Tidworth-Marlborough	59	Devizes Road
10	Salisbury-Amesbury-Upavon-Devizes	60	Wilton
11	Devizes-Urchfont	61	Waters Road
12	Devizes-Beechingstoke-Pewsey	62	Bishopdown Estate
13	Salisbury-Amesbury-Ablington-Netheravon	63	Bishopdown Estate
14	Marlborough-Great Bedwyn-Oxenwood	64	St Francis Road
16	Pewsey-Hungerford	65	Laverstock
17	Marlborough-Burbage-Oxenwood		
18	Upavon Village-Upavon RAF		
20	Tidworth-Everleigh		
21	Blandford-Blandford Camp		
22	Salisbury-Old Sarum-Porton Down		
23	Warminster-Sutton Veny		
24	Salisbury-Warminster-Trowbridge [BO]		*Andover town services to:*
25	Salisbury-Hindon-Zeals	92	Drove Estate
26	Salisbury-Fovant-Tisbury-Hindon	93	Bell Road
27	Salisbury-Fovant-Shaftesbury	94	Leigh Road
28	Salisbury-Tisbury-Shaftesbury	95	River Way
29	Salisbury-Bowerchalke-Shaftesbury	96	River Way
30	Salisbury-Odstock-Coombe Bissett	98	Gallagher's Mead
32	Salisbury-Winterslow direct	99	Picton Road
33	Salisbury-Farley-Winterslow		
34	Salisbury-Dorchester-Weymouth [WN]		
35	Salisbury-Dorchester-Weymouth [WN]		
36	Salisbury-Lockerley-Romsey		
37	Salisbury-Whiteparish-Southampton [HD]		
38	Salisbury-Ringwood-Bournemouth [HD]		
X38	Salisbury-Ringwood-Bournemouth [HD]		
40	Salisbury-Woodgreen-Fordingbridge		*Basingstoke town services:*
41	Fordingbridge-Hyde	105	Bus station-Hatch Lane
42	Salisbury-Rockbourne-Fordingbridge	106	Bus station-Hatch Lane
66	Salisbury-Romsey-Winchester [HD]	111	Sheppard Road-Park Prewett
68	Andover-Winchester [HD]	112	Sheppard Road-Park Prewett
71	Andover-Amport	113	South Ham-Popley
72	Andover-Picket Piece- Stoke	114	South Ham-Popley
73	Andover-Redenham-(Tidworth or Chute)	115	South Ham-Oakridge
75	Andover-Kimpton-Tidworth	116	South Ham-Oakridge
76	Salisbury-Andover-Basingstoke	117	Basingstoke-Winklebury (anti-clockwise)
77	Andover-Middle Wallop-Broughton	118	Kempshott-Houndmills
80	Salisbury-Andover-Newbury	119	Kempshott-Popley North
82	Andover-Vernham Dean	121	Basingstoke-Winklebury (one way)
83	Andover-Stockbridge- Romsey	211	Park Prewett-Sheppard Road
97	Fordingbridge-Cranborne-Wimborne [HD]	212	Park Prewett-Sheppard Road
101	Basingstoke-Bramley	213	Popley-South Ham
102	Andover-Longparish-Whitchurch	214	Popley-South Ham
103	Basingstoke-East Oakley	215	Oakridge-South Ham
104	Whitchurch-Overton Mills	216	Oakridge-South Ham
107	Basingstoke-Lasham-Medstead-Alton	217	Basingstoke-Winklebury (clockwise)
109	Basingstoke-Alresford-New Cheriton	218	Houndmills-Kempshott
122	Basingstoke-Kingsclere-Newbury [AV]	219	Popley North-Kempshott
130	Basingstoke-Long Sutton	220	Winklebury-Basingstoke (one way)
131	Basingstoke-Lyde Green		
132	Basingstoke-Hannington-Baughurst		
133	Baughurst-Bramley Camp		
134	Basingstoke-Silchester-Baughurst		
135	Newbury-Whitchurch		
136	Basingstoke-Baughurst-Beenham		
137	Basingstoke-Tadley-Baughurst		
138	Basingstoke-Bramley-Stratfield Saye		
470	Salisbury-Marlborough-Swindon [BO]		

Appendix C
Acquired Operators, chronological summary

¶ Wilts & Dorset only acquired part of the business.
● Business previously absorbed or taken over by the operator listed above it.

1915
16 March:
Edwin Maurice Coombes, motor engineer,
46 High St, Amesbury,
Wilts & Dorset Motor Service

100 £1 shares; E.M.
Coombes hired as
Amesbury Manager

Scout saloon; leasehold premises;
Amesbury-Salisbury bus service;
taxi and garage business

March:
A.A. Brewer, Ringwood

Not known

Scout saloon; Ringwood-Salisbury,
Ringwood- Southampton services

1921
2 August:
Salisbury & District MS Ltd, 14 Queen St, Salisbury, *The Yellow Victory*,
(Edwin Maurice Coombes, T. Kerr, James Street)
● T. Kerr, Fordingbridge

£1 for each of
10,000 shares, plus
35 £1 shares for
E.M. Coombes

7 Thornycroft, 2 Crossley buses; leasehold
garage on Fisherton St, Salisbury; Salisbury-
Wilton, Salisbury-Amesbury and Salisbury-
Fordingbridge services

1927
8 April:
Arthur James Corp,
Highbury Avenue, Salisbury,
B & C Motor Services/Bannister & Corp

£400; A.J.Corp hired
as traffic
superintendent

Leasehold garage at Bulford; two saloons
(Berliet and Chevrolet); Bulford-Salisbury
service

1 November:
¶ Hants & Dorset MS Ltd, service ex-Anna Valley
Motors Ltd, 1927, ex-Mobility Ltd, Ludgershall, 1924

(£400?)

Goodwill; Andover-Ludgershall service,
operated for only a few weeks by H&DMS

1929
31 March:
Edward J. Gulliver, Bowerchalke

Hired as driver

Goodwill; Bowerchalke-Salisbury service

March:
A. Gulliver, Bishopstone
(formerly William J. Gulliver)

Not known

Bishopstone-Salisbury service

12 April:
Harold Roy Bartley & Charles Avery,
North Tidworth Garage
The Tidworth Motor Service

£500

Four Leyland vehicles; Tidworth-Salisbury
and Tidworth-Andover services

12 April:
S. Moore, Awbridge, Hants

Hired as driver

Goodwill; Awbridge-Romsey service

1930
7 June:
Herbert Henry & Derek Leslie Wolstenholme, North
Houghton, Hants,
Andover & District Motor Services

£1,650; hired as
drivers

Three saloons – Dennis, Guy, Chevrolet;;
Andover-Romsey and -Broughton-Salisbury
services; contract carriage

1931
1 January:
Frank Holt, Hurstbourne Tarrant, Hants

£50; hired as driver

Goodwill; Vernham Dean-Hurstbourne-
Tarrant-Andover service; school contract

1 March: Harry Gregory, The Stores, Hatherden, Hants	£25; rent of garage at 17 Hatherden	Goodwill; Andover service; contract carriage
25 March: Charles Henry Haines, Charlie's Corner, Durrington, *Charlie's Car*	£650	Goodwill; school contracts
25 March: Alfred W. Fulford, Bishopstone • Cecil Martin Wort, Bishopstone, *Chalke Valley Motor Service*, 1927	£35	Goodwill; Bishopstone-Salisbury service; excursions
1932 14 January: Gilbert Walter Haines, King's Arms, Downton	£700	Goodwill; Downton-Salisbury, Downton- Southampton services; excursions
4 March: John H. Jarvis, Fovant	£100	Goodwill; Fovant-Salisbury service; excursions
4 March: ¶ Sidney Charles Shergold, Tidworth, *Allington Queen*, (continued as *Tidworth Coaches*)	£175	Goodwill; Tidworth-Salisbury, Tidworth- Andover services
12 April: ¶ Robert Elliott, The Garage, Middle Wallop, Hants, *The Iris Motor Services* • Nathaniel Thomas Southwell, Middle Wallop, by 1930	£100	Goodwill of Middle Wallop-Andover service
12 April: Ernest Walter Mare, Broughton, Hants, *Speedwell Motor Coaches*	£350	Goodwill; Broughton-Salisbury, Broughton Andover services
13 April: ¶ Lewis Austin Horne, 103 High St, Andover, *Pride of Andover*	£471	Goodwill of Andover-Newbury, Andover- Vernham Dean services
7 June: Reginald Stevens, Victoria Garage, Shaftesbury	£300; hired as driver at £3/week	Goodwill; Shaftesbury-Salisbury services
11 October: ¶ Harold I. Couchman, Codford St Mary, *Wylye Valley Motor Services*	£500	Goodwill of Salisbury-Warminster via main road service
13 October: ¶ Albert Hawkins, Durrington, rest of business to Shergold & White, see below, 1963	£250	Goodwill of Durrington-Salisbury service
25 November: Alfred White, Netheravon	£550	Netheravon-Salisbury, Netheravon-Bulford Camp services
28 November: William Charles Mortimer, Jervis Garage, Upavon, *Upavon & District* • Edwin G. Cave, *Upavon Motor Services*, 1927	£250	Goodwill; Pewsey-Salisbury. Netheravon- Devizes, Upavon-Devizes services
28 November: ¶ Edmund Stanfield, Figheldean, retained private hire and tours	£50	Goodwill; Figheldean-Salisbury service
28 November: Percival Charles John Sawyer, Netheravon	£350; hired as driver	Netheravon-Salisbury service

1933
1 July:
John Connolly, Woodfalls,
Woodfalls Motor Service

£5

Goodwill; Hale-Salisbury service

30 September:
Joseph H. Cockle, Woodford, *Cockle's Motor
Services/Blue & Yellow Cars*

£700

Goodwill; Salisbury-Amesbury, Salisbury-
Durnford, Salisbury-Old Sarum Aerodrome
services; excursions

22 November:
Charles Allen Sparrow, Sidney Alfred Sparrow &
Charles George Vincent, 79 Fisherton St, Salisbury,
Victory Motor Services
•   Archibald Curtis, West Grimstead 1930

£16,000;
employment of C.A.
Sparrow

16 vehicles; garage and office tenancies;
local services in Salisbury and Wilton,
Salisbury-East Grimstead (ex-Curtis);
excursions

1934
5 July:
¶ Albert Millson, Upper Chute

£30

Goodwill of Thruxton-Andover service

¶ Edwin Frank Piper, Thruxton, Hants, *Primrose Bus
Service*

£25

Goodwill of Thruxton-Andover service

1936
5 March:
Walter Owen Swadling, Hindon Road, Tisbury, *The
Victor Motor Services*

£3,300

Goodwill; Hindon-Salisbury, Newtown-
Salisbury, East Knoyle-Salisbury services;
contract carriage; excursions

3 April:
Joseph Charles Rose, Nomansland,
Nomansland Motor Services

£275, acquired
jointly, Hants &
Dorset share £165

Goodwill; Nomansland-Salisbury,
Nomansland-Southampton services;
contract carriage

16 April:
¶ Laurance Tom Alexander, Lydeway,
Queen of the Road

£1,000

Goodwill; Vale of Pewsey-Devizes local
services

24 April:
Edwin Bryant & Son, Coombe Bissett

£20

Goodwill; Coombe Bissett-Salisbury service

3 June:
William Charles Lewis, Barkers Hill, Donhead, *The
Chocolate Bus/Donhead Transport Co*
•   A.R. Askwith, Donhead St Andrew, 1933

£150

Goodwill; Donhead-Shaftesbury, Donhead-
Tisbury services

21 August:
¶ Reginald Geoffrey Bartlett,
East Knoyle Bus Service

£100

Goodwill; East Knoyle-Salisbury and
Hindon-Shaftesbury stage services; contract
carriage; excursions

1 October:
W. Rowland & Sons, Castle St, Salisbury
(William Edward Rowland)

£2,250

Seven coaches – 6 Leylands and a Rolls
Royce; excursions; contract carriage

30 October:
Frederick William & Reginald Bailey, Whiteparish,
Bailey Bros/Whiteparish Motor Service,

£1,500, acquired
jointly, Hants &
Dorset share £750

Goodwill of Whiteparish-Salisbury,
Whiteparish-Southampton, Whiteparish-
Romsey services; excursions

1937
2 March:
Sybil C.S. White, Minstead, Hants
White Brothers/Forest Queen

£300 share in Hants
& Dorset 1936
purchase at £2,200

White's route shared the Totton-
Southampton road with H&DMS/ W&DMS
Salisbury-Southampton

7 August:
¶ Edward W. Shergold & Bernard F. White, Porton
Down, *Silver Star Motor Services*

£1,500

Goodwill of Sling-Bulford Barracks-
Salisbury service; excursions from Bulford
Camp

29 October:
Reginald Henry & Morgan Emm, Bowerchalke

£350

Goodwill of Bowerchalke (Woodminton)-
Salisbury service

3 December: ¶ Bath Tramways Motor Co Ltd • Lavington & Devizes Motor Services Ltd, 1934, which acquired M. Hall & Sons, Orcheston, 1923	£500	Ex-Lavington & Devizes Motor Services Ltd Hindon-Salisbury (ex-M. Hall 1923) and Easterton-Devizes services only
1938 12 July: Austin William Alner & K.J. Hayward, Fordingbridge, *Victory Motor Service,* acquired jointly with Hants & Dorset	£2,375, half share of £4,750 with Hants & Dorset, which paid on 15 February	Goodwill; Fordingbridge locals and market services to Salisbury and Southampton
26 September: Edward Hastings Saunders, Verwood, *Sunflower/Verwood Motor Services*	£500 share in Hants & Dorset purchase at £1,300	stage licences in Verwood area, including Fordingbridge
27 September: Cyril Joseph Adolphus Cully, Midddleton Road, Salisbury, *Gem Coaches*	£350	Goodwill; Salisbury race days service; excursions
1939 10 March: ¶ Edward Charles H. Grant, Middle Winterslow, *Kingston Coaches*	£250	Goodwill; Winterslow-Farley-Salisbury service
10 March: Wilfred Robert Parsons, Middle Winterslow, *Blue Belle Service/Winterslow Motor Services*	£1,000	Goodwill; Winterslow-London Road- Salisbury service
30 September: Ernest William Oborn, The Vicarage Cottage, Ebbesbourne Wake	£250	Goodwill; Ebbesbourne Wake-Salisbury service; excursions
1942 28 February: ¶ Lewis Sprackling, Winterborne Stickland, Dorset, *Ivory Coaches,* rest of business to Bere Regis & District	£500	Goodwill of Blandford-Blandford Camp service
1944 31 October: ¶ Frederick James Lampard, Lampard's Garages Ltd, Pewsey, garage business continued	£1,000	Six services: Pewsey to Devizes, to Hungerford, to Tidworth, to Everleigh; Burbage to Marlborough, and to Devizes; contract carriage; excursions; leasehold property
1945 28 February: Sidney Valentine Williams, Grange Garage, Penton Mewsey, Hants	Not known	Goodwill; two Penton-Andover services
1946 21 March: Leonard George Percival Humphries, Fosbury, Wilts	£150	Goodwill; Fosbury-Andover and Fosbury- Hungerford services
1947 18 March: George Young, South End, Damerham	£250	Goodwill; Damerham-Salisbury, Damerham-Ringwood services
1949 23 July: Sidney Gould Lever & Leslie Raymond King, The Garage, Fovant, *Lever & King/Rambler Service*	£50	Goodwill; Swallowcliffe-Salisbury service; excursions; private hire

1951
1 January:
Venture Ltd, Basingstoke
- C.V. Reynolds, *Old Basing Bus*, 1933
- ¶ William Ernest Kent, Baughurst, 1937, stage services only, including ex-Fred Kent (Blue Bus), Charter Alley service acquired 1932
- Alfred Ernest Blake, Baughurst, Baughurst-Newbury, 1937
- ¶ S. Huntley & Son (Sidney & George Thomas Huntley), East Oakley, East Oakley-Basingstoke, 1948

Management agreement following Red & White sale to British Transport Commission. Business included a network of routes centred on Basingstoke, with services to Andover, Newbury, Aldermaston and Winchester; depots at Basingstoke, Baughurst and Whitchurch; fleet of 27 AEC double decks, 19 AEC and 2 Bedford single decks

19 March:
¶ Skylark Motor Services Ltd, (Horace L. Barber), 11 Butcher Row, Salisbury
- Fred & Reg Viney, Chilmark, 1947

£2,000 — Goodwill of Chilmark-Salisbury (ex-F. & R. Viney) and Redlynch-Salisbury services

30 October:
Alfred Moore, Carters Clay, Hants, *Moore Bros/ Lockerley Coaches,*

£1,500 (of which Hants & Dorset paid £400, and G.S. Sweet and A.E. Budden & Sons £250 each for excursion licences) — Lockerley-Romsey, Lockerley-Salisbury services

1952
31 December:
¶ Sidney & George Thomas Huntley, East Oakley, Basingstoke, *S. Huntley & Son*

£1,500 — Goodwill; Basingstoke-Kingsclere, Basingstoke-Hannington, and Hannington-Kingsclere services

1953
7 April:
John & Thomas Wood, Worting, Basingstoke, *J.&T. Wood/Empress Motor Service*

£1,500 — Goodwill; Basingstoke-Park Prewett and Basingstoke-Kempshott services

1963
5 June:
Silver Star Motor Services Ltd, (Edward W. Shergold & Bernard F. White), Porton Down
- Albert Hawkins, Durrington, 1932
- Martha Lee, Winterbourne Gunner, *Winterbourne & East Gomeldon Motor Service*, 1949

£65,000 — 23 vehicles; leasehold property, goodwill; Salisbury-Porton service, Armed Forces weekend express services, works services

1965
16 October:
¶ Oswald Porter, The Garage, Dummer, Hants
- Henry T. Nobbs, Preston Candover, *Nobby Bus Service*, 1945

£260 — Goodwill of Basingstoke-Cheriton service ex-H.T. Nobbs

1966
November:
¶ Odiham Motor Service Ltd,
Remainder of business to Smiths Luxury Coaches (Reading) Ltd

Replaced Basingstoke-Long Sutton service, which OMS withdrew February 1966

1969
¶ Oliver Reginald Tibble, St Mary Bourne, Hants, *Pioneer Motor Service,* ceased trading

Replaced Andover-St Mary Bourne service on cessation of business

Appendix D Fleet Summary

Year	Fleet nos.	Registration nos.	Vehicle type
1915	1-4	1B801-804 (see note 1)	Three Scout saloons, one charabanc (2)
	..	?	Ex-E.M. Coombes, Amesbury: Scout saloon
	..	?	Ex-A.A. Brewer, Ringwood: Scout saloon
1916	6	1B806	McCurd saloon
1919	7-9	CD3330/2555-2556	One AEC charabanc, one AEC & one Leyland double deck
1920	10-13	CD3177/5247-5249	AEC saloon, Leyland charabanc, AEC saloon, AEC double deck
	14	HR3186	Maxwell charabanc
1921	15-16	HR4459/4483	Leyland saloon, Leyland double deck
	17-19	HR4559/1887, AM9997	Ex-Salisbury & District: Thornycroft charabancs
	20-21	AM9721, HR3550	Ex-Salisbury & District: Thornycroft saloons
	22-23	HR1952/3037	Ex-Salisbury & District: Thornycroft double decks
	24/25	HR2275/5605	Ex-Salisbury & District: Crossley charabancs
1922	26	HR6404	Leyland G7 coach
1923	27	HR9541	Leyland G7 double deck
1924	28-29	MR994/1393	Leyland G7 coach (28), AEC 2-Ton charabus (29)
1925	30-32	MR3178-3179/4867	AEC 2-Ton saloons (30-31), Leyland SG11 saloon (32)
1926	33-35	MR6437/6636/7203	Leyland G7 coaches (33-34), G7 double deck (35)
1927	36-43	MR8635-8637/9540-9541, MW565/566/956	Dennis 30-cwt saloons
	50-54	MW112-113/567-568/823	Leyland PLSC1 Lion (50-51), PLSC3 saloons (52-54)
	..	MR1106/5671	Ex-B&C, Durrington: Berliet, Chevrolet saloons (see note 2)
1928	44-47	MW957/1510-1511/1854	Dennis 30-cwt saloons and Dennis G coach (47)
	55-62	MW1851-1853/3052/3204/3372-3374	Leyland PLSC3 Lion saloons
	14/17-20/22-23	CD6521/5221/6011/5220/5222/5215/6013	Ex-Southdown: Daimler saloons
1929	63-65	MW3850-3852	Leyland PLSC3 Lion saloons
	66-73	MW4594-4597/5799-5802	Leyland TS1 Tiger coach (66) and LT1 Lion saloons
	74-75	MW6050-1	Leyland TD1 Titan lowbridge double decks (see note 3)
	21/24-25/--	HR74/2661/4738, MR723	Ex-Bartley, Tidworth: Leyland saloons, charabancs (21/25)
1930	76-78	MW6284-6286	Leyland LT1 Lion saloons
	81-84/91-92	MW6289-6292/7052-7053	Leyland LT2 Lion coaches (81-84), saloons (91-92)
	85-86	MW6293-6294	Leyland TS1 Tiger coaches
	79-80/87-90	MW6287-6288/7048-7051	Leyland TD1 Titan lowbridge double decks
	25/48-49	XV6211, UL9607, UK8818	Ex-Andover & District: Chevrolet, Dennis G, Guy ONDF saloons

1. 1B805, another Scout, was also registered by Wilts & Dorset with Armagh County Council in May 1915, but never entered service with the company.

2. B&C Durrington: W&D board minutes record the two vehicles as being included in the acquisition of B&C, but a contemporary witness told David Pennels they ran for the company 'on a mileage basis'. They apparently did not receive fleet numbers.

3. Double decks: Up to and including the 1926 deliveries all double decks were open top. Between 1929 and 1953 Wilts & Dorset standardised on lowbridge double decks, with sunken offside gangway to reach four-abreast seating on the top deck. Most double decks acquired from other operators were highbridge, with central upper deck gangway.

Year	Fleet numbers	Description
1931	MW7054-7055/8752-8756/ 9396-9397	Leyland TD1 Titan lowbridge double decks
	MW8757-8758	Leyland TS1 Tiger coaches
	MW8759-8761/8983-8985	Morris Commercial Viceroy saloons
1932	WV647-651	Leyland Tiger TS3 coaches
	WV652-653	Morris Commercial Viceroy coaches
1933	WV2379-2384	Leyland TD2 Titan lowbridge double decks
	MR9964-9965	Ex-Sparrow & Vincent: Albion PM28 saloons
	MW912/2955	Ex-Sparrow & Vincent: Leyland PLSC3 Lion saloons
	MW1696	Ex-Sparrow & Vincent: Dennis 30-cwt saloon
	MW4028	Ex-Sparrow & Vincent: Gilford 166OT coach
	MW6528/6694	Ex-Sparrow & Vincent: Leyland LT1 Lion coaches
	MW9860	Ex-Sparrow & Vincent: Dennis Arrow coach
	WV1274/3371	Ex-Sparrow & Vincent: Albion PV70 coaches
	MR6171/3364	Ex-Sparrow & Vincent: Dennis coach, Dennis charabanc
	MR6170/HR6408	Ex-Sparrow & Vincent: Daimler coaches
	MR3214	Ex-Sparrow & Vincent: REO coach
1934	WV4922-4923	Leyland TD3 Titan lowbridge double decks
	WV5526-5527	Leyland TS6 Tiger coaches
1935	WV7333-4	Leyland KP3 Cub coaches
	WV7474-5	Leyland TD4 Titan lowbridge double decks
1936	WV9727-9728	Leyland Tiger TS7 coaches
	AHR399-400	Leyland TD4 Titan lowbridge double decks
	AHR521-522	Leyland KPZ2 Cub coaches
	WV8166, MW2750, WV5661	Ex-W. Rowland & Sons: Leyland LT7, PLSC3, LT5A Lion coaches
	MW9149-9150	Ex-W. Rowland & Sons: Leyland TS3 Tiger coaches
	MR510, R1289	Ex-W. Rowland & Sons: Leyland, Rolls Royce coaches
1937	AMW481-482	Leyland LT7 Lion dual-purpose saloons
	BAM51-52	Leyland TD5 Titan lowbridge double decks
1938	BAM798-799	Leyland LT7 Lion dual-purpose saloons
	BAM800-801	Leyland TS8 Tiger coaches
	BHR739-742	Leyland TD5 Titan lowbridge double decks
1939	BWV662-664	Leyland TD5 Titan lowbridge double decks
	BWV665-668	Leyland LT8 Lion dual-purpose saloons
	BWV669-672, CHR475/476/478/483	Leyland TS8 Tiger dual-purpose saloons
	UF4645/4662/6598/3592/4659/5064/5076/4648/5074	Ex-Southdown: Tilling-Stevens B10A2 saloons
	UF7383/7081	Ex-Southdown: Leyland TD1 Titan highbridge double decks
	TM3736, VW8823, VX822	Ex-Eastern National: Leyland TD1 Titan lowbridge double decks
	UF7395/7411/7388-7389/7078/7420/7385/7429/7410	Ex-Southdown: Leyland TD1 Titan highbridge double decks
	UF7402/7079/7393/7396/7424/7413/7430/7401/7427	Ex-Southdown: Leyland TD1 Titan highbridge double decks
	RU5031/8059, TR6147, RU8925	Ex-Hants & Dorset: Leyland PLSC3 Lion saloons
	TK2591-2592/2595, TR7463/7465, TK2596, TR7464	Ex-Hants & Dorset: Leyland TD1 Titan lowbridge double decks
	RU9490/9493/9492/9494-9495	Ex-Hants & Dorset: Leyland TD1 Titan lowbridge double decks

Year	Fleet nos.	Registration	Description
1939 contd	129	UF6808	Ex-Southdown: Tilling-Stevens B10A2 saloon
	130	UF7384	Ex-Southdown: Leyland TD1 Titan highbridge double deck
	132/4/5	KR1729/1731/1733	Ex-Maidstone & District: Leyland TD1 Titan highbridge double decks
	136/150/151	GP6237, GN6222, GW6281	Ex-Brighton, Hove & District: AEC Regent highbridge double decks
	201/203	RV1844, OU7856	Ex-Southdown: Thornycroft CD, BC saloons
	202/206-8	UF2007/2014/2020/2023	Ex-Southdown: Tilling-Stevens B9B coaches
	204-205/209-210	KR6530/1/6392/6532	Ex-Chatham & District: Leyland TD1 Titan highbridge double decks
	211-214	WH3303-3304/3306/3309	Ex-Bolton Corporation: Leyland TD1 Titan lowbridge double decks
	215-222	CK4208/4214/4225/4278/4207/4213/4222/4233	Ex-Ribble: Leyland TD1 Titan lowbridge double decks
	223-226	TY6971-6972/6974-6975	Ex-Tyneside: Leyland TD1 Titan lowbridge double decks
	227-230	TV1635/1639/1624/1625	Ex-Nottingham Corporation: AEC Regent highbridge double decks
	231-232	UF7415/7387	Ex-Southdown: Leyland TD1 Titan highbridge double decks
	233-234	VH4753/2966	Ex-Huddersfield Corporation: AEC Regent highbridge double decks
	235-241	UF7409/7416/7493-7404/7412/7425/7386	Ex-Southdown: Leyland TD1 Titan highbridge double decks
	242	CG7119	Ex-Southdown: Thornycroft CD saloon
	243-244	UF7407/7382	Ex-Southdown: Leyland TD1 Titan highbridge double decks
	245-250	CM8736-8737/8740/8725-8726/8729	Ex-Birkenhead Corporation: Leyland TD1 lowbridge double decks
	251-259	UF7390/7423/6456/7391/7399/7421/7394/7417/7419	Ex-Southdown: Leyland TD1 Titan highbridge double decks
1940	178/180-183/185-187	CHR477/479-482/484-486	Leyland Tiger TS8 dual-purpose saloons
	188-199	CHR487-498	Bristol K5G lowbridge double decks
1943	260-263	CWV778-781	Daimler CWG5 lowbridge double decks
1946	264-268	DMR836-840	Bristol K5G lowbridge double decks
1947	269-273/280-281	EAM612-614, EMW181/182/285/286	Bristol K5G and K6B (269/271) lowbridge double decks
1948	274/277	EMW183/282	Bristol L6B coaches
	282/283	EMW287/288	Bristol K5G lowbridge double decks
1949	275-276/278-279/284-286	EMW184/185/283/284, FAM1-3	Bristol L6B coaches
	287-293	FAM4-6, FMW652/653/827, GAM10	Bristol K6B and K5G (293) lowbridge double decks
1950	294/298-304/311-313	GAM11, GHR199/200/364-368, GMR26-28	Bristol K5G lowbridge double decks
	295-297/305-310	GAM214-216, GHR866-868, GMR29-31	Bristol L6B coaches (295-297) and saloons
	314-320	GMR893-894, GMW194-196/850-851	Bristol KS6B and KS5G (319-320) lowbridge double decks
	322-323	GMW912-913	Bristol LL6B saloons
1951	321	GMW911	Bristol LL6B saloon
	324-332	GWV305/929, HAM229-231/693-696	Bristol KS5G (324) and KSW5G lowbridge double decks
	333-341	HHR60-64/750-751/822-823	Bristol KSW5G lowbridge double decks
	412/434-438/439	UU6650, COT547-551, GH3815	Ex-Venture: AEC Regal saloons, coaches (436-438)
	427-428/430-431	BOU697-698/700-701	Ex-Venture: AEC Regent highbridge double decks
	441/443-445	JO5401/1624, ECG645-646	Ex-Venture: AEC Regent highbridge double decks
	463-466/468/470/472	TV6753/4958/4493/4496/4948/4490/4957	Ex-Venture: AEC Regent highbridge double decks
	475/485/488/491	HG1022, BAD30, DG9820/9819	Ex-Venture: AEC Regent highbridge double decks

Year	Fleet numbers	Registration numbers	Description
1951 contd	477-478	FOR633-634	Ex-Venture: Bedford OB coaches
	479-481/493-494/499	FOT200-202, GCG814-815, HAD745	Ex-Venture: AEC Regent III highbridge double deck
	482-484/486-487/489-490	FOT203-204, FOU719, GAA8/739/832-833	Ex-Venture AEC Regal coaches, dual-purpose saloons (482-483)
	492/495-498	GCG544/816, GHO295-297	Ex-Venture: AEC Regal III coaches
	500	EJB321	Ex-Newbury & District: AEC Regent III highbridge double deck
1952	342-358	HMR12/58-59/414-416/624/688-690/743-747/809-810	Bristol KSW5G lowbridge double decks
	359-365	HMW445-448, HWV292-294	Bristol KSW5G lowbridge double decks
	366-371	JAM419-420/933, JHR140-142	Bristol KSW5G lowbridge double decks
	516-528	HWV944-946, JAM151-152/225-227/303-306/418	Bristol LS6G dual-purpose saloons
	501-503	TR6166, BLJ394, CEL226	Ex-Hants & Dorset: Leyland TS2 (501), TS7 Tiger coaches
	504-505	BOW169, EEL800	Ex-Hants & Dorset: Bristol L5G saloons
	506-515	BFM155/172/176/178/181/204/157/165/171/185	Ex-Crosville: Leyland TS7 Tiger saloons
1953	529-534	JHR383-389/494-495/604-605	Bristol LS6G dual-purpose saloons
	535-543	JMR13/85-86/323-325/637-639	Bristol LS6G dual-purpose saloons
	544-551	JMW412-413/669-670, JWV261-262/761-762	Bristol LS6G dual-purpose saloons
	372-378	JHR883/959-960, JMW243/317/499/955	Bristol KSW5G lowbridge double decks
	379-387	JMW954/JWV263/380-383/849/978-979	Bristol KSW6B lowbridge double decks
	388-393	KAM594-595, KHR103-104/529-530	Bristol KSW6B lowbridge double decks
1954	552	KHR654	Bristol LS6G dual-purpose saloon
	600-606	KMR608-609, KMW109/345/916-917, LHR155	Bristol Lodekka LD6G, LD6B (606) (see note 4)
	553-556	KWV933-936	Bristol LWL5G saloons
	557-567	LAM107-110/278/465/743-745, LHR857-858	Bristol LWL5G saloons
1955	607-616	LMR740-742, LMW680/914-916, MMW411-413	Bristol Lodekka LD6B
	568-580	LWV844-848/964-966, NAM116-117/286-288	Bristol LS6G saloons
1956	581-583	NHR128-129/723	Bristol LS5G saloons
	617-619	NHR844-845/909	Bristol Lodekka LD6B
	584-592	OAM125/366-367/552-553, OHR389-390/587, OMR56	Bristol LS5G saloons
	620-629	OAM969, OHR57/123-124/382/509/708-709/919/918	Bristol Lodekka LD6G
1957	630-631	PMR913-914	Bristol Lodekka LD6G
1958	632-635	PWV353, RWV526, SHR441-442	Bristol Lodekka LD6G
	701-706	RHR852-853, RMR524/736/992/995	Bristol MW6G coaches
1959	707-708	SWV688-689	Bristol MW6G coaches
	636-637	TMW273, UAM941	Bristol Lodekka LD6G
1961	709-714	XMR942-947	Bristol MW6G coaches
	801-805	XMR948-952	Bristol MW6G saloons
1962	806-810	XMR953-957	Bristol MW6G saloons
	715-720	673-675AAM, 130-132AMW	Bristol MW6G coaches
	638-650	676-688AAM	Bristol Lodekka FS6G, FS6B (648-650)

4. Lodekka: All double decks taken into stock from 1954 onwards were Bristol Lodekkas, whose design achieved the lower height of a lowbridge bus (see note 3), but with central upper deck gangway.

Year	Fleet nos.	Registrations	Type
1963	651-657	689-695AAM	Bristol Lodekka FS6G
	721-722	133-134AMW	Bristol MW6G dual-purpose saloons
	658-659	467-468BMR	Bristol Lodekka FLF6G
	901-903	PHR829, PMW386, RAM620	Ex-Silver Star: Leyland PSUC1/2 Tiger Cub dual-purpose saloons
	904	HWV793	Ex-Silver Star: Leyland PSU1/15 Royal Tiger coach
	905-907	OHR280-281, SAM47	Ex-Silver Star: Leyland PSUC1/2 Tiger Cub coaches
	908-909	WAM441, WWV564	Ex-Silver Star: Leyland L1 Leopard coaches
	..	KGU263, GWV360	Ex-Silver Star: Leyland 7RT, PD2/1 Titan double decks
	..	JMR736	Ex-Silver Star: Leyland PSU1/15 Royal Tiger coach
	..	KMW643-644, LMW483, MMR552-553	Ex-Silver Star: Leyland PSUC1/2 Tiger Cub coaches
	..	NMW340	Ex-Silver Star: Commer TS3 coach
	..	TMW853, VAM944, XMW706, 1013MW	Ex-Silver Star: Leyland PDR1/1 Atlantean double decks
	..	367BAA	Ex-Silver Star: Trojan 19 minibus
1964	660-671	469-470BMR, AHR244/246B, 473-479BMR, AHR245B	Bristol Lodekka FLF6G (660-665), FS6B
1965	910-914	BMW135-139C	Bedford SB13 coaches
1966	672-681	EMR288-297D	Bristol Lodekka: two FLF6G, eight FLF6B
	723-727, 811-812	EMR298-304D	Bristol MW6G saloons (723-727 dual-purpose)
1967	915-919	HAM501-505E	Bedford VAM14 coaches
	813-814	HHR943E, HWV326E	Bedford VAM14 saloons
	682-689	JMR812-819F	Bristol Lodekka: five FLF6B, three FLF6L
1968	690-691	JMR820-821F	Bristol Lodekka FLF6L
	920-923	LMR731-734F	Bedford VAL70 coaches
	815-820	LMR735-740F	Bedford VAM70 saloons
1969	821-833	MMW351-357G, PRU63-64G, RLJ796-799H	Bristol RELL6G saloons (825-827 dual-purpose)
	924-927	PEL903-906G	Bedford VAL70 coaches
	835-840	REL746-748H, RRU692-694H	Bristol LH6L saloons
1970	834/841-844	RLJ800H, TRU225-226J/944-845J	Bristol RELL6G saloons
	928-930	SLJ756-758H	Bedford VAL70 coaches
	848-851	TRU227-228J, UEL567-568J	Bristol LH6L saloons
	593-596	KEL401-402/408/410	Ex-Hants & Dorset: Bristol LL6B saloons
1971	845-847	TRU946-948J	Bristol RELL6G dual-purpose saloons
	*62-63, 21-22	WEL802-803J, VIL413-414J	Bedford VAL70 (62-63) and YRQ (21-22) coaches
	*686/690-692	JKK197/201-203E	Ex-Maidstone & District: Leyland PSUR1/1R Panther saloons
1972	*11-12	AEL5B, FEL424D	Ex-Hants & Dorset: Bristol MW6G coaches
	*531-536	XEL835-840K	Bristol LH6L saloons
	*622-626	XLJ727-729K, AEL100/105K	Bristol RELL6G saloons (622-624 dual-purpose)
	*684-685/687-689/693-699	JKK195-196/198-200/204-210E	Ex-Maidstone & District: Leyland PSUR1/1R Panther saloons
	*783	SRU973	Ex-Hants & Dorset: Bristol LS5G saloon

*Hants & Dorset numbering scheme introduced mid-1971. Earlier Wilts & Dorset vehicles were renumbered as follows:
2-3/5-10 Bristol MW coaches, 11-20 Bedford SB and VAM coaches, 51-61 Bedford VAL, 101-128 Bristol FS, 201-226 Bristol FLF, 363-399 Bristol KSW, 401-437 Bristol LD, 501-508 Bedford VAM saloons, 521-530 Bristol LH, 601-621 Bristol RELL, 739-799 Bristol LS, 801-811/814-827/831-839 MW saloons, 994-999 ex-Silver Star Leylands.

Appendix E
Fare Systems

Up to 1930 most bus companies had a different ticket printed for every value they needed. Wilts & Dorset was no exception. Like Southdown, it had them printed by Williamson of Ashton-under-Lyne, and they closely resembled those of co-founder Douglas Mackenzie's other company.

The conductor carried his tickets in a wooden rack with rows of mousetrap-like spring clips, each holding a pack of singles or returns of a different value. He punched a hole in the ticket when issuing it, cancelling the stage number that corresponded to the start of the passenger's journey. The punch machine retained the little disc of paper punched out of each brightly coloured ticket. Should a conductor be suspected of cheating, each piece of this 'confetti' could be counted up in the office when he paid in at the end of the day's work.

By 1933, when it began to adopt more efficient systems, Wilts & Dorset needed 62 different single values and 28 returns to meet all the possible fares on its routes. Singles ranged from one halfpenny to five shillings (about 0.2p to 25p), and returns from 3d to 7/6 (1.2p-37.5p). The long Salisbury-Weymouth service, which began in 1929, called for most of these, but the five halfpenny values (up to 4½d (1.9p) were mainly confined to Salisbury city services.

The first new system employed was the TIM (Ticket Issue Machine), which printed the entire ticket on a flimsy roll of paper and saved time for both conductor and office. The conductor set the fare with a contraption on top of the machine like an old-fashioned telephone dial. The disadvantage of the TIM was that it could only cope with a relatively limited range of fares. Apart from possible experimental use at Andover, Wilts & Dorset only used it on Salisbury city services but retained it for these until about 1958.

The company adopted the TIM early on in its development, as it did with its next ticket system, the Setright, invented by a Scotsman of that serendipitous surname. This was introduced over a couple of years from 1934. The Setright stamped the fare, date and stage number on a pre-printed ticket.

Conductors on most journeys now only had to carry two or three different types of ticket, a return and one or two singles; the machines could not cope with halfpenny values so there was a single ticket with a halfpenny overprint. Extra tickets were needed on some early morning journeys when cheaper 'workmen's returns' were available. Up until at least the early 1940s a stock of punch tickets was apparently still held in case there were not enough Setright machines at specially busy times.

The Setright could cope with fares of up to eleven shillings and eleven pence (just under 60p). This was adequate for the company's stage services. In the late 1940s and early 1950s Wilts & Dorset was one of the most innovative of Setright users; it adapted some of its machines to handle higher values for excursions and express services. Luckily Venture Ltd used same system, so integrating the fare-collection system was straightforward when Wilts & Dorset took over in 1951. Even before World War II Setright had developed a new version of his machine. Like the TIM, the Setright Speed issued tickets from a roll, but this was smaller and used better paper. The company name and conditions were pre-printed on the roll so that they appeared on every ticket. Wilts & Dorset began to adopt the Setright Speed in 1954, and by the 1960s it was in general use both with conductors and fixed alongside the driver's position on one-man buses.

By the time Wilts & Dorset took them over, both Venture and Silver Star had long been insert Setright users. If they issued tickets at all, most of the other operators that Wilts & Dorset absorbed used punch tickets. Just one, O. Swadling of Tisbury, used a system better known in northern England, the Willebrew. This called for tickets with all the possible fares printed on them; on issue to a passenger a rectangular section was sliced off the ticket so that the appropriate fare was the highest one that remained.

Bibliography and Recommended Reading

Books

- Berryman, David: *Wiltshire Airfields in the Second World War,* Countryside Books, 2002
- Birmingham, Peter and Pearce, John: *Venture Limited – The Story of Basingstoke's Own Bus Company,* Holmes & Sons, Andover, 1995
- Chambers, J.D., and Mingay, G.E.: *The Agricultural Revolution 1750-1880,* Batsford, 1966
- Chandler, John: *Endless Street – A History of Salisbury and its People,* Hobnob Press, Salisbury, 1983
- Cummings, John: *Railway Motor Buses 1902-1933, Volume 2,* DPC, Oxford, 1980
- Dangerfield, George: *The Damnable Question,* Constable, 1977
- Doggett, Maurice, and Townsin, Alan: *Eastern Coach Works 1946-1965,* Venture Publications, Glossop, 1993
- Freeman, J.D.F., and Jowitt, R.E.: *King Alfred Motor Services,* Kingfisher, Southampton, 1984
- Hibbs, John: *The History of British Bus Services,* David & Charles, Newton Abbot, 1968
- Jack, Doug: *Leyland Bus, Mk 2,* Promotional Reprint Company Ltd, 1992
- James, N.D.G.: *Plain Soldiering – A history of the Armed Forces on Salisbury Plain,* Hobnob Press, Salisbury, 1987
- Klapper, Charles F, with Lee, Charles E.: *Golden Age of Buses,* RKP 1978
- Lacey, Paul: *The Independent Bus Operators of the Newbury Area, 1919-1932,* Lacey, 1985
- Lacey, Paul: *A History of Newbury & District Motor Services Ltd,* Lacey, 1987
- Morris, Colin: *British Bus Systems: Southdown,* TPC, Glossop, 1985
- Morris, Colin: *Hants & Dorset – a history,* DTS, Croydon, 1996
- Morris, Colin: *Glory Days: Royal Blue,* Ian Allan, 2000
- Pennels, D.J.N.: *The Fleet History of Wilts & Dorset Motor Services Ltd and Venture Ltd,* The PSV Circle/Omnibus Society, 1963
- Taylor, A.J.P.: *English History 1914-1945,* OUP, 1965
- Tempero, Derek J.: *Andover, a Pictorial History,* Phillimore, Chichester, 1991
- Townsin, Alan: *The Bristol Story, part 1 – 1908-1951,* Venture Publications, Glossop, 1996
- Townsin, Alan: *The Bristol Story, part 2 – 1952-1983,* Venture Publications, Glossop, 2000
- Townsin, Alan: *Thornycroft,* Ian Allan, 2001
- Waller, Andrew: *The Tickets of Wilts & Dorset Motor Services Ltd 1915-1972,* The Transport Ticket Society, 2003
- White, H.P.: *A Regional History of the Railways of Great Britain, Volume 2: Southern England,* David & Charles, Newton Abbot, 1970

Journals and magazines

- Anon: 'Organisation of Road Transport Services – Wilts & Dorset Motor Services Limited', in *Modern Transport,* 23 March 1929
- Anon: 'Serving the Agricultural Community in Wartime – Independent Bus Operation to an Important Market City', in *Modern Transport,* 20 February 1943
- Anon: 'Buses in North Hampshire – Development of Venture Limited', in *Modern Transport,* 2, 9 and 30 October 1943
- Attwood, Arthur: 'Sir John's Wonderful World of Steam', and 'Firm that Forged Fame Abroad for its Town', in *Basingstoke Gazette,* 21 November 1980 and 19 October 1990
- Batten, John: 'Bath Tramways and Salisbury Plain,' in *Omnibus Magazine,* June/July 2006
- Broatch, Stuart: 'The Scout Story' parts I and II, in *First Word,* February and March 1985
- Harper, Charles G.: 'The Salisbury Carriers', in *Motor Traction,* 10 July 1918
- Morris, Colin: 'Mobility Ltd', in *The Hampshire Magazine,* February 1974
- Pennels, D.J.N.: 'The Titans of Wilts & Dorset', in *Buses Illustrated,* February and March 1963
- Pennels, D.J.N.: 'The Silver Star Story,' in *Buses Illustrated,* January, February and March 1965
- Watkin, Iolo: 'Road Passenger Transport in South Wiltshire.', in *Omnibus Magazine,* March 1935
- Townsin, Alan: 'Bus service planning for the new Basingstoke', in *Bus & Coach,* February 1967

Contact details

Readers wishing to learn more about independent operators in the Wilts & Dorset area or other parts of the West Country are referred to a series of booklets published by Roger Grimley, details of which can be obtained from:

Old Post, Bigbury, Kingsbridge, Devon TQ7 4AP

BASINGSTOKE	OLD SARUM	DEVIZES ROAD
RELIEF	OLD CASTLE INN	HEATH ROAD
PRIVATE	PERHAM DOWN	LAVERSTOCK
SALISBURY	PEWSEY	MARKET
AMESBURY	POOLE ON HIRE TO HANTS & DORSET	MEYRICK AVENUE
ANDOVER	REDLYNCH CHURCH & P.O.	MILTON ROAD
BERWICK ST. JOHN	RINGWOOD	WATERS ROAD
BLANDFORD	ROCKBOURNE	ST. MARKS CHURCH
BLANDFORD CAMP	ROMSEY	WEST HARNHAM
BOSCOMBE DOWN	SALISBURY	WILTON
BOURNEMOUTH	SHAFTESBURY	DEVIZES ROAD EXTENSION
BOWERCHALKE	STRATFORD BRIDGE	WOODSIDE ROAD
BULFORD	SHREWTON	SKEW BRIDGE
COOMBE BISSETT	SOUTHAMPTON	RELIEF
CRANBORNE	SUTTON VENY CAMP	ST. FRANCIS ROAD
DEVIZES	TIDWORTH	
DURNFORD	TISBURY	
EAST WINTERSLOW	TROWBRIDGE	
FARLEY	WARMINSTER	
FORDINGBRIDGE	WEYMOUTH	
HALE P.O.	WHADDON	
HINDON	WHITEPARISH	
HYDE	WIMBORNE	
KNOOK CAMP	WINTERBOURNE	
LANDFORD POUND	WINCHESTER	
LARKHILL	WINTERSLOW	
LOCKERLEY	WOODFALLS	
MARLBOROUGH	WOODFORD	
MERE	YEOVIL	
MIDDLE WALLOP	ZEALS	
NETHERAVON P.O.	BISHOPDOWN ESTATE	
NETHERAVON R.A.F.	CITY CENTRE	
NETHERHAMPTON	RAILWAY STATION	
NEWTOWN	BEMERTON HEATH	
NOMANSLAND	SOMERSET ROAD	
ODSTOCK	CORONATION ROAD	
	DITCHAMPTON	

Destination blind from a Salisbury-based bus, late 1950s. Courtesy of Bob Williamson

Wilts & Dorset routes in 1949, before the management agreement with Venture Ltd

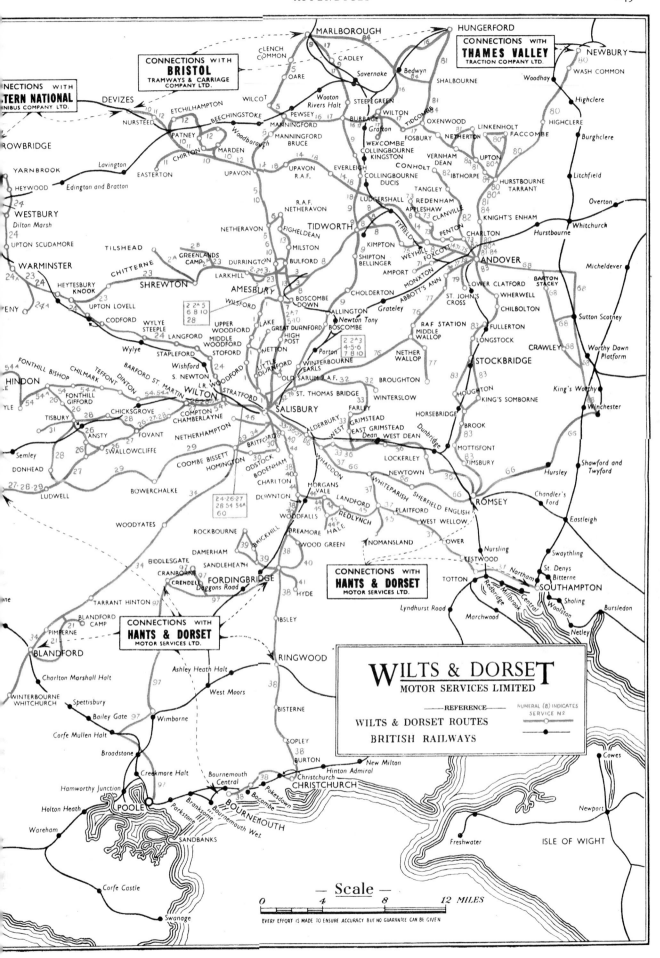

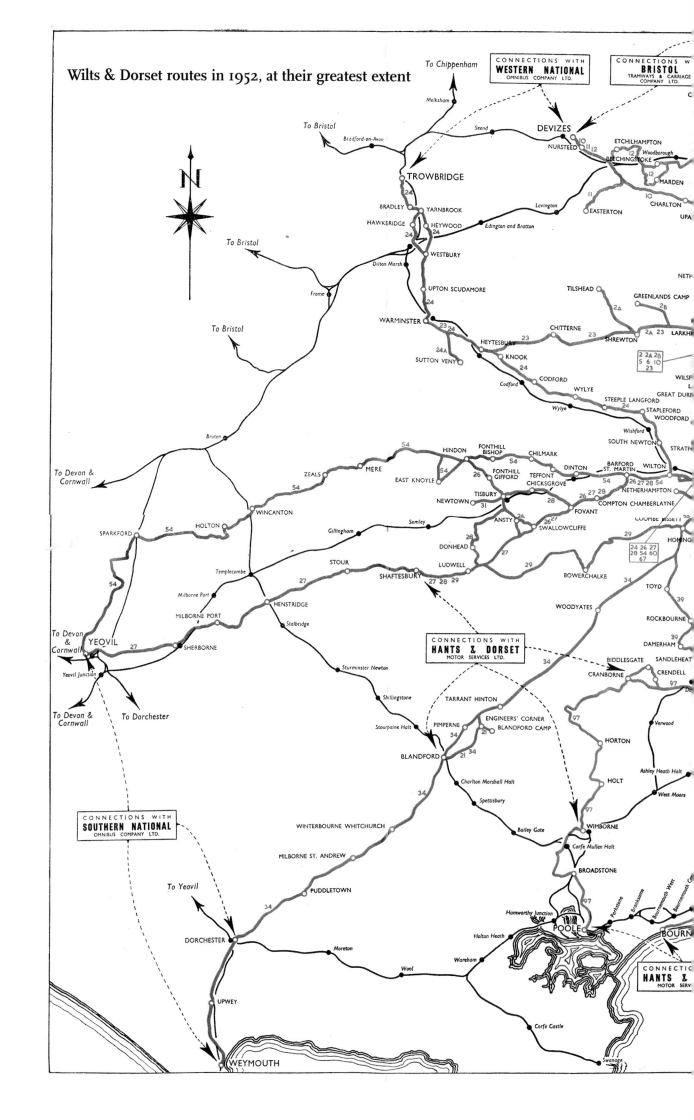

Wilts & Dorset routes in 1952, at their greatest extent

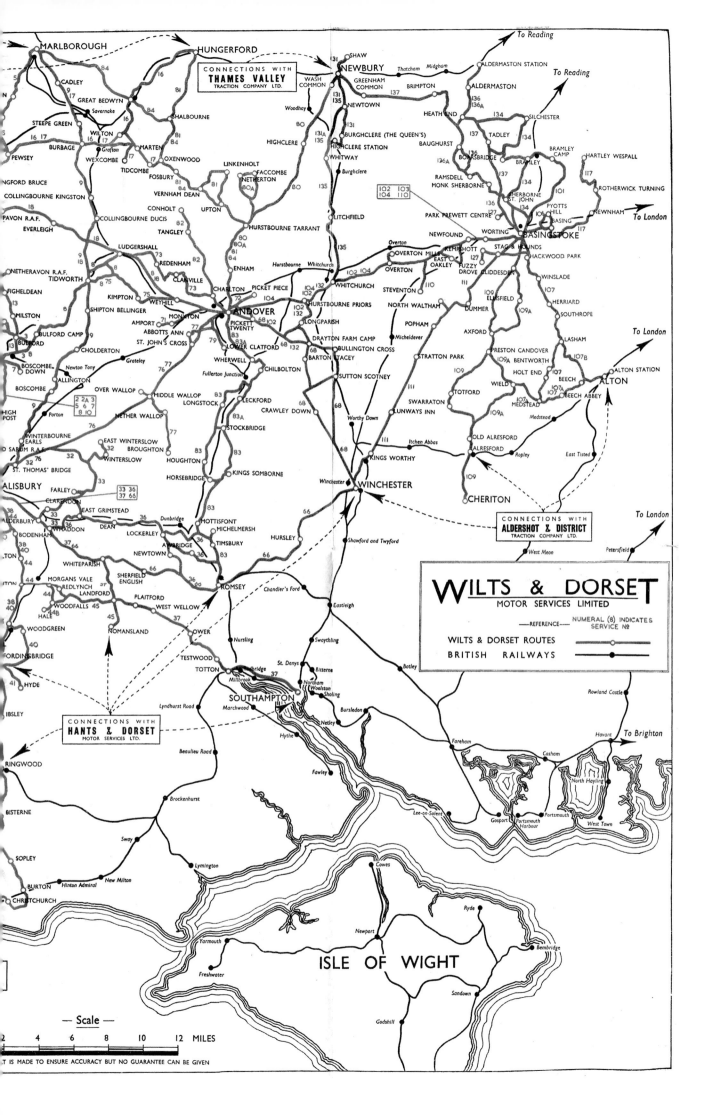

WILTS & DORSET
MOTOR SERVICES LIMITED

------ REFERENCE ------ NUMERAL (8) INDICATES SERVICE Nº

WILTS & DORSET ROUTES

BRITISH RAILWAYS

CONNECTIONS WITH
THAMES VALLEY
TRACTION COMPANY LTD.

CONNECTIONS WITH
ALDERSHOT & DISTRICT
TRACTION COMPANY LTD.

CONNECTIONS WITH
HANTS & DORSET
MOTOR SERVICES LTD.

ISLE OF WIGHT

— Scale —

2   4   6   8   10   12 MILES

...T IS MADE TO ENSURE ACCURACY BUT NO GUARANTEE CAN BE GIVEN

Index

This selective index includes individuals, companies (other than Wilts & Dorset Motor Services Ltd), relevant towns, villages, institutions, Acts of Parliament, and some specific topics, which appear in the text or captions. References to Salisbury are so frequent that it would not be helpful to cite all of them. Vehicle manufacturers are generally only listed where operators ordered chassis or bodies from them. The appendices are not indexed.

Salisbury–Woodford–Amesbury 'was and still is my number 1 bus service,' wrote Edwin Maurice Coombes in 1961. A later, and better known writer, the Nobel prizewinning novelist V.S. Naipaul, sometimes used this service, and described its passengers catching the early afternoon departure from Salisbury in his acclaimed novel, The Enigma of Arrival. 'It picked up young children from the infant schools in one direction, and then on the way back it picked up bigger children from the secondary schools.' DAVID PENNELS